MAKE IT
LEGAL

WHAT EVERY CANADIAN ENTREPRENEUR
NEEDS TO KNOW
ABOUT THE LAW

Also available in the series from

PROFIT: The Magazine for Canadian Entrepreneurs

Beyond The Banks: *Creative Financing for Canadian Entrepreneurs*, by Allan Riding and Barbara Orser (ISBN: 0-471-64208-8)

Secrets of Success from Canada's Fastest-Growing Companies by Rick Spence (ISBN: 0-471-64233-9)

Marketing Masters: The Best Ideas, Tips & Strategies From Canada's Savviest Marketeers, edited by Ian Portsmouth (ISBN: 0-471-64274-6)

MAKE IT
LEGAL

WHAT EVERY CANADIAN ENTREPRENEUR NEEDS TO KNOW ABOUT THE LAW

MARGARET KERR AND JOANN KURTZ

JOHN WILEY & SONS CANADA, LTD

Toronto • New York • Chichester • Weinheim • Brisbane • Singapore

John Wiley & Sons Canada Limited
22 Worcester Road
Etobicoke, Ontario
M9W1L1

Canadian Cataloguing in Publication Data

Kerr, Margaret Helen, 1954-
  Make it legal: what every Canadian entrepreneur needs to know about the law

On cover: Profit: the magazine for Canadian entrepreneurs.
Includes index.
ISBN 0-471-64245-2

1. Small business—Law and legislation—Canada—Popular works. 2. Business law—
Canada. I.Kurtz, JoAnn, 1951-. II. Profit (Toronto, Ont.). III. Title.

KEI658.K47 1998	346.71'0652	C98-930672-0
KF1659.K47 1998		

Production Credits
Cover & text design: Interrobang Graphic Design Inc.
Cover photography: Mir Lada
Printer: Tri-Graphic Printing

Printed in Canada
10 9 8 7 6 5 4 3 2 1

To Daniel, Jacob, Max and Ely Henry

and

To James Willis Wood

CONTENTS

ACKNOWLEDGEMENTS

We want to thank the following for their help:

Jan Oldreive, Michael Kerr, Christopher Holoboff, Elizabeth Johnson, Ruth Snowden, David Akande, Eric Gross, Ken McAvoy, Joseph Agostino, Michael Engleberg, and Robert Berkowitz, who read portions of the book for us; and Ian LeBain, John Azzarello, Belinda Sutton, the Insurance Bureau of Canada, Halifax Insurance, Hartford Insurance, the Canadian Franchise Association, Rumanek & Cooper Ltd., the Bank of Montreal, Revenue Canada, Customs and Excise, the Department of Foreign and International Affairs, the Canadian Intellectual Property Office, and the Competition Bureau, who provided information to us.

We would also like to acknowledge the role of our muses, Λυπη and Φοβος, in the writing of this book.

NOW YOU'RE IN BUSINESS

You're in business for yourself now. You may have made the jump on your own or you may have been pushed. Either way, going into business is a major undertaking and you shouldn't proceed without a lot of careful thought. You have to research your product, your market, your competition, and your potential sources of financing, but you can't stop there. We apologize for adding to your work load, but you're going to have to research the law that will affect your business as well.

Law touches on many more aspects of your business than you probably think. The law tells you:

- what area of business you can go into—some businesses require you to have special training and qualifications, some require you to have a government licence or permit

- what form of business you can choose—some businesses cannot incorporate and must be carried on as a sole proprietorship or partnership

- what name you can give your business—there are regulations about how you name your business and whether you can have a name similar to someone else's

- where you can carry on your business—municipal zoning by-laws may prevent you from setting up your business where you want

- how you can carry on your business—there may be specific laws and regulations that tell you exactly how you must perform certain activities

- how you have to go about hiring and firing employees, and what your responsibilities are as an employer

- what taxes you must pay and when

- what steps you have to take to get out of business—you can't just walk away and be done with it

And a whole lot more. And you have to know something about all of it, because there are penalties for not obeying the numerous laws that apply to you. You can't escape them by saying you didn't know about the law. That loophole was plugged centuries ago with the rule that ignorance of the law is no excuse. You need to know the law so that you don't get fined or imprisoned or shut down for doing business the wrong way. But you also *want* to know the law because it tells you the rules of your game. For example:

- Businesses are run according to sets of legal rules that explain such things as how partners share the profits of a partnership and how shareholders choose the people who will run the corporation.

- Business is carried on according to a set of rules called the law of contract. If you don't know when you've entered into a contract, what you and others are required to do under the contract, and what steps to take if the contract isn't fulfilled, you won't be in business for very long.

- Businesses collect the money that is owed them according to yet another set of legal rules that cover matters such as getting the right to take your debtor's property if the debt isn't paid and suing the debtor and turning a court judgment into cash in your hand.

In other words, at every stage of your business there are legal issues. One of the purposes of this book is to help you recognize when you're nose to nose with a legal issue. Legal issues don't necessarily mean lawyers. You don't need to consult a lawyer every time you realize that a law applies to your business, just like you don't have to have a lawyer with you whenever you go for a drive even though there are laws that apply to your driving. But there will be times when you need a lawyer. At those times, you shouldn't wait too long to get professional legal advice. That's another reason you have to know some basic law, so you'll get the help you need in time.

QUESTIONS THIS BOOK ANSWERS

Here are some of the questions this book answers:

About Lawyers

- When should you use a lawyer?
- How do lawyers charge?
- How do you make the best use of your lawyer?

About Setting Up Your Business

- What form of business organization makes the most sense for you?
- What form of business protects you best from creditors?
- What sort of permits and licences do you need for your business?
- What's involved in buying an existing business?
- What kind of security will a lender ask you for, and what happens if you don't pay back the loan?
- How is a commercial lease different from a residential lease and what happens if you don't pay your rent?
- What's a patent, copyright, trademark, and industrial design, and how do you get one?

About Running Your Business

- What can you do to limit your liability if you sell defective goods?
- What happens if one of your customers goes bankrupt?
- What are your rights and duties as an employer?
- When can you be sued for wrongful dismissal?
- How is income tax calculated when you're in business?
- When do you have to register for the GST?
- Do you need a licence to import or export goods?
- What happens if a customer is injured on your premises or by one of your products?
- Can you detain a suspected shoplifter?

About Wrapping Up Your Business

- How do you go about selling your business?
- What happens if your business goes bankrupt?

THIS BOOK CAN'T ANSWER ALL OF YOUR QUESTIONS

The cover of this book says that we're going to tell you what you need to know about the law. Let us warn you up front that we're not going to tell you absolutely *everything* you need to know about the law. We can't answer all of your questions. If we tried to do that, this book would be as big as...well, as big as a law library. Even if you could squeeze into the same room with it you would find it too detailed and complex to be useful. One of the particular things we're not going to tell you is exactly what you can expect to pay for anything. Professional fees always depend on circumstances, and government fees are always changing (and always upward).

The purpose of this book is to give you a strong background in the law you need to know to carry on business, to give it to you in language that a non-lawyer can understand, and to give it to you in a format that reflects how entrepreneurs work—not how lawyers work. It's also intended to help you to avoid problems as well as to solve problems.

Every business is different, and every business has different legal problems. There's an awful lot of law out there, and most of it is complicated, and (as if that weren't enough) it changes all the time. In addition to that, we're writing a book for all of Canada and we haven't been able to take provincial variations on every topic into account. So when you need to know about specific laws that affect your particular business, you're going to have to get legal advice that's tailored exactly for you—perhaps from a government department, perhaps from a lawyer. Don't just rely on this book.

But, speaking as your legal counsel, we strongly advise you to buy it.

CHAPTER TWO

YOU AND YOUR LAWYER

If you are an entrepreneur you need a lawyer. This is not just propaganda from a couple of lawyers, it is a fact of life. That's why in this chapter we're going to give you advice about finding and dealing with lawyers, and getting your money's worth out of them.

You may think that you can't afford a lawyer. If you are starting up a business there are probably a lot of things that you can't afford. But sometimes you can't afford *not* to have a lawyer. In this chapter we'll also try to give you some help finding legal information and advice that won't cost you much. But remember the old saying: you get what you pay for.

CAN YOU BE YOUR OWN LAWYER?

You may want to do as much of your own legal work as you can. You have the right to do most legal work for yourself, and some of it you can do quite safely. However, there are some things that by law, you cannot do. For example, in most provinces only a lawyer can represent your corporation in a legal proceeding. There are many other things that it's worth paying a lawyer to do because mistakes can be very costly. Throughout this book we will be providing you with enough background in business law to help you make an informed decision about whether you should try to do your own legal work or whether you should get professional help. We will also tell you when we think a lawyer is essential.

> **T I P**
>
> There is one very good reason not to be your own lawyer but to hire one. If you make a mistake in your legal affairs, you have no one to blame but yourself. But if your lawyer makes a mistake (which is less likely than *you* making a mistake) you can not only blame your lawyer, you can also sue her for professional negligence and receive financial compensation for the mistake.
>
> T I P

HOW DO YOU GET LEGAL HELP (WITHOUT HAVING TO GET A LAWYER)?

You can get free or inexpensive legal information and advice from government and private sources, but you will have to rely on your own interpretation and analysis of the legal issues and information.

Government Sources

Government information sources include:

- **Canada-Provincial Business Centres** can provide information about the legal requirements of setting up a business, paying taxes, importing and exporting, employing workers, and other basic matters.

- **Specific Ministries of the Federal Government** such as Industry Canada, Health Canada, Employment Canada, and Revenue Canada can give you a lot of information and help in various areas.

- **Specific Ministries or Departments of the Provincial Government** such as agriculture, consumer and commercial relations, economic development, environment and energy, labour, natural resources, transportation, trade and tourism, and workers' compensation will also help you.

- **Your Municipal Government** may have a business centre set up to provide local businesses with information about municipal requirements and to refer you to other sources of information.

- Some municipal **libraries** have business law collections. However, if you need to do in-depth legal research you will probably have to go to a law library at a law school or at a courthouse. Not all law libraries are open to the general public.

Private Sources

Private sources of information include:

- **Trade, Industry, or Professional Associations** can provide members with information about legal issues that particularly affect your area of business, and may also be able to give you access, at a special rate, to a lawyer who is familiar with those issues.

- **Local Chambers of Commerce or Boards of Trade** may be able to provide general information about doing business in your city, town, or municipality.

- **Local Merchants' Associations** may give you information about issues of interest to merchants in your immediate neighbourhood.

Paralegals

In many provinces non-lawyers offer a number of legal services that a business might need, such as registration of a business name, incorporation of a company, drafting of contracts, collections and small claims court work, and appearances before licencing boards and agencies. These people may call themselves paralegals, legal consultants, or legal services providers. You might be tempted to use their services because they are cheaper than lawyers. But you should know that in most provinces the paralegal industry is totally unregulated—there are no educational, licencing, or third-party liability insurance requirements. While some paralegals have many years of experience, others have none at all. If a paralegal does a bad job for you, there may be nobody to complain to, and it may not be worth your while to sue if the paralegal is not insured.

More important than that, in virtually every province the law only allows paralegals to represent clients on limited matters before certain lower courts, such as small claims court, residential landlord and tenant court, and provincial offences court, and before some administrative boards and agencies, such as licencing commissions. It is against the law for paralegals to give legal advice or do legal work in other matters, although many openly advertise their services in these areas because the law is rarely enforced. (When the law is enforced, it's the paralegal, not the client, who will get into trouble.)

WHEN SHOULD YOU USE A LAWYER?

What do you call 50 lawyers at the bottom of the ocean? A good start.

That's a joke by the way. (Don't tell it to your lawyer, or you may find a 10 per cent lawyer joke surcharge on your bill.) Lots of entrepreneurs suspect that life could go on just fine without lawyers, and that might be true if there were no lawyers at all. However, you can be pretty sure that the government has a lawyer. And your competitor. And your customer. And your employee. Probably even your mother-in-law has a lawyer. So you need one too. But even when you don't need a lawyer to protect you from someone else's, you'll find that having a lawyer is useful because almost everything that happens in the business world has a legal dimension. A lawyer can guide you through all kinds of minefields at every stage of your business.

When you're setting up a business a lawyer can:

• help you decide whether your business should be a sole proprietorship, partnership, or corporation

• draft a partnership agreement or incorporate your company

• review documents a lender may require you to sign

- review leases of premises and equipment
- act for you in the purchase of property (in Quebec and British Columbia, a **notary** can act for you instead)
- review franchise agreements
- draft standard form contracts for use in your business
- advise you how best to protect your ideas, processes, trademarks, and designs

After a lawyer has helped you to get your business set up, you may breathe a sigh of relief that you don't have to contend with lawyers—and legal fees—ever again. But you still need a lawyer when your business is up and running. At this stage, your lawyer can:

- help you negotiate contracts and put them in writing
- help you collect unpaid bills
- defend any lawsuits that are brought against you
- advise you on the hiring and firing of employees
- advise you about taxes
- advise you about doing business in other provinces and countries

Whenever you run into a problem, your lawyer should do whatever is possible to solve it and then follow up by recommending action to prevent something similar from happening in the future. For example, if you're sued by a customer over a standard form contract you use, your lawyer will not only handle the lawsuit but will also redraft the contract so the same situation won't arise again.

If you decide to get out of business, you need a lawyer to help you:

- sell your business
- arrange for the transfer of the business to your children
- dissolve or wind down a corporation

So if you can possibly afford it, you should make a lawyer an important member of your business team from the very outset. Stay in touch with your lawyer, don't wait until you're in trouble. By getting advice about problems that look small and harmless, you can often prevent major crises. If you can't afford a lawyer as a permanent team member, you should still budget for occasional legal advice, not just for crisis management, but for crisis *prevention*.

WHAT KIND OF LAWYER DO YOU WANT?

All lawyers are not created equal. When you are deciding which one you want, you should consider:

• the area or areas of law in which you need expertise

• the size of law firm

• the personality of the individual lawyer

• the amount the lawyer will charge

Area of Expertise

Over the life of your business you may need a lawyer with expertise in corporate or partnership law, negotiating and drafting commercial contracts or leases, employment law, commercial litigation, estate planning, or bankruptcy law. Ideally, you want to find someone with knowledge and experience in all these areas. Unfortunately you're not likely to.

For most businesses a lawyer with general corporate-commercial experience will be able to provide the routine services you need, and when you need more specialized expertise, your lawyer should be able to direct you to a specialist. Whatever your legal needs, you want a lawyer with actual knowledge and experience in the area, not merely a willingness to educate herself and take a stab at it.

A company had a lawyer who specialized in corporate-commercial law. The lawyer had handled the incorporation of the company and all of the legal work in getting the business set up, and had done an excellent job. After a year in business, the company was sued by a disgruntled customer. The client consulted the lawyer. The lawyer, who had long wanted to dabble in litigation matters, suggested that he handle the lawsuit, even though he had never appeared in court before. Because of his lack of litigation experience the lawyer presented the case in court very poorly, and the judge's decision went against the client.

Size of Law Firm

Law firms range in size from locally based sole practitioners to large international firms employing hundreds of lawyers. While it is impossible to generalize, we're going to anyway.

People go to sole practitioners because their fees tend to be lower than those of the large law firms, and because there's never any question about who will be doing the work. Sole practitioners may specialize in one area of law only, but often they carry on a general practice. The more you do something the better you get at it. Therefore, if you choose a sole practitioner, make sure that she is able to do the required work well.

The other end of the spectrum from a small practitioner is the big, well-known firm with dozens, if not hundreds, of lawyers. People choose these firms because they are usually full-service and can provide the right expert at the right time. There is also some prestige in being represented by the biggest firm in the city. However, big law firms usually charge big fees. As an added consideration, you may not develop a close working relationship with one particular lawyer if your work is always done by specialists. Or you may develop a close relationship with one lawyer only to find that your work is being done by three or four young and inexperienced lawyers you've never met.

In between these two extremes are small to mid-size firms, usually made up of lawyers who specialize in different areas of the law. One lawyer might have the expertise that best suits your needs, but will be able to call upon others in the firm if necessary. You get the benefits of a broader range of expertise, while the smaller size allows one lawyer to have a personal relationship with you, and to keep overall track of everything that happens with your business. Legal fees of small to mid-size firms may be a bit higher than those of sole practitioners, but will generally be lower than those of the big firms.

Personality

Don't be afraid to let personal style sway your choice. After all, you may end up spending a lot of time with your lawyer. You may feel more comfortable if you have a formal, strictly business relationship, or you may prefer a more casual relationship. While there are exceptions, the general rule is that the larger the firm, the more formal the lawyers will be.

Whether your relationship is formal or casual, you want to feel that you can talk freely to your lawyer about your problems. You want a lawyer whose judgement you trust. And perhaps most important, you should have absolutely no doubt about the honesty and integrity of your lawyer.

What the Lawyer Will Charge

There is no such thing as a schedule of fees that lawyers are allowed to charge, and the fee for the same services can vary widely from lawyer to lawyer. Fee levels are affected by such things as the lawyer's years of experience, reputation, location, and the size of the lawyer's firm.

HOW DO LAWYERS CHARGE FOR THEIR SERVICES?

Lawyers can charge for their services in different ways (but one way or another they *will* charge for them). They can:

- bill at an hourly rate for the time they spend working for you
- charge a flat rate for a particular matter
- charge a contingency fee (in some provinces)
- provide a range of specified services for a fixed monthly or annual fee

However their fees are calculated, lawyers are required to charge GST.

In addition to their fees, lawyers will also bill for **disbursements**, such as long distance telephone calls, photocopies, document filing fees, experts' reports, and travel, among many possibilities. (A warning about photocopy fees: lawyers usually charge a lot more per page than your local copy shop.) Some disbursements are also subject to GST. Be aware that disbursements can add up to a significant amount of money—hundreds or even thousands of dollars.

> **T I P**
>
> If you feel that you have been overcharged either for fees or disbursements, don't just fume silently, do something about it. It is not a good idea simply to ignore the bill. Your lawyer will sue you (it comes naturally), and may have the right to refuse to give you some parts of your **file** (the collection of documents related to your case). What you should do is speak or write to your lawyer. He should be able to explain why the bill is as high as it is, or may be willing to reduce the amount. If you are not satisfied after a discussion, you have the right to have the bill reviewed by an officer of the court. If the officer agrees that you have been overcharged, the bill will be reduced. This procedure is called **assessment** or **taxation** of a lawyer's account.
>
> T I P

Billing at an Hourly Rate

Lawyers, like most professionals but unlike most entrepreneurs, usually charge for every minute spent doing your work, although the charge is stated in terms of an hourly rate. When you hire a lawyer be sure to ask what the hourly rate will be: you have the right to know. If you think that rate is unreasonably high, you can try to negotiate a lower one, or you can take your business elsewhere. If your lawyer later wishes to raise the stated hourly rate, you must be advised of the change in advance, and must agree to it. If your lawyer raises the hourly rate without telling you or without your consent, the account will be reduced to the original hourly rate if you have the bill assessed or taxed.

Before any work is done on a particular matter, if you are being billed at an hourly rate you should ask your lawyer for an estimate of how many hours the work will take. If it later turns out that the work is going to take longer, your lawyer must tell you before proceeding further.

A client was given an estimate by her lawyer for the cost of negotiating a contract. The negotiations dragged on and on because the other party was being unreasonable. The lawyer's final bill was a lot more than the estimate. The client was horrified and had the bill assessed. The assessment officer, while agreeing that all of the work done was necessary, reduced the account to the original estimate, stating that the lawyer should have notified the client when it became clear that the work was going to take longer than estimated.

Your lawyer will bill you for everything done, including meetings and telephone conversations with you and with others on your behalf, drafting of documents, and preparation of letters to you and others. The lawyer will also bill you for reading letters and documents received from you or others, doing research, reviewing the file (reading through the file to remember what's in it before actually getting down to work), and returning telephone calls—even when the other party isn't there to answer. If you have a conversation with your lawyer, you may be billed for the length of the entire conversation, even the time spent schmoozing about golf or the kids. Generally, you should be billed only for the business part of the conversation, although perhaps not if you are the one who chooses to use the lawyer's time in this way. Lawyers divide every hour into tenths, and will bill for as little as .1 of an hour—six minutes! A phone call to your voice mail would be billed as .1. (This hourly billing business sounds like quite a racket, doesn't it? But remember, lawyers are in the business of selling their time, and this is their form of inventory control.)

Before your lawyer does any work for you, he will ask for a **retainer**, which is a deposit to be applied against the bill. The requested retainer is usually enough to cover either all or a substantial part of the estimated work. The lawyer must hold the money in a special trust account until the work is done and a bill has been prepared for you. If the retainer is used up before work is finished, you will be asked for a further retainer. Sorry, there's no legal limit to the number of times your lawyer can ask you for a further retainer. That's why it's a good idea to get an estimate before your lawyer starts the work.

**T
I
P**

When billing at an hourly rate, your lawyer should give you an account that shows not just the total number of hours but also a detailed breakdown of how the time billed was spent. If the bill does not contain enough detail, ask for more. If the work is of an ongoing nature, your lawyer should not wait until everything is finished to bill you, but should send you interim bills on a monthly basis. While it's a bit of a pain to receive legal bills every month, it's far better than being unpleasantly surprised with a huge legal bill at the end. Interim bills also help you keep tabs on what your lawyer is doing for you. Speak up if you want more done or less.

T I P

Charging a Flat Rate

Lawyers are willing to quote a flat fee for certain kinds of work such as incorporations, real estate transactions, and other kinds of work where they can predict how long the work will take. Disbursements will usually be charged over and above the flat fee. Since these can be quite hefty, be sure to ask how much they will cost. As when billing hourly, the lawyer will ask for a retainer.

Monthly Retainer

Just to confuse you, the word "retainer" has more than one meaning. It can also mean an agreement that the lawyer will provide you with whatever advice you need, whenever you need it, for a fixed monthly rate. (Retainer agreements can also be made on an annual basis.) Such a fee usually covers questions or matters that can be quickly dealt with and that do not require the opening of a new file (starting a separate collection of documents related to the matter). If a contract has to be negotiated or a lawsuit started or defended, or if any other major matter comes up, those legal services would not be covered under the retainer agreement. The lawyer would bill for those matters at either an hourly or flat rate.

> **T**
> **I**
> **P**
> A monthly retainer may make sense if you regularly need legal information in your business such as advice about contract terms, suggestions about how to deal with employees, or updates on regulatory law that affects you. It makes legal fees more predictable and encourages regular communication with your lawyer.
>
> T I P

Contingency Fee

In some provinces a lawyer is allowed to charge a **contingency fee** for suing someone on your behalf. The lawyer's fee will be a stated percentage of the amount of money you collect from the other party to the lawsuit. If you don't win or if you win and don't collect any money, you don't have to pay the lawyer's fees, although you usually still have to pay the disbursements. A lawyer will only agree to a contingency fee if you have a good chance of winning and collecting. A contingency fee allows a client with a good case but no money to start a lawsuit.

> **T**
> **I**
> **P**
> What if you have a good case but no money, and you live in a province where contingency fees are not allowed? Many lawyers will agree to postpone billing you until after your case is finished. They may or may not require you to pay disbursements as the case proceeds. You'll still have to pay legal fees, even if you lose, but they won't be as high as if you win.
>
>

HOW DO YOU FIND THE RIGHT LAWYER?

Well, you don't find your lawyer by opening up the Yellow Pages to "Lawyers" and calling the first listing, "AAA Advocates." Don't bother watching for lawyers' ads on TV either. You have to choose your lawyer as carefully as you choose your partner. There are three main steps in finding a lawyer:

- get several recommendations
- investigate the recommended lawyers and narrow your choices
- interview the finalists before making your decision

Get several recommendations by:

- asking friends, relatives, or associates with a business, your accountant, or bank manager for the names of lawyers they know and trust and haven't been shockingly overcharged by
- asking your provincial law society for a list of corporate-commercial lawyers in your area

Investigate the recommended lawyers by:

- finding out the size of the firm each lawyer practices in
- comparing the fees that each lawyer charges
- finding out the location of each lawyer's office

Once you have narrowed down your choices, meet with the finalists to find out:

- how much experience the lawyer has in corporate-commercial law (and in any other kind of law that is important to your business)
- in what circumstances you will be billed at an hourly rate and at a flat rate, and what those rates are
- whether a monthly retainer arrangement is possible
- whether your work will be handled by the lawyer personally or by others
- whether you can work comfortably with this person

WHAT DO YOU DO ONCE YOU'VE FOUND A LAWYER?

When you find the lawyer you want to use, you must formally retain his services. Many lawyers will ask you to sign a written agreement called a retainer (yes, there's that word again—and with yet another meaning). Even if your lawyer doesn't suggest it, you should.

The retainer should include at a minimum:

- a description of the work the lawyer has been retained to do

- the name of any lawyers who will do work on your file

- how and how much you will be billed for the work—by the hour, at a flat fee, on contingency, etc.

- if you are being billed at an hourly rate, an estimate of what the total fee will be, and a promise to tell you before doing any more work if the fee will be higher

- how frequently the lawyer will send you bills

WHAT SHOULD YOU EXPECT OF YOUR LAWYER?

Lawyers in all provinces are governed by rules of professional conduct that require them to:

- act with integrity and honesty

- perform any legal services competently and promptly, and ensure that anyone who assists the lawyer is also competent

- keep confidential all information about the client and the client's affairs

- represent only the interests of the client and avoid any conflicts of interest

- keep the client thoroughly advised of all work being done and all developments in the matter

- act only on the client's instructions

In addition, because lawyers are in a service industry, you should expect good service. As a smart business person your lawyer should:

- not keep you waiting for appointments
- return your telephone calls within 24 hours
- generally treat you with courtesy and respect

A lawyer habitually kept her client waiting, took phone calls from other clients during meetings, and grew impatient when she had to spend any length of time answering questions. The lawyer seemed to believe that she looked more important if she didn't have much time for the client. Even though the lawyer did excellent work, the client finally got fed up and found another lawyer who showed that he was more anxious to keep the client's business.

You should feel confident that you are getting good quality legal services at a reasonable price and that you are being well treated. If you don't, find another lawyer.

HOW DO YOU GET THE MOST OUT OF YOUR LAWYER?

There are things you can do that will help your lawyer do a better job for you, and there are also things you can do that will help keep your legal fees down.

In order to help your lawyer do the best possible job for you:

- Consult your lawyer sooner rather than later: an ounce of legal prevention is worth a pound of legal bills. Many problems can be prevented altogether if you get the right legal advice at the right time. For example, a well-drafted contract can prevent disputes from arising. Even after problems arise, they can often be solved much more quickly and cheaply if dealt with early.

- Tell your lawyer the absolute truth about your situation. You may want to show the strongest side of your case, but your lawyer has to know the full story (including weaknesses) in order to represent you properly. The chances are very good that your opposition will know all about any weaknesses anyway, and it's better for your lawyer to find out about them from you than from the lawyer for the other side.

- Collect *all* the information and documents on the matter in question. Only you know what information you have. Not everything may turn out to be relevant, but let your lawyer be the judge of that.

- Make yourself available to the lawyer. You must be easily reachable and must answer telephone calls and letters promptly. Sometimes your physical presence may be required as well, so if you're in the middle of litigation or a business deal, don't leave town without consulting your lawyer first. To minimize the amount of time you sit around waiting for your lawyer to get back to you, ask if there's a certain time of day when she usually returns calls. Or make sure you have a way for the lawyer to get a detailed message to you—a secretary, e-mail, fax, or voice mail.

You want your lawyer to do a good job for you, but you also want the job done efficiently so that your legal fees are kept down. You can help your lawyer work efficiently if you:

- Do your homework. If you understand something about the law concerning your particular matter, you will be better able to identify what facts and documents are relevant and to talk about them in a logical manner. Also, the more you know about the law, the less time your lawyer will have to spend explaining it all to you. That's where this book will come in handy.

- Give clear instructions. Your lawyer cannot do anything without them. It is your lawyer's job to tell you what your options are and what the consequences of different courses of action might be, and perhaps even to recommend a particular course of action, but only *you* can make the final decision. Once you've done that, be sure to tell your lawyer exactly what you have decided—don't assume he will know what you want done.

- Keep copies of any documents you give to or receive from your lawyer. That way, you won't have to ask for additional copies and be reminded of what's already been done or decided.

- Make the best use of telecommunications. Many clients call their lawyers and leave messages that simply say "please call" without explaining why. If it takes several attempts for your lawyer to contact you, your legal bill will rise. (Remember you are charged for each telephone call, even if you can't be reached.) More importantly, your lawyer won't be able to do what you want before connecting with you. It is far better to leave a detailed message in the first place—either with a secretary or law clerk, or on voice mail, by fax, or e-mail. Some clients are reluctant to discuss their business with a secretary, but the secretary will be working on your file and will know all about it anyway. In addition, law firms require all employees to keep client information confidential.

WHAT IF YOU'RE NOT HAPPY WITH YOUR LAWYER?

If you've chosen your lawyer carefully, you shouldn't run into too many problems. But if, as time goes by, you become unhappy with any aspect of your relationship, what should you do?

If you are generally pleased with your lawyer's work, discuss problems as they come up. Talk about matters such as phone calls that are not returned in a reasonable time or a bill that you don't fully understand. But if you've lost confidence in your lawyer, or no longer feel comfortable working with her, find another lawyer. It's wise to choose the new one before parting ways with the old one. Your new lawyer should be able to smooth over transitional matters like getting your file so that you never have to confront the lawyer you're firing.

If your concerns are of a more serious nature, such as professional negligence or misconduct, seek advice from another lawyer or contact your provincial law society. Lawyers are insured against professional negligence, so if a lawyer's mistake has cost you money, you should be able to recover something from the lawyer's insurer. Lawyers can be disciplined by the provincial law society if they are guilty of professional misconduct such as never returning your phone calls or answering your letters, not following your instructions, or lying to you about the status of your matter. The law society has the power to reprimand lawyers, suspend them from practice for a time, or even disbar them. In serious cases of deliberate misconduct, such as taking your money and disappearing, lawyers may be subject to criminal charges as well. In addition, provincial law societies have a compensation fund available to clients who have suffered losses because of their lawyer's deliberate misconduct (rather than a mere mistake).

AN INTRODUCTION TO THE LAW OF CONTRACTS

You have to understand something about contracts in order to do business. Contracts are everywhere—they are not just multi-page documents filled with small print and incomprehensible language. From a business point of view, a contract is any agreement that a court will enforce. It does not have to be in writing, and it doesn't matter how long it is. The same legal rules apply to all contracts whether short or long, simple or complex, in writing or not.

You need to know about contract law so that you:

- will know when you are in a contract situation
- understand why you need a lawyer to deal with many contract situations
- will be able to communicate effectively with your lawyer
- can recognize the underlying legal reasons for some of the steps that experienced entrepreneurs take in their dealings with others

BUSINESS IMPLICATIONS OF CONTRACT LAW

Just in case you're tempted to skip this chapter and go on to something more exciting, like bankruptcy, we're going to explain in a little more detail why it's not just legally necessary, but extremely useful from a business point of view to have a good grasp of contracts.

All of the parties to a contract must know what is required of them—what they actually have to do—and what can happen if they don't do it. This reinforces the importance of taking the proper precautions at the formation stage of the contract. Successful entrepreneurs who understand that the formation stage is the most important usually:

- check out the other party to the contract to make sure that he has enough assets or insurance to satisfy a judgment in case it's necessary to sue

- structure the deal so that it's fair, so that both parties *want* to perform the terms of the contract

- schedule payments so that they match performance at any stage of the contract (this way the loss is minimized if the other party fails to perform)

- consider including a term in the contract requiring the parties to go to arbitration or mediation, as an alternative to litigation, if there is a contract dispute

- get their lawyer involved (at least in drafting, and possibly in negotiating) if the contract has to do with a lot of money or work, if it is a long-term commitment, or if it is a standard form contract that will be used over and over

When negotiating a contract successful entrepreneurs:

- keep in mind that even a pre-printed contract can sometimes be negotiated. It's just a contract drafted by the other party's lawyer (to favour that party) and printed up to look important and unchangeable.

- consult a lawyer before entering into negotiations, even if the entrepreneurs are conducting the negotiations themselves. It may be too late for a lawyer to fix things at the drafting stage, when the deal is being converted into legal language, if negotiations have already resulted in an agreement.

And when negotiations are completed, they put the agreement in writing. This is a lawyer's job, but savvy entrepreneurs know that the precise wording used in a contract is important.

> **T**
> **I**
> **P**
>
> **D**on't think your lawyer is being unnecessarily picky about the words used in the contract and don't worry about the possible reaction of the other party. It is vitally important that everyone know what is expected when the time comes for performing the contract. Neither party should be insulted by the desire for a carefully drafted contract, and you should be suspicious of someone who is.
>
> T I P

But don't be suspicious of this chapter. Come on in.

HOW CONTRACTS ARE FORMED

To be enforceable a contract must have all of the following elements at the time it is formed:

- consideration
- offer and acceptance
- legal capacity of the parties
- (in some cases) compliance with legal formalities

Consideration

In a contract each party must give something of value (the legal term is **consideration**) to the other party. Consideration can be money, services, goods, or even a promise to do something in the future. In contract law, no one gives something for nothing. If you do promise to give something for nothing it is considered "a gratuitous promise"—in other words, a promise to give a gift— and a court will not force you to go through with it.

The courts do not recognize as consideration money or goods given, services performed, or promises made by either party before there is an agreement between the parties. The legal maxim is "past consideration is no consideration at all."

You decide to set up a gardening and landscaping business. You mow a potential customer's lawn while the homeowner is away at work, and leave a bill for $25 in the mailbox. You stop by the house later that evening and ask to be paid. The homeowner says, "I'll pay you tomorrow." You return the next evening and the homeowner refuses to pay you. By contract law there is nothing you can do to force payment, because you gave your consideration (mowing the lawn) before the homeowner agreed to pay.

The courts also do not recognize as consideration anything that is illegal. If the consideration on one side is an illegal or wrongful act, the contract is not enforceable. For example, if you agree to buy stolen merchandise, no court will help you make the seller deliver the merchandise, even if you've already paid for it.

Offer and Acceptance

For there to be a contract, one party must make an **offer** that the other **accepts**. You won't be surprised to learn that this isn't as straightforward as it sounds.

You may offer to perform a service for a client if he will pay you money. You don't have a contract until the client agrees to (in legal terms, accepts) your offer. If you perform the service before the client agrees, no court will make him pay you for it. When you make your offer you can say that the other party only has a limited time in which to accept it. If the other party doesn't accept your offer within that time, your offer expires—it can no longer be accepted. If you do not specify a time for acceptance, your offer will expire after a reasonable time. In addition, you can **revoke** or withdraw your offer at any time before it is accepted by telling the other party the offer is no longer open. If the other party accepts your offer before it expires or you revoke it, then there is a contract.

There's a legal rule that says, "Silence is not acceptance." You cannot say in your offer that there is a contract unless the other side tells you no. Silence can only mean acceptance if an existing contract between the parties says so.

A coffee company you've never heard of delivers a carton of coffee to your office, with a note stating that you will be billed for the coffee if it is not returned within seven days. No court will make you either pay for the coffee or return it. A party making an offer cannot say that your failure to do or say something is your acceptance. On the other hand, you can have an agreement with your regular coffee company that you must pay for any coffee they deliver and you don't return.

The person making an offer may state specifically how acceptance is to be communicated. If that is done, only acceptance in that manner will create a contract. For example, if an offer made to you says that acceptance must be in writing, there is no contract if you telephone the other party to say that you accept the offer. If no method of acceptance is set out in the offer, you may accept the offer in any way that is reasonable.

If the offer can be accepted by mail, unless the person making the offer specifies otherwise, the law states that the offer is accepted when the letter of acceptance is put in the mail. This rule is called the **postal acceptance rule**.

You put in an application to a school to enroll in a training program. You receive a letter offering you a place in the program, and stating that you must accept the position in writing within four days. As long as you mail your letter of acceptance within four days, you have a contract. If, however, the letter offering you the place states that your written acceptance must be *received* by the school within four days, you have to make sure that your written acceptance is actually at the school within the four days. The school has overridden the postal acceptance rule.

If you make an offer and the other party rejects it, your offer no longer exists: the other party cannot later try to accept it. If you make an offer, the other side must accept it exactly as it is made. If the other party changes your offer in any way, in law that amounts to a rejection of your original offer and the making of a **counter-offer**. Now it's up to you to accept or reject the counter-offer.

You may think that you now understand offer and acceptance, but we must warn you that there is something lurking in the tall grass that looks like an offer but is not. This is known as an **invitation to treat**. It is not an offer, but merely a request for others to make an offer on suggested terms. You've seen many invitations to treat (although you didn't know it at the time), such as store displays and advertisements.

You go to a computer store and pick up a box of computer disks displayed under a sign saying $8.95 per box. You take the disks to the cash register to pay. You may think that you are accepting the store's offer to sell those disks to you when you hand over your $8.95. In fact, you are making an offer to the store to buy the disks at that price when you hand over your money. (As a matter of good business, the store owner is not going to reject your offer to pay $8.95, but in contract law, he could.) The display was not an offer to sell the disks to you, but was merely an invitation to treat.

You see an ad in the newspaper saying that a second-hand fax machine is for sale for $100. You immediately call up the seller and say, "I'll take it!" The seller tells you that he's changed his mind and wants to keep it. No court will say that you have a contract. The advertisement was merely an invitation to treat, and your offer to buy the fax machine was not accepted.

Legal Capacity of the Parties

For a contract to be legally binding the parties must have full **legal capacity**. A party has legal capacity if:

- he or she is a human individual who has reached the age of majority and is mentally competent, or
- it is a corporation

Legal capacity is actually a lot more complicated than this, but most of the complications will not affect you in the ordinary course of business. If you are thinking about entering into a contract with a minor or someone who is not of sound mind, you should first seek the advice of your lawyer.

Formalities

Most contracts are enforceable whether they are oral or written. Usually the only reason to have a written contract is because it provides the best evidence of your agreement. However, there are some contracts that must, by statute, meet certain **formal** requirements to be enforceable. In other words, the contracts must be in a certain form. In most provinces the following contracts must be in writing and signed by the parties:

- a guarantee
- a contract that will not be fully performed within one year from the date that it is made
- contracts involving land—sale, lease, or mortgage
- contracts for the sale of goods worth more than $40, if the goods aren't taken and the money isn't paid at the time the contract is made
- contracts for services worth more than $50, if the services aren't performed and the money isn't paid at the time the contract is made

We've left out some of the complications and details about formalities. If you'd like a rule of thumb, make sure your contract is in writing and signed by both parties. It makes good business sense to do this anyway.

Contracts in Writing

Whenever you sign a written contract (whether the law required it to be in writing or not) you are presumed in law to have read it, understood it, and to have agreed to all the terms in it—even if you have not in fact read, understood, or agreed. You are "bound" by the contract even though you may not have paid attention to all of it. However, if the contract contained terms that were especially unfavourable to you and no effort was made to bring them to your notice (by putting them in larger print or by someone actually pointing them out to you), you may not be bound by those particular unfavourable terms.

Y ou are on a business trip and are late for a very important meeting. You go to an airport car rental counter, and rent a car for $75 a day. Because you are in a hurry, you sign the rental company's standard pre-printed contract without reading it. When you return the car three days later, in addition to the $75 daily rental charge, the bill contains an extra charge of $50 each day for collision insurance. When you question this extra charge, the rental agent points out a clause in very small type in the pre-printed contract. A court would not make you pay this extra charge unless it had been pointed out to you by the rental company at the time you signed the contract.

Even lawyers don't read and understand every word of every contract they sign. But they know that that's no defence if the other party sues to enforce the contract. Get into the habit of looking over contracts before you sign them, and don't feel you have to sign if you don't like the look of the small print.

Failure to Create an Enforceable Contract

You can have consideration, you can have offer and acceptance, you can have parties with legal capacity, and you can meet all the formalities, and you may still not have an enforceable contract. This will happen if there has been:

• misrepresentation

• duress or undue influence

• unconscionability

If there has been **misrepresentation** by a party during the contract negotiations, the contract can be set aside by the court. Misrepresentation is a false statement by one party about an important fact related to the contract. The other party must have relied on that statement in deciding to enter into the contract. Similarly, a contract can be set aside for **duress** if one party enters the contract because of violence or threats of violence or of criminal prosecution made by the other party. A contract can also be set aside for **undue influence**, which arises out of a relationship between the parties in which one is very dominant over the other. For example, a court will presume that there was undue influence if a lawyer persuades a client to enter into a contract that is outside the sphere of their ordinary solicitor-client relationship and if the client later wants out of the contract. The court would set aside the contract unless the lawyer could show that she had taken no advantage of the client. A court may also be willing to set aside a contract that is **unconscionable** (extremely unfair to one party).

HOW CONTRACTS ARE PERFORMED

Once there is a contract the parties have to **perform** it by doing what they promised to do. When each party has done what was promised the contract is said to be **discharged**, and is then successfully finished. A contract is also discharged if a party substantially performs what was promised. **Substantial performance** means performance that is reasonably complete although not exactly what was promised. For example, a restaurant that offers a *prix fixe* dinner performs fully if the waiter serves a diner the advertised soup, main course, dessert, and coffee, and it still performs substantially if the waiter happens to forget the coffee, or brings tea instead. The vast majority of contracts are successfully discharged by performance by the parties.

You are responsible for performing any promise you make under a contract. If you promised to provide goods or services, *you* are responsible for providing them. If you promised to pay money, *you* are responsible for paying it. If you get someone else to perform your contractual obligations for you, you still remain responsible for the performance of those obligations.

You have a contract to deliver flowers to a hotel, but you have too many orders to fill so you give the order to a friend who is also in the flower business. If your friend delivers dead flowers, *you* are responsible to the hotel, not your friend.

There are certain kinds of obligations that you cannot have performed by someone else without the consent of the other party to the contract. These obligations are ones that involve your own personal skill or knowledge.

You are an interior decorator, and enter into a contract to decorate a client's living room. You yourself must choose the colour scheme and materials. You can't get someone else to do the work for you without the client's permission.

Sometimes after a contract has been made, the parties decide that they want to change their agreement. In order to do so they must **amend** the contract by going through the same process of consideration and offer and acceptance that they went through to make the original contract. In other words, an amendment to a contract is a new contract in itself. You can even amend a contract to end it without either party having to perform.

Call Your Lawyer

Even the most carefully thought out and expertly negotiated contract can run into trouble in the performance stage. You should contact your lawyer if:

- you have any question about exactly what you have to do to perform your part of the contract.

- you have any question about exactly what the other party has to do to perform.

- you want to make any changes to the contract before or during performance, to ensure that any changes are validly made and properly drafted.

BREACH OF CONTRACT

It is a **breach of contract** if a party does not at least substantially perform his obligations under the contract. The big question for a business person is whether you still have to perform your contractual obligations after the other party has breached the contract. The short answer is sometimes yes and sometimes no. The long answer is more involved and we will try to explain some of it to you. But first back to the short answer. If you are ever in a situation where the other party breaches its contract with you, contact your lawyer right away.

If the other party breached a very important term of the contract (called a **condition** in contract law) then you probably no longer have to perform your obligations. If the other party breached a less important term of the contract (called a **warranty** in contract law) then you probably still have to perform your obligations.

You make a contract with a local company to deliver five tons of gravel to your premises on Friday, June 21st. The company delivers the five tons of gravel on Saturday, June 22nd. Unless the contract stated that delivery on the 21st was essential, you must accept delivery of the gravel and pay for it. On the other hand, if the company delivers five tons of top soil on Friday, June 21st, you do not have to accept delivery or pay for it.

Whether a term is a condition or a warranty is a legal question as much as a business one, which is why you should get legal advice about whether you must perform your contractual obligations. Another reason you need legal advice is this: if a breach is serious enough to end your obligations to perform your part of the contract, it is important for you to take the proper steps to preserve all of your rights under the contract. You should also contact your lawyer if the other party to a contract tells you in advance that she will not perform.

If a party to a contract is unable to perform for reasons totally beyond his control, the contract is said to be **frustrated**. In the event of frustration, special rules apply. In general, neither party has to perform the contract, and neither party can force the other to perform. However, if a party to a contract has made it impossible for himself to perform obligations under the contract, that is a breach of contract, not frustration.

Y**ou make a contract on May 10 with a small delivery company to deliver a shipment of your birdseed to a local pet store on May 12. On May 11, a tornado picks up the company's only truck and dumps it somewhat later in Kansas, smashed beyond recognition. The delivery company tells you that it is now unable to perform its contract. This contract is frustrated, and you cannot insist on performance or successfully sue the delivery company. If, on the other hand, on May 11 the delivery company sells its truck, and tells you that it is now unable to perform its contract, the contract is not frustrated; it has been breached, and you *can* sue successfully.**

RIGHTING CONTRACT WRONGS

If you end up in a major contract dispute, you may be sued by the other party or you may want to sue. If you are involved in a lawsuit for any significant sum of money, you should have a lawyer represent you. If a lawsuit over a contract is not settled and it goes to court, the judge will interpret the contract, decide who was at fault, determine the losses of the party not at fault, and grant a remedy. There are a number of remedies available to help the innocent party if the other party breaches the contract, and the one(s) you ask for will depend on the circumstances of your case. The remedies include:

- rescission (in Quebec, annulment)
- damages
- specific performance
- injunction

The most common remedy in contract situations is damages.

Rescission

As we told you earlier, if you enter into a contract because of misrepresentation, duress, undue influence, or if the contract is unconscionable, you can get out of it. To do so, you have to start a court action for **rescission**. If you win the lawsuit, the court will set aside (rescind) the contract. When a contract is rescinded the court tries to put the parties into the position they would have been in if the contract had never been made. If that is impossible to do, the contract cannot be rescinded. (You may be able to get an alternative remedy such as damages, though.)

Y ou are a swimsuit manufacturer who enters into a contract to buy certain fabric because the seller represented that it is colour fast. In fact the fabric is not colour fast, and the seller knew it. After taking delivery, you test a small piece of the fabric, and discover that the colour bleeds. This contract can be rescinded, the fabric returned to the seller, and any money paid for it returned to you. However, if you do not discover that the fabric bleeds until after the swimsuits have been made, the contract cannot be rescinded. Although the money can be returned, the fabric cannot. You'll have to ask for damages instead of rescission.

Damages

If the other party breaches the contract, you can sue for **damages**. If you win the lawsuit, the court will order the other party to pay you money to compensate you for the losses you suffer because of the breach. The amount you receive in damages is supposed to put you in the position you would have been in if the contract had been properly performed.

Y ou own a cookie business. A customer orders 1000 dozen macadamia nut cookies. Your expected profit on this order is $3000. You
order the macadamia nuts at a cost of $250. When the macadamia
nuts arrive, you can't use them because they are rotten, and it is too late
for you to get more in time to fill the order. The customer goes elsewhere.
You can sue the nut supplier for the $3000 profit that you have lost.

When the other side has breached the contract, you are required
to **mitigate your damages**, which means that you have to take all
reasonable steps to keep your losses to a minimum. If you don't
try to mitigate your damages, the court will act as if you had, by
giving you only the amount of damages you would have received
if you had made a successful effort to reduce your losses.

I n the example above, if you are able to find another source of
macadamia nuts for $500 and still fill the customer's order in time, you
must do so. Afterwards you can sue the original supplier for the extra
cost of the nuts—$250. You cannot just sit back and lose the order and
then expect the supplier to pay the entire amount of your lost profit.

Sometimes a contract specifies exactly what you will have to
pay in damages if you breach the contract. It may be that you
will lose a deposit, or you may have to make all the remaining
payments under the contract. Sometimes a court will award
damages in this specified amount if it feels the amount is a gen-
uine pre-estimate of the losses that will actually be suffered. But
if a court feels that the amount is much higher than the proba-
ble damages, and that the amount is calculated to frighten you
into performing the contract, it will call this contract provision a
penalty clause, and will refuse to enforce it. While the court may
still order damages paid, the amount will reflect the real loss.

Specific Performance and Injunction

If the court thinks that damages will not sufficiently compensate
you for your loss, it has other options as well. If the other party

has refused to go through with the contract at all, the court may order **specific performance** and force the other side to perform the contract. Specific performance will only be ordered if the subject matter of the contract is unique. A court would not order specific performance of a contract to sell you a car off the assembly line because it is not unique, but would probably order specific performance of a contract to sell you an original oil painting, because it *is* unique. The law also usually considers every piece of real estate to be unique. A court will not order specific performance of a contract for personal services. If you enter into a contract with a singer to give a concert in your theatre and he decides to perform in another theatre instead, no court will order the singer to appear in your theatre.

If the other party has refused to perform a particular part of the contract with you, or is doing something that is a breach of the contract, the court may grant you an **injunction** and require the other party either to do something or to stop doing something. In the example of the singer above, the court has the power to grant an injunction preventing the singer from performing in another theatre on the date he was supposed to perform in your theatre.

DOING BUSINESS IN MORE THAN ONE PLACE

Many businesses in Canada have a home base in one province but do business in other provinces or in other countries. The law of contract is similar but not exactly the same in every province, and it is not necessarily similar at all in other countries. If a business in a certain province enters into a contract with a customer in the same province and a dispute arises, the law of that province applies and the parties sue each other in the courts of that province. But what happens if the business is in one province and the customer in another province—or another country? Where do you go to court? And which law applies, that of the business's province or that of the customer's province (or country)? These questions are addressed in a legal field known as **conflict of laws**. Here are some general principles that apply to contracts that cross provincial or national borders.

- The parties to a contract can state in the contract which law applies and where a lawsuit can be started. The law chosen does not have to be the law of the place where the lawsuit can be started.
- If the parties did not state in the contract which law applies:
  - if the subject matter of the contract is real property (land and buildings), the law of the place where the real property is located applies
  - if the subject matter is not real property, the law that has the closest connection with the contract applies. To determie which law this is, a court will look at where the contract was made, wherewas to be performed, and where the parties are resident, among other things.
- If the parties did not state in the contract where a lawsuit can be started, it can be started where either party resides. However, the court where one party resides may refuse to hear the case if it thinks there is not a close enough connection between the dispute and the province, state, or country the court is located in.

If you are doing business outside your province, consult your lawyer to find out whether a clause should be added to the contract specifying where and under what law the parties can sue each other.

CONCLUSION

What you have just read is a brief and simplified (although by no means simple) summary of the law of contracts. In law school a student spends a full semester studying basic contract law—so it's OK to be confused by some of this. We'll return to contracts in Chapter 13 (when you get there, it will do nothing to change your mind about 13 being an unlucky number), where we'll talk much more specifically about contracts to buy and sell goods and services.

CHOOSING A FORM OF BUSINESS ORGANIZATION

There are three main forms of business organization in Canada: sole proprietorship, partnership, and corporation. A sole proprietorship involves only one person; partnership involves two or more; and a corporation may involve only one person or a cast of thousands. (Whichever form you choose, you can hire employees. Taking on employees does not affect the form of business organization.) The kind of organization you choose for your business will depend on a number of things: how much you want to spend on setting up and running it, how rigidly structured you want your organization to be, and whether you want your business to be legally separate from you as an individual. You can change the form of your business organization to meet your changing needs.

Books about setting up a business usually talk about which form of business organization you should choose, but in fact the form of business organization is just as likely to choose you. If you, all by yourself, start doing business, your business is *automatically* a sole proprietorship, and you are a sole proprietor. If you and at least one other person start carrying on business activities together with the intention of making a profit, your business is *automatically* a partnership and each of you is a partner. Sole proprietors and partners don't have a legal identity separate from their business. If you want your business to have a separate legal identity, you must carry on your business as a corporation, and that *doesn't* happen automatically. You must take certain steps to create a corporation.

For the most part, the choice of business organization is yours. However, in some provinces certain kinds of businesses can only be a sole proprietorship or a partnership and cannot be a corporation. These are usually the practices of professionals such as doctors, lawyers, dentists, accountants, and so on. In fact, most partnerships in Canada are professional partnerships. Certain other kinds of businesses may need government approval before being allowed to incorporate. These include a real estate brokerage, an insurance agency, or a money lending business.

In order to make an intelligent choice about the form you want your business to take, you need to understand the legal consequences of forming a sole proprietorship, partnership, or corporation.

SOLE PROPRIETORSHIP

Because it happens automatically, sole proprietorship is an easy and inexpensive form of business to set up. The only formal requirement might be provincial registration of your business name.

If you carry on business as a sole proprietorship, there is no distinction in law between you and your business:

- the assets of the business are your personal assets
- the liabilities and losses of the business are your personal liabilities and losses, so that you can be forced to pay your business debts out of your personal, non-business assets
- the income of the business is taxed as part of your personal income, at your personal taxation rate (so if the business's income exceeds about $59,000, it, through you, is taxed at the highest personal rate)

The advantage of a sole proprietorship, besides simplicity and low cost, is that if the business is losing money, you can deduct its losses from your other income. If your income, including that from your business, is small, the tax you pay on your business income will be low.

The disadvantages of a sole proprietorship come into play if your business does really well or really badly. If your taxable income, including your business income, is higher than about $59,000 you will pay tax on the income over $59,000 at the highest personal rate. If the business flops, you can be forced to pay its debts out of your personal assets. That's why sole proprietors (and partners) sometimes put their personal assets such as real property and cars into a spouse's name. The business's creditors then can't reach any of the assets, but the sole proprietor may not be able to reach the assets either if love, loyalty, and spouse fly out the door.

PARTNERSHIP

Partnership can also be an easy and inexpensive form of business to set up. In some respects a partnership is very much like a sole proprietorship:

- your share of the partnership assets is included among your personal assets
- partnership liabilities are personal liabilities of the individual partners
- your share of the partnership income is taxed as part of your personal income

Partnerships, also called **firms**, are subject to specific legislation in each province. If you start carrying on business with another person with the intention of making a profit, you will automatically be considered partners under provincial law. So you don't *have* to go to any expense or trouble to create your partnership, although you may have to register your business name.

Provincial Laws on Partnership

The partnership legislation of your province states what the terms of your partnership are. These include the following rules:

- all partners have an equal say in management
- all partners are entitled to an equal share of partnership income
- all partners are entitled to an equal share of partnership assets
- partners may not compete with the partnership
- all partners have an equal share in the liabilities and debts of the partnership (even after leaving the firm, if the debts were incurred while a person was a partner)
- the partnership must repay any partner who makes a payment or incurs a debt or liability on behalf of the partnership in the usual course of business
- the partnership automatically dissolves if just one partner dies, goes bankrupt, or withdraws from the partnership
- a new partner can only be admitted to the partnership with the consent of all of the existing partners
- each individual partner is liable for any wrongful act or omission of any other partner in the course of business
- if any partner makes a contract with a third party in the usual course of business, all of the members of the partnership are responsible for that contract; and if the partnership has a debt, any of the partners can be required to pay it

If the provincial law of partnership does not reflect the way you want your partnership to work, you can enter into a partnership agreement with your partner(s) to change the rules that apply. However, a partnership agreement cannot be used to override the last two rules, which involve the liability of the partners and the partnership to third parties. For more information about partnership agreements see p. 56 in Chapter 5.

The law of partnership is a bit different in Quebec, where there are two forms of partnership: general (declared) and undeclared. A general partnership is created by filing a declaration of partnership with the government. The laws relating to a general partnership are similar to those described above, but a general partnership does not dissolve if a partner goes bankrupt or dies. The laws relating to an undeclared partnership are also similar to those described above. The main difference is that the property each partner brings into the business does not necessarily become partnership property, and a partner is not necessarily responsible for the contracts and liabilities of the other partners.

The advantages of a partnership are similar to those of a sole proprietorship. It is easy and inexpensive to set up, a set of rules for running it already exists, and business losses of the partnership can generally be deducted from your other income. If your combined income from the partnership and other sources is small, your tax rate will be low.

The disadvantages of a partnership are also similar to those of a sole proprietorship. If your taxable income, including that from your partnership, is higher than about $59,000, you will pay tax on the income over $59,000 at the highest personal rate. If business stinks, you can be forced to pay partnership debts out of your personal assets.

Limited Partnership

A limited partnership is for the most part like any other partnership, but it has one characteristic of a corporation—limited liability of *some* partners.

In a limited partnership there are "general" partners (who are exactly like the partners in an ordinary partnership) and "limited" partners. The limited partners contribute money but do not participate in management. Unlike the general partners, who are fully liable (to the extent of all of their personal assets) to third parties for partnership debts and liabilities, the limited partners' liability is limited to the amount of their investment in the partnership.

Limited partnerships are used most commonly for tax shelters. They can give the limited partners the tax benefit of loss deduction that is associated with an ordinary partnership, together with the protection against liability that a corporation provides for a shareholder.

Management Companies

Even if you have to carry on your actual business as a partnership (or as a sole proprietorship), you can incorporate a company to:

- own or lease the office equipment that the firm uses
- employ support staff
- enter into the lease for the firm's office
- provide the equipment, staff, or premises to the firm for a fee

Often the spouses of the partners are the shareholders, directors, and officers of the management company. In the past these companies have been used to try to reduce the tax the partners have to pay. They may be useful to limit the partners' liability on the leases for premises and equipment. They may also make it easier for new partners to be admitted to the partnership because the new partners will not have to buy a share of extensive partnership assets. The tax laws that deal with management companies are complex. Get an accountant's advice before setting up a management company, to find out if it will be worth the trouble and expense.

CORPORATION

A corporation is a legal being with an identity separate from that of the individuals who create it by the process of incorporation, own it through shares, and run it as directors and officers. Because it has no physical existence, it must act through humans. It cannot "die" in the sense that human beings die, because it has "perpetual existence." Even though it is not human, a corporation has many of the legal powers, rights, and duties of Canadian residents.

A corporation is created by preparing and filing articles of incorporation (or in certain provinces a memorandum of association, or an application for letters patent), paying a fee, and receiving government approval. The government fees for incorporation are a few hundred dollars, and to this you may have to add lawyers' fees. A corporation can be created either provincially (or territorially) or federally. Incorporate provincially if you intend to do all of your business in one province, federally if you intend to do business in more than one province or outside Canada.

The owners of a corporation are shareholders, and they buy into the corporation by providing money, goods, or services to the corporation in exchange for shares. The money and goods become assets of the corporation and are used to carry on the business. The shareholders do not own the assets of the corporation and are generally not responsible for any of its debts or liabilities. If the corporation runs into serious trouble, the shares may lose their value, and the shareholders' investment may disappear, but that is pretty much the extent of the shareholders' risk. Creditors of the corporation cannot normally look to the shareholders to pay off corporate debts or liabilities.

Corporations can be public or private. A public (or "offering") corporation can issue its shares to the general public. A public share offering is a major and very expensive undertaking and is subject to a great deal of scrutiny from the provincial securities commission. The great majority of corporations in Canada are private (or "non-offering") corporations and their ability to sell their shares to the general public is severely restricted. Their shareholders are also restricted in their right to resell shares either publicly or privately.

ADVANTAGES OF INCORPORATION

The traditional reasons for choosing to incorporate a business are:

- limited liability
- ease of raising capital
- ease of transferring an interest in the business
- tax advantages

While these reasons look good on paper, not all of them have much meaning in real life.

Limited Liability

By incorporating, entrepreneurs hope to limit their personal liability in the event that the business runs into trouble, but they may not be able to do so. In practice, most corporations are very closely identified with the people who created them and run them—its shareholders, directors, officers, and employees. If a corporation without big assets borrows money, most lenders will demand a **personal guarantee** from the individuals behind the corporation; then, if the corporation can't repay the loan, the guarantors must. If the corporation buys materials on credit, the corporation's suppliers may also want a personal guarantee.

In many corporations, the shareholders will probably also be its directors and officers. The directors and officers of a corporation are not completely protected from liability for debts and acts of the corporation. For example, directors may be liable for unpaid wages of employees if the corporation becomes insolvent. They can also be held responsible for the corporation's breaches of tax statutes and other legislation.

An entrepreneur was a director, officer, and shareholder of a corporation that was set up to run a pub. The entrepreneur's involvement with the business was limited to getting the initial liquor licence and giving some advice about management, and he was not involved in the corporation's day-to-day operations, which were handled exclusively by the other major shareholder. He and the other shareholder fell out, and he had nothing further to do with the corporation. More than a year passed, and he received a notice of assessment from Revenue Canada saying that as a director he was required to pay employees' source deductions since they had not been remitted by the corporation. He appealed the assessment, arguing that he was not in fact a director because he had no influence over the affairs of the corporation. He also argued that he had had no way of knowing that source deductions had not been remitted since he was not kept informed of the corporation's affairs. He was held liable to pay the assessment because he was a director both in law and in fact. He had never tried to resign, had never been relieved of his duties as a director, and had never disposed of his shares in the corporation. He had not stopped being a director simply because he no influence over the affairs of the corporation or because he had no knowledge of what was going on in the corporation.

Raising Capital

While publicly traded companies, if attractive to investors, may be able to raise large amounts of capital by selling shares to the general public, that is not true for a private corporation. A private corporation is going to have to raise money by borrowing, and a private corporation with modest assets is not going to have an easier time of it than a sole proprietorship or a partnership with similar assets. A lender is going to scrutinize the people behind the corporation and will likely demand personal guarantees from them.

Ease of Transferring Interest

In fact it is not very easy to transfer an interest in a private corporation by transferring shares. If a business wishes to remain classified as a private corporation, most provinces require tight restrictions on transfer of its shares. Normally, the consent of the majority of the shareholders or directors is required. Quite apart from that, there is an extremely limited market for anything less than 100 per cent of the shares of most private corporations.

Tax Advantages

This is an area where some of the perceived advantages of incorporation can be real. Incorporating your business does not give you or your business automatic protection from taxes, although there may be some advantages. The taxes an incorporated business pays can be lower than those an unincorporated business pays. However, there's more to consider than that, because a corporation can't pay taxes for employees on salary or benefits received, or for shareholders on dividends taken.

Corporate and Personal Income Tax Rates

All taxpayers, whether individuals or corporations, pay income taxes to both the federal and provincial governments. Corporations are taxed on their profits at a flat rate. Compare that with the way an individual is taxed. The combined rate of federal and provincial tax a person pays goes up in steps as the person's taxable income goes up. The lowest combined personal tax rate is zero if a person's taxable income is less than about $6,500, and the highest combined personal tax rate is over 50 per cent on income in excess of approximately $59,000.

The actual combined provincial and federal flat tax rate for a corporation will depend on a number of factors:

• the province in which the corporation does business

• the kind of business the corporation carries on

• whether the business qualifies for the Small Business Deduction as a Canadian Controlled Private Corporation

The highest flat rate of combined corporate tax is about 45 per cent. However, there is a federal Small Business Deduction that reduces the flat tax rate for a Canadian Controlled Private Corporation to between approximately 18 and 23 per cent, depending on the province. This tax rate deduction applies to the first $200,000 of taxable income. As a business grows, however, the tax advantages decline. If the taxable income of the corporation is over $200,000, the combined tax rate goes back up to the mid-40 per cent range for the income in excess of $200,000. Corporations in a manufacturing business still get a tax break to keep them in the 30 to 40 per cent tax range.

A corporation can pay salary out of its income to its directors, officers, and employees. If you are paid a salary by your corporation, you will be taxed on your salary at your personal rate, and the corporation will be taxed on any remaining profits at the corporate rate. If you want to take some or all of the profits out, you can do so by having the corporation pay dividends to you as a shareholder. Dividends are taxed in your hands at your personal tax rate but only to a maximum rate of about 35 per cent. The rate is lower because the profit has already been taxed once in the hands of the corporation before the dividend is paid.

Timing

If your business is incorporated, you can control when you receive income for tax purposes by:

- choosing the date of the corporation's year end
- deciding when to pay yourself an employee bonus
- deciding when to declare a dividend for shareholders

Tax Planning: To Incorporate or Not to Incorporate?

To decide whether incorporating your business will reduce your taxes, you must calculate what you would pay in taxes if all of the profits were taxed in your hands (as they would be if you were a sole proprietor or partner). Then you must calculate what *you* would pay in taxes on your salary and on any dividends plus what *the corporation* would pay on its profits. Compare the two to see which results in a lower overall tax payment. In the first few years of business, if your business is making little profit, you may pay less tax as a sole proprietor or partner than you would if your business were incorporated. If your business operates at a loss (as it may in the early stages) you won't pay taxes whatever the business organization. But if the business is a corporation you will not be able to deduct any of the business's losses from any other income that you may have. The tax laws are written so that, in theory, whether you're incorporated or not there shouldn't be a significant difference in the overall taxes paid. However, in practice, there may well be a difference, especially if the business's taxable income is either very low or over $200,000.

If you have a corporation that is really just you providing services to a third party, and you would be regarded as the third party's employee if it weren't for the corporation, you won't gain any tax advantage by incorporating because the *Income Tax Act* won't allow such a **personal services corporation** to benefit from the Small Business Deduction in order to reduce your personal taxes. Get professional advice before incorporating if you think that your corporation may turn out to be a personal services corporation.

Tax planning for your business is crucial, and should be done in consultation with your accountant and/or tax lawyer. They will do the calculations and let you know whether it makes sense from a tax point of view to incorporate at any given stage of your business.

Other Advantages of Incorporation

There are advantages to incorporation besides the four perceived ones discussed above. They include:

- meeting the expectations of your clients or customers—an incorporated business may appear more impressive.

- avoiding responsibility for the acts or omissions of your associates in the business—the owners (shareholders) of a corporation are not responsible for each others' acts the way partners are.

- profit sharing with employees—shares can be given to employees in lieu of higher salaries or bonuses. Employees who own shares in the company may have a greater interest in seeing that the business prospers, and these shares can be designed to give them an ownership interest without a management say.

- estate planning—you may be able to use a corporation to pass assets to family members in a way that allows you to maintain control over the assets in your lifetime while minimizing taxable capital gains on your death (see p. 323 in Chapter 23). This kind of estate planning requires expert legal and accounting advice.

DISADVANTAGES OF INCORPORATION

As we showed above, there can be tax disadvantages to incorporation. There are other disadvantages as well:

- It can be expensive to set up and run a corporation. It costs a few hundred dollars in government fees alone to incorporate, and to that you have to add lawyers' fees. Corporations are required to make various filings with the government, to maintain corporate records, and they may have to have their financial statements audited annually. A corporation that does not meet such obligations can be **dissolved** or cancelled by the government.

- There are residency requirements for directors. Federally, and in Alberta, British Columbia, Manitoba, Ontario and Saskatchewan, a majority of the directors of the corporation must be resident Canadian citizens or landed immigrants (but only landed immigrants who have not waited for more than one year to apply for citizenship after becoming eligible for citizenship). In Alberta, British Columbia and Saskatchewan, at least one director must be resident in the province. This can be a problem if a majority of the people who run your business are not Canadian or if all of them live out of the province.

JOINT VENTURE

Different people use the expression **joint venture** to mean different things. Some people use it to mean a partnership; others use it to mean a business association of two or more people that is *not* a partnership. It can also refer to any pooling of resources for a commercial arrangement or project, in which case it could be simple co-ownership of property, or a partnership, or a limited partnership, or a corporation. Now that you've made it almost to the end of this chapter, you know that there are important differences among the forms of business organization. So before you suggest a joint venture to someone, or agree to one, make sure you understand exactly what the expression is supposed to mean.

SO HOW DO YOU DECIDE?

Before choosing a form of business organization, examine the advantages and disadvantages of each as they relate to your particular business. Don't incorporate a business just because that's what everybody seems to do. Don't become a sole proprietorship or partnership just by default. Get advice from a lawyer and an accountant. Make an educated choice and then take the appropriate steps to make sure that your business, whatever its form, is properly set up.

CHAPTER FIVE

GETTING YOUR BUSINESS UP AND RUNNING

The form of business organization you have chosen will dictate what you must do to get your business going, as well as the amount of work and expense involved.

SETTING UP AND RUNNING A SOLE PROPRIETORSHIP

Because this is such a simple form of business, you don't have to do very much. The only real requirement in most provinces is that you may have to register your business name with the provincial government. Registration of a business name is not intended to protect your right to use the name but rather to let creditors know whom to sue (since they have to sue the person behind the business, not the business).

Once your business is running, it is important to keep track of your business income and expenses, separately from your personal income and expenses. When you file your annual personal income tax return, you will have to provide a separate statement of the income and expenses of your business. Any profit shown on that statement is part of your personal income, and any business loss can be deducted from other income.

SETTING UP AND RUNNING A PARTNERSHIP

You don't *have* to do very much to form a partnership either. In most provinces, you may have to register the partnership's business name with the provincial government.

> **T**
> **I**
> **P**
>
> We recommend that you and your partners have a partnership agreement. For the majority of businesses, the terms of the partnership that are created by the provincial legislation are not adequate (see p. 44 in Chapter 4). Some of the matters that you and your partner(s) should think about and that your partnership agreement should cover are discussed in the section below.
>
> T I P

Partnership Agreements

If you want to change the terms that provincial law imposes on your partnership, you and your partner(s) will need a partnership agreement to set your own terms. In the agreement you may wish to:

- have partners divide the profits unequally, for example a 25-75 split instead of a 50-50 split between two partners. Some partnerships have very complicated formulas to divide profits. These may take into account factors such as money generated by each individual partner, the number of clients or customers the partner finds, or promotional or other outside work the partner does for the benefit of the partnership.

- allow the partners to draw an advance against their share of the profits (take a "draw"), sort of like taking a salary

- allow the partners to divide the assets unequally, because different partners may have contributed assets of different value to the partnership

- divide responsibility for debts unequally. Such an agreement would only affect accounting between the partners, and not the responsibility of each individual partner to pay debts owed to third parties. A partner cannot change that responsibility, but would be entitled to reimbursement from the other partner(s) for paying partnership debts.

- give some partners a greater right than others to make management decisions or to decide to admit new partners

- provide for partners' meetings and a method for dealing with management deadlocks

- have the partnership continue even if one partner dies, retires, or goes bankrupt

- set up a method to buy back the interest of a partner who leaves or dies

- provide a method for expelling a partner

- give each partner the right to force the other(s) either to sell their interest to her or else buy her out (a buy-sell clause)

Two entrepreneurs, both accountants, had known each other socially for a number of years before they agreed to set up a partnership. They discussed the terms of their partnership and were under the impression they were in complete agreement—but they never got around to putting their partnership agreement into writing. At the end of their first year of partnership, they found out that there was a serious misunderstanding between them about how profits were to be shared. They had originally agreed that the first partner was entitled to a full 50 per cent of the profits if she generated "$100,000 in billings net of bad debts." It now turned out that the first partner had thought that meant "if she billed $100,000 without taking bad debts into account," while the second partner had thought that meant "if she billed $100,000 after deducting bad debts." Although they eventually reached a financial settlement about that year's profits, their fight over this matter ended the partnership. Chances are, they would still be together and generating great billings if they'd taken that extra step and put their agreement in writing. If they'd had to define the terms of their partnership in writing, they probably would have realized then that they hadn't actually come to an agreement about profit-sharing.

Going beyond this, partnership legislation does not address a number of important matters that the partners should agree on. You may want your partnership agreement to deal with:

- the nature of the business
- the firm name
- the financial contribution of each partner
- a definition of what will constitute partnership income
- the division of labour among partners
- bank accounts
- accounting and tax matters
- insuring assets
- insuring the partners (life and disability)
- the disability of a partner
- use of partnership property by individual partners
- methods to resolve disputes among partners

If you're going to the trouble of making a partnership agreement, it should probably deal (at a minimum) with all of the issues discussed above. The agreement should be prepared by a lawyer. If the partnership has chosen a lawyer for the new business, it's a good idea for you to have the agreement reviewed by your own lawyer before you sign it to make sure that the agreement is fair to you. If the partnership lawyer is the only corporate-commercial lawyer you know, he can direct each of the partners to other lawyers for this independent legal advice.

> **T**
> **I**
> **P**
> f you can't afford a lawyer, it is probably better not to try to draft a partnership agreement at all. It would be safer to live with the statutory terms for your partnership than to risk the confusion that might result from a poorly drafted agreement.
>
> T I P

Financial Matters

You must keep track of the business income and expenses of the partnership. At the end of each year, a financial statement for the partnership must be prepared to show income and expenses, and division of the net income or loss among the individual partners in accordance with the partnership legislation or partnership agreement. The partnership does not file a separate income tax return (although partnerships of six or more must file a partnership information return). Instead, the partners include their own shares of the net partnership income on their individual tax returns, and each partner must attach a statement of income and expenses for the partnership. A partner's share of any partnership loss can be deducted from that partner's other income.

Partnership Meetings

There should be regular communication among the partners. Even if you have a very small partnership it is probably a good idea to schedule regular partners' meetings to discuss matters of importance to the partnership such as:

• matters of new clients or customers

• strategies for finding new clients or customers

• what the competition is up to

• actual and anticipated income

• actual and anticipated expenses

• distribution of work among the partners

• office management

SETTING UP A CORPORATION

A corporation is much more complicated and expensive to set up than either a sole proprietorship or a partnership. You may incorporate your business federally or in any of the provinces or territories. You will have to file incorporating documents and pay fees to the government.

The information that actually goes into the incorporating documents is relatively simple. The forms are readily available, and almost anybody can fill them out, but there are implications to the choices you make in doing so. Only someone with a full understanding of the underlying legal issues will know the implications.

You may be able to acquire that level of understanding, but if you can't, you would be very wise to use the services of a lawyer when you incorporate your business. Once you make a choice in your incorporating document (such as the number of directors, or restrictions on transfer of shares), it can be difficult to change things later because all the shareholders will have to be consulted and at least a majority of them will have to agree to the change. Keep in mind that no government official is going to check your documents over to make sure that you've set things up right. If you make mistakes, they're your problem.

INCORPORATION DOCUMENTS

Incorporating documents vary somewhat, but generally they address the following matters:

- name of the corporation
- address of the registered office of the corporation
- the shares of the corporation
- the director(s) of the corporation
- the business the corporation may carry on
- the powers of the corporation
- the name(s) of the incorporator(s)

What follows is a brief discussion of the information required in an incorporating document and of some of the underlying legal and practical issues.

Name of the Corporation

A corporation is automatically assigned a number when it is incorporated, and this number can also be the "name" of the corporation (which is then known as a **numbered company**). If you want a real name for your company, one consisting of words instead of numbers, you have to follow certain rules in choosing the name. The rules about corporate names are somewhat different under the various statutes for Canada and the provinces and territories, so find out the rules that apply to you before you start thinking up a name. In the meantime, here is a general guide about some of the common rules.

The name cannot be confusingly similar to that of an existing corporation or business in the jurisdiction (provincial, territorial, or federal) where you are incorporating, especially to one that carries on similar activities. In order to make sure that the name you have chosen is sufficiently different, you will have to pay to have a NUANS (New Updated Automatic Name Search) search done of the name. (In Quebec, the search is called CIDREQ rather than NUANS.) This is a computer search of previously registered corporate and business names. It can be very difficult to find a corporate name that is not similar to the name of an existing corporation or business, and if you can't, the government will not allow the incorporation to go through in the name you have chosen. You'll have to search for another name. Or you can just have a numbered company. Then once the business is incorporated, you can carry on business under the name you want. You will have to register that business name with the province.

Other rules include: the name cannot be obscene; it cannot contain words to suggest any connection with the government, words like "royal," "crown," "federal," "provincial," or "municipal," unless you have government permission; it can't contain words like "university," "bank," and "stock exchange" unless it actually is a university, bank, or stock exchange that has been properly set up under the applicable legislation; and it can't be misleading about the corporation's business or connections. The corporation's name cannot include the name of a specific person unless that person is involved in the business or has agreed in writing to the use of his or her name or has been dead for more than 30 years (if the person has been dead for less than 30 years the consent of the estate is needed).

There is something that the corporation's name *must* include, and that is a word that indicates that the business is a corporation. You can choose any one of: Limited, Ltd., Incorporated, Inc., Corporation, Corp. (in Quebec, Limitée or Ltée.).

Address of the Corporation

A provincially incorporated business must have a registered office within the province of incorporation, and a federally incorporated business must have a registered office within Canada, but the address of the registered office does not have to be the place where business is actually carried on. Many businesses use their lawyer's address as the corporation's address, because they want government correspondence to go directly to their lawyer. This is especially true of businesses that have their lawyer do their corporate record keeping.

Shares of the Corporation

The shareholders, as you recall, own the corporation by holding shares in it. At the time of incorporation you should consider:

- how many classes of shares the corporation will have and the rights and conditions that will attach to each class
- what restrictions there should be on the right of shareholders to transfer their shares
- the maximum number of shares there should be in each class and how many shares of each class the corporation should issue

Classes of Shares

There are two kinds of shares. **Common shares** normally give a shareholder a right to vote at shareholders' meetings, in particular to elect the directors. They also give the shareholder the right to receive a share of the corporation's property if the corporation closes down. Common shares may also entitle a shareholder to receive a portion of the corporation's profits in the form of dividends. **Preferred shares** (also called "preference" or "special" shares, or "pref" shares if you're cool) have special conditions attached to them. Preferred shareholders may or may not be given the right to vote at shareholders' meetings, but have the right to receive dividends before common shareholders do. If you decide to have only one kind of shares, they are all automatically common shares, and they all carry the same and equal rights.

If you don't want all of the shareholders' to have the same rights to vote or the same rights to receive dividends, then you want more than one **class** of shares. (For example, you might create three classes: common, preference "A", and preference "B.") You must define the rights that attach to the different classes of shares. By doing so you can give a particular class of shareholders:

- the right to elect directors, and therefore to control the corporation
- the exclusive right to receive dividends, or the right to receive them before other classes of shareholders do
- the exclusive right to receive a share in the assets of the corporation if it closes down
- the right to demand that the corporation buy back (**redeem**) their shares, or the obligation to sell back their shares to the corporation on demand
- the right to convert their shares into shares of another class

Restrictions on the Right to Transfer Shares

Most entrepreneurs will want to set restrictions on the transfer of shares by the shareholders in the corporation. There are a number of reasons for this. First of all, you want control over who has an interest in your corporation. You don't want a fellow shareholder to sell her shares to a third party without your consent. Secondly, you need to set restrictions on the transfer of shares if you want to qualify as a Canadian Controlled Private Corporation (CCPC). Only a CCPC qualifies for the Small Business Deduction for income tax that we discussed in Chapter 4. In addition, restrictions on transfer may be necessary to keep your corporation private (non-offering) and to prevent the provincial securities commission from taking an interest in the sale of shares of your corporation.

Maximum Number of Shares

You must decide if you want to set a maximum number of shares that the corporation can issue, or if the number is to be unlimited. However, the incorporating document does not require you to state how many shareholders there are, who they are, how many shares are actually being issued, or what the shareholders are paying for the shares. These are matters, though, that you should decide before you incorporate your company.

Shareholders' Agreements

In a business corporation where the owners of the business are essentially partners, it is very wise to have a shareholders' agreement to set out their mutual rights and obligations. The shareholders' agreement can deal with the election of directors and resolution of deadlock votes, or an agreement among all the shareholders (a **unanimous shareholders' agreement**) can even allow the shareholders rather than the directors to run the corporation. A shareholders' agreement can also have a buy-sell clause that allows any shareholder to buy a co-owner's shares or be bought out. It can also deal with matters similar to those in a partnership agreement, including what happens if an owner-shareholder dies. Shareholders' agreements are prepared separately from the incorporating documents and are not filed with the government.

Directors of the Corporation

Every private corporation must have at least one director. The role of a director is to manage the affairs of the corporation. A director must be a person (as opposed to another corporation), at least 18 years old, not bankrupt, and of sound mind. In addition, federally, and in most provinces, a majority of the directors must be Canadian citizens resident in Canada. In some provinces at least one director must also be a resident of the province. In many businesses, the director(s) and shareholder(s) will be the same, unless a shareholder cannot be a director because of residency requirements.

A director of a corporation has special legal duties to the corporation and its shareholders. First of all, in managing the corporation, a director must be reasonably careful and must exercise reasonable skill. Secondly, a director must act honestly and in good faith, with a view to the best interests of the corporation (this is called a **fiduciary duty**). This means that a director should never get into a conflict-of-interest situation with the corporation, and that if a director gets any personal benefit or profit at the expense of the corporation, the director may have to pay it to the corporation.

A small Canadian corporation specialized in aerial map-making for mining exploration projects. Two directors of the corporation were working on a bid for a project in South America. Before the bid was finalized, the directors resigned from the corporation, formed their own new corporation, and put in a competing bid. The new corporation was given the contract. The original corporation sued for breach of fiduciary duty. The court made the former directors and their new corporation pay their profits to the original corporation.

Directors can sometimes be held liable for the debts of the corporation. For example, a director may have to pay:

- employees' wages if the corporation becomes insolvent and can't pay them
- income tax, sales tax, GST, Employment Insurance, and Canada Pension Plan remittances that the corporation was required to pay but did not

Furthermore, a director can be held responsible for the actions of the corporation and convicted of an offence if the director authorized or participated in the commission of a criminal or provincial offence (such as an offence against environmental protection laws) by the corporation.

You must name at least one director (called a **first director**) in the incorporating document. The job of a first director is to get the corporation running. A first director may or may not become a real director of the corporation. The real or permanent directors are elected at the first shareholders' meeting after the business is incorporated.

The Business of the Corporation

In most provinces you don't have to state the corporation's business in the incorporating document. A corporation can carry on any kind of business (as long as it's legal) unless the incorporating document sets out restrictions. It's wise not to limit the kind of business the corporation can carry on, in case you want to change the nature of the business in the future.

The Powers of the Corporation

The incorporating document does not require you to set out what the legal powers of the corporation will be, such as the ability to enter into contracts and to sue and be sued. The legal powers of a corporation are set out in the legislation of each jurisdiction. Federally, and in most provinces, the powers are defined to be the same as those of a human individual, while in Nova Scotia, Prince Edward Island, and Quebec the powers are broad, but are specifically listed. In some provinces you can restrict the powers by noting the limitations in the incorporating documents.

The Names of the Incorporators

The incorporators are the people who are applying for the incorporation and who sign the documents. They are often the actual owners of the business, but, for convenience, they may simply be members or employees of the law firm handling the incorporation.

Other Matters

If you want to make sure that your corporation is considered a private corporation for tax and securities purposes, it is not enough simply to restrict the ability of the shareholders to transfer their shares. You must also include provisions in the incorporating documents that the corporation is prohibited from offering its shares to the public, and that the number of shareholders in the corporation is limited to 50 (apart from past or present employees).

INITIAL ORGANIZATION OF A CORPORATION

A corporation comes into existence after the government receives the incorporating documents and fees and issues a **certificate of incorporation** (or, in Quebec and Prince Edward Island, grants a **charter by letters patent**).

The corporation cannot start to carry on business until it has had a **first directors' meeting**. At this meeting the first directors pass the corporation's **by-laws**, which are the rules governing how the corporation will be run. The by-laws deal with such things as:

- how directors are elected and how long they may hold office
- how meetings are called and held
- the powers of the directors to borrow money
- where the corporation will bank
- what officers the corporation may have, and their duties

In addition, the first directors may pass **resolutions** that:

- appoint the **officers** of the corporation, for example a president, secretary, and treasurer. The officers run the corporation on a day-to-day basis by carrying out the orders of the directors
- appoint an auditor to hold office until the first shareholders' meeting
- adopt pre-incorporation contracts
- adopt the forms of share certificates, set share prices, and issue shares to the shareholders

If you use a lawyer to incorporate your business, as part of the fee the lawyer will take care of the first directors' meeting and by-laws and resolutions. If you're doing the incorporation yourself, you can buy pre-printed forms that contain standard by-laws and resolutions.

Within a specified number of months after the certificate of incorporation is issued the corporation must hold the **first shareholders' meeting**. At that meeting, the shareholders confirm the by-laws passed by the first directors, elect the permanent directors of the corporation, and may appoint an auditor.

RUNNING A CORPORATION

If your business is incorporated, you have to remember that you are not only running your business—you are also running a corporation. It's easy to lose sight of the fact that the corporation is a legal entity separate from you and the others who are running the business. You have to follow certain procedures to make sure that your business decisions and actions are those of the corporation. This requires:

- regular directors' meetings
- annual shareholders' meetings
- the keeping of complete corporate records
- the filing of required documents with the government

Directors' Meetings

Directors meet as required to make decisions about the affairs of the corporation. A **quorum** (a specified minimum number) of directors is required for a meeting to be held. Meetings can take place in person or by telephone (by conference call if there are more than two directors). Directors' decisions are made in the form of resolutions. Generally, a majority of the directors present must agree in order for a resolution to be passed, and after it has been passed it must be recorded in writing. Resolutions can also be made in writing in the first place, without the necessity of a meeting. In that case, *all* directors must agree to and sign the written resolution.

<table>
<tr><td>T
I
P</td><td>As you run your business you will be making decisions on a daily basis. Remember that any decision involving major corporate actions (such as buying property or entering into a lease) must be documented in the form of a directors' resolution.</td></tr>
</table>

T I P

Shareholders' Meetings

Corporations are required to hold annual shareholders' meetings to:

• elect directors

• appoint an auditor or dispense with an auditor

• review the corporation's financial statements

Other matters requiring shareholders' approval can also be dealt with at the annual meeting or at a special meeting called for that purpose.

For a shareholders' meeting to proceed there must be a quorum, and most decisions are made by simple majority vote. The decisions of the shareholders, called shareholders' resolutions, must be recorded in writing. An annual **shareholders' meeting** does not have to be held if the shareholders deal with all of the necessary matters in a resolution in writing signed by all of the shareholders.

One-Person Corporations

Many smaller corporations have only one shareholder and one director. These corporations must still fulfill all of the requirements for director's and shareholder's resolutions. Since there's only one person involved, meetings can be held very flexibly. For example, the shareholder can meet to elect the director while brushing his teeth in the morning. However, rather than holding one-person meetings, the director/shareholder normally makes resolutions in writing.

Corporate Record Keeping

Federal, and most provincial, corporations are required by statute to keep many different records, including:

- the incorporating documents
- by-laws of the corporation
- any unanimous shareholders' agreements the directors are aware of
- minutes of shareholders' meetings and resolutions in writing of the shareholders
- a directors' register containing their names and residential addresses
- a shareholders' register containing their names and addresses
- a register containing the names of warrant-holders (people with a right to acquire specific kinds of shares) of the corporation
- a register containing the names of holders of debt obligations of the corporation
- a register of transfers of shares from the corporation to shareholders and from one shareholder to another
- a capital account (showing how much in total has been paid by shareholders for each class of shares that has been issued)

In addition, most corporations also keep the following records:

- sample share certificates for each class of shares
- minutes of directors' meetings and resolutions in writing of directors
- a register of officers

Most of these records are kept in a corporate **minute book**. You can pay your lawyer to be responsible for keeping all of your corporate records up-to-date, including documenting all meetings and resolutions of directors and shareholders. And, no, your lawyer doesn't have to attend the meetings to perform this service for you.

Filing Requirements

In some provinces a corporation is required to file annual notices about its status, including such things as its address and the names of the directors. In other provinces the corporation need only file notices when there is a change in status.

Taxes

It will be necessary to file an annual income tax return for the corporation plus one for yourself setting out your income derived from salary, dividends, and other amounts received from the corporation as well as your income from other sources.

SETTING UP IN A NEW PROVINCE

If you incorporate in one province and wish to do business in another province as well, or if you incorporate federally and you wish to do business in a province, there are certain steps you must take in the province you target for business. The steps vary from province to province but they may include some or all of the following:

- searching and reserving a corporate name in the province
- registering your corporation and (sometimes) obtaining a licence
- registering a business name
- appointing an agent or attorney in the province with whom the provincial corporations branch can communicate

Your corporation will have to file required documents and information in that province, and will have to pay provincial corporate taxes there too.

MORE WORK

As you can see, there's a lot to know about setting up and running a corporation or even a partnership—and we've only told you the bare minimum. We advise you to get a copy of the federal *Business Corporations Act* (if you're incorporating federally) or the provincial or territorial act that governs corporations (if you're incorporating provincially or territorially). Don't just slip it under your pillow as a lucky charm. Read it and get to know it, because you have to play by the book now. Read the by-laws of your corporation too (they're mostly taken from the legislation), and any shareholders' agreement. If your business is a partnership, get a copy of the provincial or territorial act governing partnerships and make yourself familiar with it. If you have a partnership agreement, get to know it as well. Yes, it's more work, but look at it this way: if you read a couple of pages of a *Business Corporations Act* or a *Partnerships Act* every night before you go to bed, you will never need sleeping pills.

CHAPTER SIX

PERMITS, LICENCES, AND OTHER GOVERNMENT REQUIREMENTS

If you're in business, the odds are very good that some regulatory scheme, either federal or provincial or municipal, will apply to you. This means that for many businesses it's not enough to choose a form of business organization and then set it up. You may have to get government permission to carry on the business or else face a fine. Once you've got permission, you may have to comply with certain government regulations or else risk being fined or shut down. To get permission, you may just need to fill in some forms and wait a while, or you may have to go through a long and complicated hearing process. You may be relieved of only a few dollars or you may be forced to spend thousands. Once you've got permission you may not have to deal with the government again—or you may be under continuing supervision to ensure compliance with regulations. Compliance, like permission, may cost you little or nothing, or it may cost you a lot.

In any one province there may be hundreds of laws establishing regulatory schemes and nearly as many government boards, agencies, and tribunals to administer them. And regulatory schemes are constantly changing. As a result, we can't tell you precisely what the requirements will be for your particular business. What we will try to do in this chapter is to give you some idea of the broad scope of government regulatory interference in business and the kinds of things the government is likely to require of a business. You will have to identify all the regulatory requirements for your particular business yourself: you will have to find out if you need a federal, provincial, or municipal permit for your business, if your product has to meet certain government standards, or if it has to be packaged and labelled in a certain way. You can find these things out by consulting a lawyer, your Canada-Provincial Business Centre, a trade or industry association, or by contacting the different levels of government directly (good luck, especially if you don't know exactly which government departments to contact).

PERMITS AND LICENCES

Depending on your business, you may need a permit or licence from the federal, provincial, and/or municipal government. If you need a permit or licence, you will have to apply for it, and you may have to meet certain standards to get it. If you do get it you will have to pay for it, and the cost of some licences and permits is very high. Once you have the licence or permit, you will probably have to renew it regularly (and pay again). Your licence or permit can be revoked if you don't continue to meet all government requirements.

A family had run a bar for many years and had never had problems when the liquor inspectors made regular visits. So they didn't bother to read the liquor licence laws on a regular basis and to review their operations to make sure they complied fully with them. A new inspector visited and noted several minor breaches of the liquor licencing regulations that the previous inspectors had never paid any attention to—and that the family had never thought about before. The business was fined several thousand dollars, and ordered to shut down for a month and to post a sign during that time saying that it had been shut down by order of the liquor licencing commission. After the business reopened, inspectors made more frequent visits than they had before and enforced the liquor licence regulations very strictly.

Federal Government

If you are carrying on business in one of the following areas you may need a federal licence or permit:

- telecommunications
- aeronautics
- navigation and shipping
- energy and natural resources
- agriculture (but only for products that cross provincial boundaries or are exported)
- fisheries
- cultural resources
- importing and exporting

To find out more, contact the relevant federal government department.

Provincial Government

Individuals must meet provincial qualifications to carry on certain businesses. For example, in most provinces:

- professionals such as lawyers, doctors, dentists, pharmacists, nurses, teachers, architects, and engineers must meet educational standards and be accredited by and satisfy ongoing requirements of their governing professional body
- others such as real estate brokers, mortgage brokers, travel agents, and debt collectors must pass examinations and be registered by the province
- skilled tradespeople such as electricians, plumbers, and mechanics must also meet training requirements and be licenced by the province

If you are carrying on business in one of the following areas, a provincial licence or permit or provincial registration may be required:

- door-to-door sales
- consumer finance, including moneylending
- consumer (credit) reporting
- providing lodging
- selling or distributing tobacco
- selling or serving liquor
- food processing or handling
- agricultural production within the province
- motor vehicle sales
- transportation of goods or persons within the province
- natural resources (forests, minerals, water)
- businesses done on provincially owned land, such as parks and beaches

Contact the relevant provincial government department for more information.

Municipal Government

Most municipalities require certain kinds of businesses carried on within their boundaries to be licenced. The following kinds of businesses frequently require municipal licences:

- Retail sales
  - adult books and magazines
  - restaurants, cafes, doughnut shops
  - bake shops
  - delicatessens
  - butcher shops, and fish and seafood sellers
  - grocery stores, supermarkets, convenience stores, fruit markets
  - variety stores, and cigarette and cigar retailers
  - department stores

– second-hand goods dealers
– old gold and jewellery sellers
– pet shops

- Services
  – service stations, gas stations, and car washes
  – driving schools
  – taxis
  – trucking, including tow trucks
  – school buses
  – rental cars, trucks, and recreational vehicles
  – fuel supply and delivery
  – salvage
  – laundry and dry cleaning
  – hair salons and barber shops
  – kennels

- Trades
  – renovators and building contractors
  – building cleaners
  – auctioneers
  – taxi drivers
  – truck drivers
  – driving instructors
  – sign painters
  – distributors and posters of bills
  – hawkers and pedlars
  – masseurs

- Recreation
  – amusement parks, carnivals, circuses, carousels, or merry-go-rounds
  – theatres and cinemas
  – roller skating rinks
  – swimming pools
  – bowling alleys
  – billiards halls
  – boats for hire
  – horse-drawn carriage tours

Contact the municipality where you intend to carry on your business for more information.

PRODUCT STANDARDS

If you are manufacturing a product, it may have to meet certain federal or provincial government standards. For example:

- if you are producing food, drugs, medical devices, or cosmetics, your product will have to meet standards set out in the federal *Food and Drugs Act* and regulations.

- if you are importing or manufacturing children's products such as clothing, toys, or cribs, they will have to meet standards set out in the federal *Hazardous Products Act*.

- if you are selling agricultural products (such as milk, poultry, beef, wheat, soya beans—you name it), you may have to meet the standards of a provincial marketing board or commission that may also have the power to establish production quotas, collect fees, and control marketing.

- if you are selling food or drink, your product and your premises will have to meet provincial and municipal inspection standards.

- if you are manufacturing or importing motor vehicles of any kind, your vehicles will have to meet standards set out in the federal *Motor Vehicle Safety Act* and regulations.

- if your business involves the use of motor vehicles, they will have to meet operational standards set out by the provincial government.

- if you make jewellery, silverware, or anything made with precious metals you will have to meet minimum quality standards set out in the federal *Precious Metals Marking Act*.

- if your business uses weighing equipment, the equipment will have to be inspected by the federal government's Weights and Measures Branch.

- if you are manufacturing or importing electrical goods, they must meet the standards of the Canadian General Standards Board and must be inspected by the Canadian Standards Association Testing Laboratories.

- if you are manufacturing or importing fire protection products (such as fire extinguishers or fire-resistant building materials), your products must be inspected by the Underwriters Laboratories of Canada.

- if you are building or renovating buildings, your work must meet provincial building code standards, and must be inspected by municipal building inspectors.

- if your business involves advertising or promoting products, services, or events, you may have to meet standards set by the provincial government.

- if you are making, distributing, or displaying films or videos, they will have to be reviewed by a provincial film board.

In addition, there are many provincial statutes that regulate production and sales of various things, including bread, fur, vegetables, hearing aids, bees and honey, edible oils and imitation diary products, and wild rice.

As exhausting as this list is it is not exhaustive or complete. Once you've recovered from reading it, you can ask your lawyer what government standards apply to your business, or you can contact your Canada-Provincial Business Centre, or the relevant federal, provincial, or municipal government department.

PACKAGING AND LABELLING

Ready for more? Okay, here we go. If you are manufacturing or selling a product, you may have to meet certain federal or provincial government requirements for packaging and labelling. For example, under the federal *Consumer Packaging and Labelling Act*:

- any prepackaged consumer product (edible or not) is subject to packaging regulations that include requirements that the product be labelled in English and French with:
  - the product's net quantity, in metric units (any other unit of measurement is optional)
  - the identity of the product—its common name or its function, and for certain products information about characteristics of the product
  - the identity and principal place of business of the manufacturer or person for whom the product was manufactured
- containers cannot be shaped in a misleading manner—for some products specific packaging requirements have been established

There are exceptions to the French-English labelling requirement for products that are distributed locally, specialty products, and test market products.

The federal *Food and Drugs Act* regulates the labelling of food, drugs, cosmetics, and medical devices. The labelling must include ingredients lists, lot numbers, and expiry dates for food; warnings, directions, expiry dates, and lot numbers for drugs; and warning signs on pressurized containers.

In addition:

- hazardous or dangerous products must be marked as required by the federal *Hazardous Products Act*.

- "consumer textile articles" must be labelled as required by the federal *Textile Labelling Act* and your business may have to register for a CA Identification Number.

- upholstered and stuffed articles may have to be labelled (and made with) "New Material Only" as required by provincial statutes, and may be subject to inspection.

- in some provinces, beverage containers must meet special requirements for shape or labelling.

GOOD NEWS

Here's some good news to end the chapter. The rumour that you need to ask the federal, provincial, and municipal governments if it's okay to sneeze is not true. However, there's this regulation made under the *Sneezing and Hiccupping Standards Act....*

BUYING AN EXISTING BUSINESS

You may want to acquire an existing business, as an alternative to starting a business from scratch, or in order to expand your own business. You can acquire a business either by buying into it or by buying it outright.

There are many reasons why you might want to buy a business instead of starting your own. You may have strong management skills but no creative ideas, and buying an existing business will allow you to take advantage of someone else's good idea. You may find it easier to get financing to buy a business than to start up your own. And whether you're just starting up or you're expanding, you'll get the benefit of all the work the original owner(s) put in. And you don't have to wait and see whether the business will be successful.

Of course there can be drawbacks to buying a business too. You're buying someone else's creation, and you may find it hard to make any changes you want without alienating customers, suppliers, or employees. If you buy into a business and become a co-owner (as a partner or a shareholder), the relationship may not work out for personal reasons. If you do buy out the existing owner, you may find that you don't have the temperament, knowledge, or experience to run that particular business and that you've bitten off more than you can chew. Or it may take a lot of time and hard work (and maybe even money) to correct mistakes that the former owner made in setting up the administrative end of the business, or in hiring and training the staff.

In the short run it will probably cost you more to buy or buy into an established business than to set up or expand your own. You're willing to pay more because you believe (after a careful look) that the business's current level of income will continue or even increase, and that it will provide you with an adequate return on your investment. (An adequate return is enough income for you to turn a profit after paying interest on money you borrowed, or, if you didn't have to borrow, as much money as you would have earned by investing elsewhere.) By contrast, you can't tell how much income a brand-new business will produce, or how much money it will swallow before it becomes successful—if it ever does.

The decisions whether or not to buy a business, and how much to pay for it, will be business decisions. The mechanics of the actual acquisition will depend on the form of business you are buying or buying into.

BUYING (INTO) A BUSINESS

You may be interested in buying (into) a business that is presently being run as a sole proprietorship, partnership, or corporation. Whatever form it's presently in, and whether you're planning to buy into the business or to buy it out, you have to decide on the price you're willing to pay. Reaching this decision will involve a careful investigation. You will have to look at the business's:

- net income (its income after expenses and before taxes)
- accounts receivable (what is owed to it for goods and services)
- fixed assets (land and buildings)
- movable assets (machinery, equipment, and furnishings)
- intangible assets (licences, patents, industrial designs, copyrights, trademarks, and business names)

- employees
- inventory
- customer lists

You will also have to look at its:

- accounts payable (what it owes for goods and services)
- debt financing arrangements (how much it owes to the bank and other lenders)

These things can be examined by looking at the business's records—its audited financial statements and tax returns, its contracts, and documents—and its premises and their contents. But you also need to know what the future will bring, so you have to look at the business's **goodwill**.

Putting a price on goodwill is difficult. In fact, even putting a definition on goodwill is difficult, because people explain it in different ways. Some people define goodwill as the difference in value between what all the business's physical assets are worth and what someone would pay for the business over and above those assets. Others define it as the likelihood that customers will keep coming back. Maybe they both mean the same thing. In order to value the business's goodwill, you will have to look at its:

- established customer base
- age and reputation, including its business name and any trademarks or trade names
- location
- special benefits, such as exclusive rights to sell a popular product
- employees
- suppliers
- competition
- prospects for the future—will the service or product still be in demand two years from now? Ten years from now? Will the business's location stay attractive or will it turn into a liability?

You don't have to do all the work of putting a price on the business yourself. A business valuator or broker can help you to arrive at a fair price, taking into account all the business's assets (including goodwill) and liabilities. Your accountant will go over the financial records to determine whether they are credible and whether they show a business in good health or otherwise.

BUYING (INTO) A SOLE PROPRIETORSHIP

If the business that interests you is being carried on as a sole proprietorship, you can either buy into the business or you can buy the whole business. If you buy into the business, you and the current owner will become partners. In either case you are buying (all or part of) the assets and goodwill of the existing business.

If you become a partner you have to think about all of the partnership issues we discussed in Chapters 4 and 5. If you buy the whole business you do so through an **asset purchase**, which we discuss more fully on at p. 89. You may want the current owner to stay on with the business for a while, in which case you should negotiate a **consulting contract** with her. In any event you should negotiate a **non-competition agreement** as part of the purchase of the business, to make sure that after selling you the business the current owner doesn't undermine it by attracting away the customers you've paid for. Consulting contracts and non-competition agreements are also discussed more fully on p. 95.

BUYING (INTO) A PARTNERSHIP

If the business that interests you is being carried on as a partnership, you can become a new partner in the existing partnership, you can buy out the partnership interest of one partner, or you can buy the whole business. If you are buying into the partnership you have to consider what terms you want in your partnership agreement. If you are taking over the entire partnership, you have to deal with all that's involved in an asset purchase and negotiate a consulting contract and/or a non-competition agreement with the sellers.

BUYING (INTO) A CORPORATION

If you want to buy a business that is incorporated, you can buy some or all of the shares in the corporation through a **share purchase**, or you can buy the assets of the corporation through an asset purchase.

If you buy (into) a corporation by buying its shares, you have to decide how much to pay. In a publicly traded corporation the market determines what the shares are worth. You are not likely to be buying a controlling interest in a publicly traded company (unless you win the lottery). You might, however, buy a private corporation. In a private corporation, the value of the assets (including goodwill) determines the price of the shares. If you buy only some of the shares you should consider negotiating a shareholder's agreement with the existing shareholders. If you buy a corporation through an asset purchase, the value of the assets again determines the price you'll pay. If you are buying either the assets or all of the shares, you may want to negotiate a consulting contract and/or a non-competition agreement with the vendors.

An asset purchase or a share purchase is not something you can or should do yourself. You must use both an accountant and a lawyer to help you decide which way to proceed and to carry out the purchase. Read on for some background about what's involved in the purchase of a corporation. It will help you understand why we say that you need a lawyer *and* an accountant.

Share Purchase

If you buy all of the shares of a corporation then you own it. It continues to exist just as before with all of its assets, and all of its debts and liabilities, including its tax liabilities. All of the corporation's contracts theoretically continue as well. However, some of them may contain a clause that allows the other party to withdraw from the contract if there's a change in corporate control. If these contracts are beneficial to the corporation, the corporation's value for your purposes is tied to the continuation of these contracts. So when you are valuing the corporation, you not only have to determine the value of its assets and the extent of its debts and liabilities, you also have to find out whether its beneficial contracts will continue.

A share purchase may sound very simple—all you do is pay for the shares, and the corporation is yours. But in fact a lot of careful work has to go into tailoring the deal to make sure that you'll get exactly what you're bargaining for. The agreement to purchase the shares must be drafted to give you the right to investigate all aspects of the corporation's legal and financial status—and then those investigations must be carried out. For example, you want to make sure that:

- the corporation is validly incorporated and is in compliance with all corporate laws.

- the corporation is presently in compliance with any other applicable laws (such as tax and environmental protection).

- all shareholders have been properly identified and all interests are in fact being sold to you.

- there are no existing or anticipated lawsuits against the corporation.

- the corporation has good title to all of its assets and that there are no undisclosed claims against the assets.

Asset Purchase

Instead of buying the corporation itself through a share purchase, you can buy some or all of its property through an asset purchase. A corporation's assets might include land and buildings, equipment, machinery, inventory, office furniture, leases, and customer lists. If you buy the assets of a corporation, you will own only the assets you buy, and you will have no relationship with the corporation itself. The corporation may or may not continue to exist. The debts and liabilities of the corporation remain with it except for the ones you agree to take over (for example, you may choose to assume a mortgage on real property or on a piece of equipment that you are buying). The contracts of the corporation also remain with the corporation unless it assigns them to you (the consent of the other party to the contract will usually be required).

The mechanics of an asset purchase are very complex for three reasons. First of all, the deal has to be negotiated and structured with future tax consequences (for both the buyer and the seller) in mind. Secondly, each asset has to be transferred individually. Finally, the sale must satisfy the statutory requirements of the province that protect the creditors of a business (incorporated or not) that sells substantially all of its assets.

The details of an asset purchase are discussed more fully on p. 89.

Share Purchase or Asset Purchase: How Do You Decide?

The standard wisdom about choosing between a share purchase and an asset purchase is that purchasers prefer asset purchases while vendors prefer share purchases. The main reason for this is taxes: the vendor is concerned about the immediate tax consequences of the sale while the purchaser is concerned about the long-term tax consequences. Another important reason is that a vendor who is getting out of business wants to unload the whole business, while a purchaser would prefer to pick and choose the good stuff without having to take the junk. It's wise, then, to keep in mind that you are going to be trying to negotiate a deal with someone whose interests may be exactly opposite to yours.

The usual advantages of an asset purchase to you as a purchaser include:

- you can buy the best assets and leave the rest—this may be truer in theory than in practice, though, because the vendor may refuse to sell you the good assets unless you agree to take some or all of the bad ones.

- you do not automatically assume the debts and liabilities of the business, although you may wish to assume *some* debts (for example, a favourable mortgage as a way to help finance the purchase of a particular asset) and *some* liabilities (for example, warranty responsibilities to encourage customer loyalty).

- you can negotiate the value assigned to each asset so that in the future you will be able to claim the highest possible income tax deduction for depreciation (**capital cost allowance**) of that asset.

(See p. 237 in Chapter 17 for an explanation of capital cost allowance.) Unfortunately, these are the very assets that the vendor will want to assign the lowest value to, because of the immediate tax consequences for him.

Despite the standard wisdom, there are disadvantages as well as advantages for you as a purchaser in an asset purchase. They include:

- there can be a lot of legal paperwork because each asset has to be identified individually and transferred to you separately, and because the purchase must comply with provincial legislation to protect creditors of the business.
- you will have to pay GST and provincial retail sales tax on the personal property, and GST and land transfer tax on the real property you buy.
- you have to establish a new employment relationship with the employees you want to keep on.
- there may be assets that cannot be sold to you without the consent of a third party. For example, the landlord's consent may be required before you can assume the lease for the business premises.

Again, despite the standard wisdom, there can be advantages to a share purchase for you as purchaser:

- there can be less paperwork than in an asset purchase, but that doesn't mean that your legal fees will be lower because there has to be a thorough investigation of the corporation and its ownership of the assets.
- retail sales tax and land transfer tax are generally eliminated on a share purchase.
- when you purchase the shares of a corporation there is no change in the employment relationship between employees and the corporation, although employees you'd like to keep may choose to leave because of the change in ownership.
- because there is no change in ownership of the assets, no third

party has to consent to the sale; some leases, however, may contain a condition that the lease ends if there is change in ownership of the corporation.

• purchase of the entire corporation may be the only way for you to acquire a licence or contract that by its terms cannot be assigned by the corporation.

• the corporation may have lost money in past years and therefore now has a loss carryforward that can be applied against its future profits to reduce income taxes. (This will only work if you know how to turn the business around!)

THE MECHANICS OF AN ASSET PURCHASE

You've heard a lot about asset purchases from us now, and you probably can hardly contain your curiosity about how they actually work. We will keep you in suspense no longer. There are four stages in an asset purchase. First you have to identify the assets you wish to purchase. Next you and the vendor must negotiate the overall price for the assets and the value that will be assigned to each particular asset. Then you must put your agreement with the seller in writing. Finally, the assets have to be transferred to you in a way that complies with all legal requirements for each asset.

Identifying the Assets You Want to Purchase

If you're contemplating an asset purchase, you are trying to acquire the business as a going concern. You're not just shopping for some pieces of machinery or office equipment. Of course you do want the machinery and office equipment, but you also want the business's name, reputation, and customers. These last three things are assets that you can buy too, and buying them is what gives you a whole business that is greater than the sum of its parts.

The physical assets of a business may include:

• land
• buildings
• vehicles

- machinery and equipment
- office furniture and equipment
- computer hardware and software
- inventory

The intangible assets of a business may include:

- leases
- franchises, licences, and distributorships
- accounts receivable
- business names, trademarks, patents, industrial designs, and copyrights
- regulatory licences and permits
- goodwill, customer lists, and mailing lists

Probably the most important and most intangible, of the intangible assets is the goodwill. You'll pay a substantial amount for it, but it's not something physical that you can grab and hold on to. Keeping the business's name and location and getting its customer list are some of the things that will help you preserve the goodwill of the business, but there's no guarantee that customers of the old business will want to continue to do business with you. Even if there are customers or contracts in existence, they're not automatically transferred to you. Customers can walk away when they realize there's new management, and they have the right to get out of existing contracts.

Negotiating the Price You Are Willing to Pay

There are two parts to negotiating a price for an asset purchase. The first is to determine the overall price that you think the business is worth and to come to an agreement with the vendor. The second, and more difficult, part is to **allocate** the purchase price among the various assets included in the sale (that is, to assign each asset a price). This must be done keeping the future income tax consequences in mind.

Everyone's guiding principle when it comes to tax is to pay as little as possible. One way to reduce the tax you pay on your business income is to increase your deductions. When you buy the assets of a business, you want to structure the deal so that in future years you will have deductions from income that are as high as possible. The assets of a business are **capital property** (property with long-term value that you buy intending to keep), and you can't deduct the full cost of capital property against income in the year that you buy it. Instead you are allowed annual deductions for depreciation of capital property (called capital cost allowance or **deduction for eligible capital property**, depending on the nature of the property). The price allocated to each asset determines the asset's **adjusted cost base**, which is the figure used to calculate capital cost allowance or deduction for eligible capital property. Each year you can claim as a deduction a percentage of the value of the particular asset. There are different percentage rates for different assets. What you want to do is to allocate a higher price to assets that depreciate at a higher percentage rate (that have a higher rate of capital cost allowance) and a lower price to assets that depreciate at a lower percentage rate (that have a lower rate of capital cost allowance).

For example, the following classes of assets have a low rate of depreciation, and so you will want them to be assigned a low value:

- land cannot be depreciated at all
- buildings are depreciated at 4 per cent per year
- eligible capital property (for example, goodwill, client lists, and licences for an unlimited period) is depreciated at 7 per cent per year (but only on ¾ of the cost)
- roads, parking lots, and sidewalks are depreciated at 8 per cent per year

The following classes of assets have a higher rate of depreciation, and so you will want them to be assigned a higher value:

- furniture, appliances, fixtures, machinery, and equipment (including photocopiers, telephones, and fax machines) are depreciated at 20 per cent per year

- computer hardware and systems software are depreciated at 30 per cent per year

- passenger vehicles are depreciated at 30 per cent per year (but the starting maximum value of a passenger vehicle is capped)

- patents, franchises, and licences for a limited period are depreciated down to zero in an equal percentage each year spread out over the life of the property

The following classes of assets have an annual depreciation rate of 100 per cent, and so you will want them to be assigned a very high value:

- computer software apart from systems software

- uniforms

- dies, jigs, moulds, and cutting or shaping parts of a machine

- tools that cost under $200

Everything we've told you so far applies to capital property only. **Inventory**, property that a business has on hand in order to resell, is treated differently. The cost of all inventory purchased can be fully claimed as an expense in the year it is purchased. As a result you will also want to assign a very high value to inventory.

To sum up, you will probably want to allocate the purchase price to assets in the following order, starting with the biggest allocation:

1. inventory

2. depreciable capital property that has a high rate of depreciation

3. eligible capital property

4. depreciable capital property that has a very low rate of depreciation

5. non-depreciable capital property

But there's a fly in the ointment. The vendor will want to allocate the purchase price in *exactly the reverse order*. That's because:

- the amount allocated to inventory will be considered income in the vendor's hands and taxed fully (as opposed to being considered a capital gain, only 3/4 of which is taxable).

- if the sale price allocated to an asset is higher than the depreciated value of the asset, the extra amount of depreciation that has been claimed is added back to the vendor's income as **recaptured capital cost allowance** and taxed fully. For example, supposing the vendor purchased a car for $24,000 and its depreciated value at the time of the asset sale is $11,760. If the value allocated to the car for the purposes of the asset sale is $15,000, the sum of $3,240 will be added to the vendor's income and taxed fully.

Because the vendor and purchaser normally have such conflicting interests, Revenue Canada usually accepts without question the allocation of the purchase price that the parties have agreed on.

Putting Your Agreement in Writing

Once you have agreed with the vendor on the assets that you are buying, the overall price, and the allocation of the price among the various assets, your lawyer should put your agreement into writing. The agreement should:

- set a closing date for the sale
- identify the assets being purchased
- specify the amount being paid for the purchase and the terms of payment
- allocate the purchase price among the various assets
- provide warranties as to the ownership of, and outstanding liabilities attached to, the various assets
- provide warranties as to the condition of the various assets
- specify who carries the risk of damage to the assets before closing
- state any liabilities being assumed
- state whether or not the purchaser agrees to offer employment to any of the vendor's employees

- set out the terms of any consulting contract
- set out the terms of any non-competition agreement
- assign responsibility for the payment of GST, retail sales tax, and land transfer tax related to the asset purchase
- require compliance with the provincial statute that protects creditors of the business (commonly called a *Bulk Sales Act*)

TIP

When a business sells all or substantially all of its assets, the provisions of the province's *Bulk Sales Act* apply. If adequate steps are not taken to make sure that the creditors get paid out of the proceeds of sale, the purchaser may have to pay the creditors. Therefore, if you're the purchaser, it's important to make sure that the Act has been complied with. Some vendors and purchasers agree not to comply with the *Bulk Sales Act,* but as a purchaser you're running a risk if you do that.

TIP

Transferring the Assets

Between the time the agreement is signed and the closing date, your lawyer will carry out an investigation to make sure that when the deal closes you will get exactly what was promised in the agreement. For example, each asset must be investigated to make sure that the vendor is legally the owner, and that there are no creditors' claims on it.

At the time of the closing, when the assets are transferred to you, each one must be dealt with separately. It may be necessary to do one or more of the following:

- prepare and register documents that transfer ownership
- register the change of ownership of the business name
- register assignment of ownership of any trademarks
- obtain consents from lenders, landlords, regulatory authorities, or other interested parties.
- give notice to employees, customers, and parties who have contracts with the vendor

- make adjustments to the purchase price to take into account expenses prepaid by the vendor such as property taxes, mortgage payments, rent, and insurance premiums

- ensure that arrangements are made for all appropriate taxes to be paid

CONSULTING CONTRACTS AND NON-COMPETITION AGREEMENTS

Whether you are buying a sole proprietorship, a partnership, or a corporation, you may want the former owner of the business to stay on at the business for a limited period of time after the sale, as a consultant. An obvious reason is that he will be able to give you advice about running the business if you don't have experience in this type of business yourself. Also, the former owner's continued presence may encourage customers to keep on dealing with the business and give them an opportunity to get to know you and transfer their loyalties to you.

> **TIP**
>
> A consulting contract can also be used even when the former owner will not continue to play an active role in the new business. It's a way of turning some of the purchase price into consulting fees, and spreading it out over the length of the consulting contract. This can be an advantage to both the purchaser and the vendor, because the purchaser does not have to come up with the full purchase price at the time of the sale, and the vendor gets to spread the profit from the sale—and more importantly the taxes on those profits—over two or more taxation years. Whatever the purpose of the consulting contract, the fees paid to the former owner must be reasonable, and the vendor must be available to do the work required.

When you buy an existing business, you want to keep the customers, so the last thing you want is for the vendor of the business to set up a competing business next door. To make sure that doesn't happen you must have a non-competition agreement with the vendor. If you don't have such an agreement, there's no law to stop the vendor from competing with you and taking your customers away. Non-competition agreements are tricky things, though. You may want to prevent the vendor from ever setting up a competing business anywhere south of the Arctic Circle and east of Alaska, but you can't do that. The law balances your right not to have competition from the vendor with the vendor's right to earn a living, and a court will only enforce your non-competition agreement if it is reasonable. That means that you can only prevent the vendor from setting up a business or going to work for a competitor of yours for a reasonable period of time and within a reasonable distance of your business location.

What is reasonable in time and distance will depend on the nature of the business. For instance, if you bought a small grocery store, you couldn't prevent the vendor from operating a competing store *absolutely anywhere* in the city. It's only reasonable to prevent the vendor from competing within the neighbourhood where your customers come from. On the other hand if you buy a company that develops computer software for sale throughout Canada and the United States, it might be reasonable to prevent the vendor from competing with you anywhere in Canada or the United States, although only for a very limited period of time. If a judge decides that your non-competition agreement is unreasonable in either time or location, she will not change the agreement to make it reasonable but will simply refuse to enforce the agreement at all. So make sure that your non-competition agreement is reasonable in the first place.

Another way of discouraging the vendor from competing with you is to structure the deal so that the vendor has a stake in the continued success of your business. For example, the vendor can help finance the sale by taking back a mortgage or promissory note for part of the purchase price. Or part of the purchase price can be payable at a future time, and can be tied to the business's income.

FRANCHISES, DISTRIBUTORSHIPS, AND LICENCES

In the last chapter we talked about taking advantage of someone else's success by acquiring an existing business. There are other ways to get the benefit of someone else's good ideas (other ways than industrial espionage, that is). You can buy a franchise, which gives you a pre-packaged business concept. You can get a distributorship, which gives you the right to sell someone else's product. Or you can get a licence to use someone else's name, trademark, or patented process in your business.

FRANCHISES

What businessperson hasn't wished that he had bought one of the earliest franchises from McDonald's? If you want to buy a McDonald's franchise today, it would cost you hundreds of thousands of dollars. You probably haven't got that kind of money, so you may settle for an established but less well-known franchise, one that's fairly successful but more affordable. Or you may be willing to take a gamble on a brand-new franchise, one that's totally untested but cheap, hoping that in 10 years' time people will be looking enviously at you, wishing they had bought in when you did.

Franchising started in the United States. Since World War II this approach to running a business has grown to the point where there are thousands of businesses in North America offering franchise opportunities and millions of people working in franchise operations. There are franchises available in many retail goods and service businesses, such as:

- restaurants and coffee shops
- photocopy shops
- clothing stores
- beauty shops
- computer stores
- pet food supplies
- travel agencies
- interior decorating
- video rentals
- auto repairs
- shipping and packaging
- car rentals
- lawn care
- plumbing
- tax preparation
- cleaning services
- tutoring services
- child care

No matter what your area of expertise or interest, there could be a franchise that's attractive to you.

When you buy a franchise you operate your own business, but you operate it as if it were part of a chain with one name and with standardized products, design, service, and operations. You get the benefits of belonging to a large organization, while still being your own boss. These benefits include:

- name recognition—probably the single most important thing a successful franchise has to offer
- a developed concept
- product research and development
- centralized advertising and sophisticated marketing
- assistance, training, and support in both management and production
- assistance in choice of business location
- centralized purchasing of supplies

Standardized operations can be comforting to someone with little business experience, but if you're creative or a lone wolf you may find the standardization stifling.

How Do You Choose a Franchise?

The first thing you should do is decide what kind of business you want to be in. Don't just base your choice on what you think will be most profitable. You should choose an area that fits your education, abilities, interests, and temperament. If you don't have a head for numbers, don't go into the tax preparation business. If you hate children, don't open a day care centre. Once you've decided on a general area of business, do as much research as you can about it, to see if there is a potential for long-term growth. When you've settled on a particular type of business, see what franchises are available. There are a number of books and magazines that advertise available franchises, or you can look in the business opportunities section of your newspaper. You can also contact the Canadian Franchise Association, which is a voluntary association of franchisors, or attend franchise seminars, shows, and conferences.

If you find a franchise that looks interesting, investigate it carefully before signing on. You should:

- find out how long the franchise business has been in existence—
  are there existing successful franchises? How many of them are
  there and how long have they been in operation? How many franchises have been closed within the past two years?

- find out something about the people who are running the franchise
  business—who are the directors, officers, and major shareholders
  of the corporation? What is their business experience? What is
  their previous involvement with franchises, either successful or
  (especially) unsuccessful? Has any of them ever gone bankrupt?
  Has any of them ever been convicted of a criminal offence?

- find out what investment is required of you.

- find out whether any financing is available through the franchisor, and on what terms.

- try to determine how profitable the franchise will be:
  - find out what earnings the franchisor claims you will make, and
    find out what facts or assumptions the franchisor is basing the
    claim on.
  - compare the earnings claims that the franchisor is making to
    the investment required from you. Is the promised return on
    your investment adequate?
  - find out if the earnings claims are likely to be realized, by
    speaking to other franchisees.

- check the reputation of the franchisor with the local Chamber of
  Commerce, Better Business Bureau, and your provincial department of consumer and commercial affairs.

- do a credit check on the franchisor.

- get a list of franchisees from the franchisor (with their addresses
  and telephone numbers) and speak to a number of them, not
  only about how much money they're making but about their relationship with the franchisor and general level of satisfaction.
  Make sure that you don't just talk to franchisees chosen for you
  by the franchisor.

- check whether the franchisor has been involved in lawsuits with
  franchisees.

• find out what locations are available now—how close are other competing businesses? How close are other franchises? How close by will the nearest franchise be allowed in the future?

The Canadian Franchise Association has drawn up a code of ethics for franchisors which includes a requirement to give written disclosure of most of the things in the list above to prospective franchisees. You may have to rant, rave, and nag to get disclosure of all of these things from the franchisor, however, and you'll also have to verify the truth of what the franchisor tells you. Once you decide on a franchise, the franchisor may want to check *you* out too. In addition to checking your financial resources, the franchisor may also want to interview you and assess your suitability as a franchisee.

Ultimately, the success of your individual franchise will depend not only on the overall success of the franchisor and on your own abilities and the location of your franchise. It will also depend to a great extent on the terms of the franchise agreement you sign.

The Franchise Agreement

When you buy a franchise you will enter into a contract with the **franchisor**, the company that created and developed the business. In the contract you are called the **franchisee**. A franchise agreement is a contract like any other, and the relationship between the franchisor and franchisee is governed by that contract. You will probably be presented with a pre-printed standard form contract prepared by the franchisor's lawyers, and there will be very little room for you to negotiate better terms for yourself. Before you sign anything have your lawyer review the contract. Your lawyer will explain the contract to you and warn you if there are clauses that are very unfavourable to you. You might be wise to walk away from the deal if it's unfair.

Most franchise agreements cover the same topics. A franchise agreement will contain terms that benefit the franchisee and terms that benefit the franchisor, but most of them benefit the franchisor.

Terms that benefit the franchisee may include:

- the right to use the franchisor's trade name and specific products, methods, and equipment.
- the right to get professional help from the franchisor to set up and run the business, in such things as:
  - choice of location
  - construction of the premises
  - selection of equipment
  - inventory control and bookkeeping
  - advertising and promotion
  - employee training
- the franchisor's promise not to sell the rights to another franchisee within a fixed distance of your franchise without your permission, or to compensate you if it does.
- the franchisor's promise to provide advertising and marketing.

Terms that benefit the franchisor may include requirements that you as franchisee:

- pay various fees such as:
  - a franchise or initiation fee and other start-up fees
  - a percentage of the income from the franchise
  - advertising fees
  - training fees
- purchase supplies and equipment from the franchisor or from suppliers approved by the franchisor. This benefits the franchisor if the goods are sold at a mark-up or if the franchisor receives a payment from the approved suppliers (but it can benefit the franchisee if this arrangement results in volume discounts).
- operate your business to the franchisor's standards
- devote your full time and attention to the franchise
- agree not to run a competing business during or after the term of the franchise agreement
- agree not to reveal trade secrets of the franchisor
- keep accounts and provide financial information to the franchisor on a regular basis

- keep on operating the business for a fixed period of time (usually one year) even if you are losing money

There may be other terms that benefit the franchisor, such as:

- the agreement will expire on a given date unless the franchisor chooses to renew it
- the franchisor has the right to terminate the franchise or to buy the franchise back at any time

A franchise agreement included a term that the franchisor could terminate the agreement immediately if the franchisee failed to make any payment to the franchisor when it was due. The agreement also stated that on termination the franchisor could take over the franchisee's lease and purchase the franchisee's fixed assets at book value. The franchisee made late payments on a few occasions, but the franchisor always accepted them without complaint. However, one month when the franchisee was two days late with a payment the franchisor delivered a letter terminating the lease. The franchisee immediately offered the overdue payment but the franchisor refused to withdraw the termination. The franchisee went to court for an injunction preventing the franchisor from terminating the agreement, but the court sided with the franchisor. The judge said that the franchisor had not agreed to give up its right to terminate by accepting late payments in the past, and that the franchisor did not have to give the franchisee notice that it intended to rely on the agreement on this occasion.

Franchising Problems and Solutions

Franchising has potential for lots of problems because:

- franchises are attractive to people without a great deal of business experience, and there are some unscrupulous franchisors
- standard form franchising agreements are always drafted to favour the franchisor over the franchisee
- in almost every province there is no specific legislation to protect franchisees, so the parties are governed by the general laws of contract

The particular problems that franchisees have can vary widely, but many of them fall into just a few areas. Often the root of
the problem is the way the franchise agreement is drafted. That's
why it's important to have your lawyer go over the agreement
before you sign anything.

- Having to buy supplies and equipment from the franchisor can
  chain a franchisee to suppliers who charge more than the going
  market rate. This is especially frustrating since one of the major
  attractions of a franchise is the prospect of access to supplies at
  a discount. However, there's little you can do about this unless
  the franchisor's insistence that you buy from it leads to reduced
  competition in the marketplace generally. Then the federal Competition Bureau may listen to a complaint about this **tied selling**
  and order the franchisor to stop.

- If the franchisor opens an excessive number of franchises in one
  area, or even one franchise that's too close to yours, it can dras-
  tically reduce your profits. Your profits can also fall if the franchisor starts to distribute through other sources (like mail order
  catalogues or the Internet) the products your store carries. You
  can't prevent this unless it's specifically mentioned in the franchise agreement.

> **TIP**
>
> Put a clause in the agreement stating that the franchisor won't open
> more than a certain number of franchises in your market area, or any
> single franchise within a certain distance of yours, and also (if it's a
> possibility) that the franchisor won't market the products by other means.
> The clause should also state what your rights are if the franchisor does.

- The franchisor may lease the premises where your franchise will
  be located and then sub-lease the premises to you. This can lead
  to a couple of problems. One is that the franchisor may charge
  you more for the sub-lease than the landlord is charging the franchisor for the lease. Another is that the franchisor may take advantage of the landlord and tenant relationship to characterize as rent
  any payments that you are required to make to the franchisor. The
  franchisor has much greater rights against you for failure to pay

your rent than it has against you for failure to make payments due under the franchise agreement. The franchisor can lock you out of your premises without notice if you fail to pay rent.

> **T I P**
>
> The franchise agreement should say that you will enter into any lease with the landlord directly and not through the franchisor. If you do have to lease through the franchisor, the agreement should contain the franchisor's promise not to charge you more than it is charged for rent. In addition, the agreement should state that any payments of a percentage of your income should be made under the franchise agreement and not under the lease.
>
> T I P

- Many franchisees complain that they are required to pay substantial amounts for advertising and yet see little or nothing for their money. There's not much you can do about this unless the franchise agreement contains specific promises by the franchisor about the nature and frequency of the advertising that it will buy.

- Franchisees also often complain that they are given inadequate training and support. Support and training provisions in franchise agreements are usually worded so generally that it's hard to prove that the franchisor hasn't given the franchisee what was promised. The best solution here is to choose wisely when you choose a franchisor—look for one who has an excellent track record in this area.

DISTRIBUTORSHIPS AND LICENCES

In a distributorship, a manufacturer gives a wholesaler or retailer the right to sell a product within a specified geographical area. A wholesale distributor may grant distributorships to retailers as well. An exclusive distributorship is more valuable than one that also allows others to sell the product in the same area. A distributor often has to buy the product from the manufacturer or wholesaler and then resell it (with luck, at a profit). In some cases, however, the distributor takes the goods on **consignment** and does not pay for them unless and until they are sold. In return for the right to sell the product, you may be required to follow specific marketing procedures and to meet minimum sales targets.

The manufacturer or wholesale distributor who gives you your distributorship may think it has the right to make up whatever terms it likes, but it doesn't. There are some practices that are common but that may be against the federal *Competition Act*. These include insisting that their products not be discounted, or sold for less than a specified price (see p. 275 in Chapter 19 for more about the offence of **price maintenance**), and requiring distributors to stock only or mainly their product (see p. 275 in Chapter 19) for more about the reviewable practice of **exclusive dealing**, which the Competition Tribunal can order stopped if it is substantially reducing competition in the market).

In a licence, the owner of a patent, trademark, copyright, industrial design, or name (the **licensor**) grants the **licencee** a right to use one of those things for a specific purpose and a specific length of time (and sometimes within a specific geographic area) in return for a royalty payment. For example, some famous clothing designers have granted licences to manufacturers of sunglasses or perfume and the like to use their name and logo on their products. Film studios licence the rights to use their cartoon and other characters in the manufacture of toys, stationery, clothing, books, dog dishes—the list is endless (but your attention span probably is not). The licensor may or may not be interested in controlling the quality of the licencee's product.

A distributorship agreement or a licencing agreement can be short and sweet, or complicated as all get-out. It just depends on the nature of the business involved and the person offering you the deal. (And possibly on the number of lawyers who have already had their fingers in the pie.) As with any contract that's important to your business, an agreement for a distributorship or a licence should be carefully reviewed by your lawyer before you sign it.

CHAPTER NINE

FINANCING
A BUSINESS

Every business needs money—seed money to start, money to cover operating expenses, and capital to expand. You may be lucky enough to have the money that you need to get started, either from your own funds or through gifts or loans from friends and relations. You may take on a partner who makes a financial contribution or sell shares in your corporation (see Chapter 4) to get equity financing. Your business may be successful and produce enough income to cover your operating expenses and enough profit to allow you to grow. But more likely you will have to find outside money for some or all of these things. Unless you've got a fairy godmother you'll have to borrow the money.

The thought of borrowing money can be very frightening, and for good reason. Some of the fear comes from a lack of understanding of the financing process. The purpose of this chapter is to provide you with enough information so that ungrounded fears won't prevent you from borrowing when you should. But this chapter should also give you enough healthy respect for the borrowing process that you won't overextend yourself financially.

WHERE CAN YOU BORROW MONEY?

The sources of money (apart from your own assets, and doting family and friends) include banks, trust companies, credit unions, and (in Quebec) caisses populaires. If you've been turned down by these institutional lenders, you can try the Business Development Bank of Canada, federal, provincial, or municipal government departments with small business financing programs, private venture capital companies, and private foundations.

If you are buying property, equipment, or machinery, you may be able to finance the purchase through a loan from the vendor, a conditional sales arrangement, or a lease. You may be able to get financing for the purchase of inventory and supplies from suppliers through a credit arrangement, a loan, or a sale on consignment. You may be able to get your clients or customers to finance the work you do for them by structuring your deal so that you get a deposit and/or instalment payments. Although you may be tempted to finance your business through your credit cards or private loan companies that specialize in lending to people who can't get a bank loan, we don't recommend either option because of the higher interest rates charged.

For more information about where to look for money and how to go about extracting it from its keeper, we suggest that you read Allan Riding and Barbara Orser's *Beyond the Banks: Creative Financing for Canadian Entrepreneurs*, also in the PROFIT series.

THE ESSENTIAL ELEMENTS OF A LOAN

Every loan is a contract under which the lender agrees to advance money to the borrower, who agrees to repay the money on certain terms. Most loan contracts address the following matters:

- the principal amount of the loan
- the interest rate
- the terms of repayment
- any security for the loan

The discussion of loans in this chapter is directed towards institutional loans rather than those from family and friends. That doesn't mean that there shouldn't be a written loan contract between you and your mother or your best friend since Grade three if they're lending you money. It doesn't have to run to 10 pages of small print like a contract with a bank, but it should adequately cover the four matters above (a promissory note may be enough—see p. 119). You may want to have your lawyer review or even draft the contract, particularly if it's for a large amount or if you are giving security.

see p. 119

**T
I
P**

Your mother or best friend should probably have independent legal advice before agreeing to the terms of the loan. If the agreement is very unfair to the lender, she may be able to get it cancelled (see p. 33 in Chapter 3), and that's the kind of uncertainty that you don't want hanging over your business.

see p. 33 in Chapter 3

Principal and Interest

The **principal**, or principal amount of the loan, is the amount of money being borrowed. As the loan is repaid, the outstanding principal (the amount still to be paid) goes down. With most loans it is not enough to simply repay the principal, the borrower must also pay **interest** on it. Interest is the fee charged by the lender for the use of the money borrowed, over the life of the loan. It is calculated as a percentage of the outstanding principal of the loan, so as the outstanding principal gets smaller, the amount you pay in interest does too.

The interest rate may be **fixed** for the term of the loan, which means that the rate doesn't change, or it may be **variable** over the term of the loan, which means that it will go up and down, usually in relation to the bank's **prime lending rate**. That is the interest rate at which the bank lends money to its best customers. Trust us: you will not start off as one of the bank's best customers! You will be one of its other customers, all of whom pay some amount over prime. The actual amount will depend on how much is being borrowed and how reliable the customer is. What the rate is at any time depends on general economic conditions. In recent memory, interest rates have ranged from a low of about 4 per cent to a high of over 20 per cent.

Under the federal *Interest Act*, if the interest rate is not expressed in annual terms (such as 6.75 per cent "per annum" or "p.a." or "annually" or "yearly"), as opposed to in daily, weekly, or monthly terms (such as "6.75 per cent payable monthly"), the maximum annual rate that can be charged is 5 per cent. In commercial loans, unlike consumer loans, there is no requirement for the lender to disclose the total amount of interest payable over the life of the loan (the **cost of borrowing**).

Terms of Repayment

The loan agreement will specify the terms on which the loan must be repaid. Two ordinary kinds of loan are the **demand loan** and the **term loan**. A demand loan has no set repayment schedule, and the lender can demand repayment of the outstanding principal plus interest at any time. A term loan is repayable in regular instalments of principal and interest over a stated period of time. With a term loan, you could be required to pay a fixed amount of principal every month plus interest on the outstanding principal. Your payments will go down every month because the interest owed goes down as the principal amount of the loan is paid down. Alternatively you may be required to make equal monthly payments, which blend principal and interest. In that case, your payments, which will remain the same over the life of the loan, are calculated so that by the end of the loan you will have repaid the entire principal amount of the loan and will have paid all the interest you owed. You will not be able to pay off a term loan early unless the loan agreement specifically gives you that right. So if interest rates go down before the term of your loan is up, you won't be able to borrow money at the lower rate and pay off the loan.

Security for the Loan

You are contractually obligated to repay the loan and pay the interest as you promised. If you don't, the lender can sue you and get a judgment against you for the amount of money that you owe. Because lawsuits are expensive and slow and because it can be difficult to collect on a judgment, lenders (suspicious and untrusting as they are) generally are not satisfied simply with the borrower's promise to repay. They usually require some form of **security** or **collateral** to give them another way to collect on the loan if the borrower **defaults** (doesn't pay as promised).

When a lender takes security for a loan, the lender has the right to take specific property from the borrower if the borrower doesn't pay back the loan. The lender uses the property to pay the loan, and can still go after the borrower for any amount that remains unpaid. Lenders can take security on different kinds of property, depending on the type of the loan being made. For example on:

• real property

• personal property

• accounts receivable (money that you are owed by your clients or customers)

• inventory

Besides (or instead of) taking security on property, a lender may demand a **guarantee**—a promise by someone other than the borrower to repay the loan if the borrower does not. If the borrower is not able to make the regular loan payments, and doesn't have enough assets to use to repay the debt, the lender can go after the **guarantor** for payment. For example, if the borrower is a sole proprietor, the lender may want a guarantee from a spouse or parent. (Isn't that nice? You can make owing money to the bank a family enterprise.) If the borrower is a corporation, a lender may ask for a guarantee from the shareholders or directors. The lender can insist on having security on the assets of the guarantor as well.

A corporation approached its bank for credit, but the bank was unwilling to advance any money unless it was assured that the corporation's parent company would continue to support it financially. The directors and officers of the corporation provided the bank with a "comfort letter" to this effect and the bank advanced the money. After several months the corporation's finances began to deteriorate and its parent company told it not to expect any help. The corporation asked the bank for an increase in credit and received it, but did not let the bank know that its parent company would no longer accept financial responsibility for the corporation. The corporation went bankrupt, leaving the bank as an unsecured creditor. The bank sued the directors and officers personally who had signed the comfort letter. The bank won. The directors and officers were held personally liable for their misrepresentation to the bank, even though they had been acting for the corporation and not for themselves.

DIFFERENT TYPES OF LOANS

The type of loan you get will depend on your reason for borrowing the money. Loans fall into two major categories—**capital loans** and **operating loans**. Capital loans finance purchases of business assets, while operating loans help cover the ongoing costs of doing business. Financial institutions have several forms of each of these loans, and the names of the different loans will vary from institution to institution.

Capital Loans

You may need a capital loan to cover the costs of starting up your business, including buying machinery and equipment and your initial inventory and supplies, buying or renting premises and fixing them up, and paying legal and other fees. After being in business for a few years you may need a capital loan to buy more machinery or equipment or to move to new premises. Capital loans are generally term loans (see above on p. 110), and the lender will typically want security on the property you are buying, but the form that the security takes will depend on the property. For example, a mortgage would be used if you are buying land; a chattel mortgage if you are buying equipment.

Operating Loans

An operating loan is one that allows you to borrow money as you need it to pay your ongoing expenses, and to repay what you've borrowed as your business revenue comes in. This kind of loan usually takes the form of a **line of credit** or **overdraft protection** that is tied to your business chequing account. For that reason, you will have to maintain your business bank accounts at the lending institution. With this kind of loan in place, you can write cheques to pay your bills, and if you don't have enough money in your account, the bank will lend you the money (up to a predetermined maximum amount). When you deposit money into your account it is automatically applied to pay down the loan. In some cases, you may be required to make regular payments as well and/or ensure that the overdraft in your account is repaid within a fixed period of time. As a rule, the bank will want some form of security for this kind of loan, usually over your business's accounts receivable and inventory. Don't be surprised if you are also asked to give a personal guarantee backed by a collateral mortgage on your home (and possibly on your first-born child as well).

DIFFERENT FORMS OF SECURITY

There are quite a few different forms of security, and the form that a lender will use will depend on the type of property involved. Just to reassure you up front, it is no longer possible for a lender to force you into slavery.

Real Estate Mortgage, Charge, or Hypothec

If the lender wants security on land you own, you will have to sign a **mortgage** or **charge** (in Quebec a **hypothec**), which will be registered on the title to the property. The mortgage will give the lender the right to seize the property if you default on your loan. The precise rights of the lender vary from province to province, and depend on the province's mortgage legislation. These remedies are discussed on p. 309 in Chapter 22.

Usually the mortgage will contain a schedule for the repayment of the loan. If the loan is given as additional security for another debt, the mortgage will be called a **collateral mortgage** and will be payable on demand (although demand will not normally be made unless you default on the loan). The lender will register its mortgage on the title to the property, so that any future buyer or lender will know about it.

Chattel Mortgage, Conditional Sales Agreement, or Lease with Option to Purchase

If you borrow money and use the money to buy a vehicle, piece of machinery, or equipment, the lender may want to take security for the loan on that vehicle, piece of machinery, or equipment, and will make you sign a **chattel mortgage** (in some provinces it is called a **specific security agreement**). The chattel mortgage will give the lender the right to seize the piece of property if you default on your loan.

If you buy a vehicle or equipment and get financing directly from the seller, the seller can get security through a **conditional sales agreement**. If you sign a conditional sales agreement the seller remains the owner of the asset until you make your final payment, at which time you become the legal owner. You get the use of the asset while you are paying for it, but the seller can take it back if you default in your payments. A lease that includes an **option to purchase** the property at the end of the lease is very similar to a conditional sales agreement.

Purchase Money Security Agreement

If you buy personal property (such as inventory) on credit from a manufacturer, retailer, or other supplier, the seller may want security over the property you are buying through an agreement that gives a **purchase money security interest**. If you don't pay, the seller can seize the property.

Security Under Section 427 of the *Bank Act*

If the lender wants security over the inventory of your business, it can take security under section 427 of the *Bank Act* if the lender is a chartered bank and if you are in business as a wholesale or retail purchaser, manufacturer, shipper, dealer, farmer, fisher, or forestry producer. If you default on your loan, the bank can seize and sell your inventory.

Assignment of Accounts Receivable

You may provide security for your debt by assigning some or all of your accounts receivable (sometimes called **book debts**) to the lender. If you assign your accounts receivable and you default on your loan payments, the lender has the right to collect any money owing to you. The lender also has the right to give notice of the assignment of accounts receivable to your customers and clients at any time. Normally, the lender will not notify your customers and clients unless you default on your loan.

General Security Agreement

In some provinces a lender may be able to get security over almost all of the borrower's present and future assets, including equipment, vehicles, machinery, inventory, and accounts receivable, by using a **general security agreement**. (A general security agreement does not usually cover real property.) The borrower is allowed to buy and sell its assets in the usual course of business. But if the borrower defaults on the loan, the lender has the right to seize and sell any or all of the assets to pay off the loan, or to have a **receiver and manager** appointed to do this.

Debenture

A debenture is similar to a general security agreement. The main differences are that only a corporation can give a debenture as security for a loan, and that a debenture usually covers all assets including real property. A debenture can cover both specific assets (a **fixed charge**) and generally described classes of assets both present and future (a **floating charge**). The corporation can deal in the normal course of business with the assets covered by the floating charge. If the corporation defaults under the loan, the floating charge **crystallizes** and freezes all assets owned by the corporation at that time, and they can then be seized by the lender.

Pledge of Shares

As additional security, the lender may require a **pledge** of shares, bonds, or debentures, which are the personal assets of the borrower or guarantor. If the borrower is a private corporation, the lender may require a pledge of the shares of the corporation from the shareholders so that the lender can have control of the corporation if the borrower defaults.

Security Over a Combination of Assets

If you are borrowing money to buy a single asset, the lender will usually ask for security on that asset only. If you are borrowing money for general business purposes, the lender will want security over as many of your assets as possible. While there are different ways for a lender to get security over the same assets, the lender will choose the way that involves the least expense and the fewest documents. Both the lender and the borrower will want to use an approach that won't require the borrower to get the lender's permission for every single transaction made in the course of business. For example, if a bank is lending money to a manufacturer that is buying more equipment, increasing its inventory, buying a new warehouse, and looking to cover extra operating expenses of the expanded business, the bank will want security over the new building and equipment, the inventory, and the accounts receivable. The bank *could* ask for a mortgage on the building, a chattel mortgage on each individual piece of machinery, *Bank Act* security on the inventory, and an assignment of accounts receivable. Or it could get security over all the same assets either through a mortgage on the premises and a general security agreement, or through a debenture.

Registration of Security Interests:
The *Personal Property Security Act*

Almost every province has a *Personal Property Security Act* (PPSA) that governs many aspects of the relationship between a lender and a borrower when security is given against personal property. With the exception of land mortgages (and sometimes security under the *Bank Act*), all of the different types of security discussed above come under the PPSA, under which every lender registers notice of its security interest by means of a **financing statement**. Anybody who wants to buy or take security on any of your personal property will check to see whether a financing statement has been registered. (A similar, but separate, registration system exists for interests in land, including mortgages.)

The PPSA also sets out what rights the lender has to take, keep, or sell the property and what obligations it has to the borrower if it does so. These rights and obligations are discussed on p. 307 in Chapter 22.

WHAT DOCUMENTS WILL YOU HAVE TO SIGN?

You may have to sign many documents as part of your loan transaction, depending on the type of loan and the security you give. For example, you may have to sign:

• a loan agreement

• promissory note(s)

• guarantee(s)

• documents to provide security over assets

TIP

All of these documents are prepared by the lender's lawyers and are drafted to favour the lender in language that is largely incomprehensible. The lender may suggest that you get independent legal advice, and we strongly recommend that you have a lawyer review and explain any loan documents before you sign them. While you or your lawyer may not be able to change the documents in any way, you will at least know what you're agreeing to.

TIP

The Loan Agreement

Every loan transaction will have some form of loan agreement that sets out the contractual arrangements between the lender and the borrower. The agreement may cover just one loan, or it may cover several at once. The length and complexity of the document will depend on the size of the loan(s) and the degree of risk to the lender. A loan agreement will deal with all or some of the following matters:

- the principal amount of the loan
- the lender's obligation to advance funds—if the money is not given to the borrower all at once, the lender is only required to continue to give you money if you meet certain conditions
- the interest rate
- repayment terms and any right to pay off the loan early
- the kind of security to be provided
- representations and warranties (statements that the borrower intends the lender to rely on as true) made by the borrower to the lender, including:
  - if the borrower is a corporation, that it is in good standing
  - that the borrower has the authority to borrow
  - that the borrower owns the assets on which security is being given and that they are not already subject to a security agreement
  - that the business is in good financial health
- covenants (promises) of the borrower, including:
  - that it won't **encumber** assets of the business by entering into other security agreements that cover the same assets
  - that it won't dispose of any major assets of the business
  - that there will be no change in control of the business
  - that there will be no change in the nature of the business
  - that it will provide financial information to the lender on a regular basis and as the lender requests
  - that it will pay the lender's legal fees associated with the loan
  - that it will maintain adequate insurance on its assets and business
  - that it will sign additional security agreements if the lender requires

- what constitutes default under the loan (and will cause the loan to be immediately due and payable), such as:
  - any covenant is breached
  - any payment is not made in full and on time
  - a representation turns out to have been false or misleading
  - the auditor is unwilling to give an unqualified opinion on the borrower's financial statements
  - the borrower or its owner becomes insolvent or goes bankrupt
  - someone gets a judgment larger than a certain amount of money against the borrower
  - the borrower doesn't pay its other debts as they come due
- what the lender may do if the borrower defaults—in particular, appoint a receiver and manager to take charge of assets covered by any security agreements.

Promissory Note

A promissory note is a written document, signed by the borrower, containing the borrower's promise to pay a specified amount of money to the lender either at a fixed time or on demand. The note may also include an interest rate and a schedule of payments. In a very simple loan transaction, where there is no security given, a promissory note can be the entire loan agreement. However, in most business loan situations, a promissory note will be just one of the loan documents. If the loan is a line of credit, the borrower will be required to sign promissory notes periodically as the amount borrowed goes up, as an acknowledgment of how much money has been advanced. If the loan is advanced in instalments, the borrower may have to sign a promissory note before each instalment is paid out.

Guarantees

A guarantee is a written document signed by a person other than the borrower and promising to pay the borrower's debt to the lender, if the borrower does not. A guarantee is not valid unless it is given in writing (and in Alberta it must also be signed before a notary public).

Sometimes a lender will ask a person other than the borrower to **co-sign** on the loan. This is different from guaranteeing the loan, because a co-signor can be required to pay the debt at any time, whether the borrower is able to pay or not.

Security Documents

We've discussed above the different kinds of security that a lender may require. Each kind requires the borrower to sign one or more documents. For example, a mortgage is used if the security is land, a chattel mortgage, conditional sales agreement, or purchase money security agreement if the security is personal property, and a general security agreement if the security is a large number of the business's assets.

WHAT HAPPENS IF YOU DON'T PAY BACK YOUR LOAN?

If you don't pay your loan, or if you default in any other way, there are different things that the lender can do to you (none of them pleasant). See Chapter 22 for the gory details. Fortunately, debtors' prison has been abolished for some time now.

CHAPTER TEN

YOUR PLACE OF BUSINESS

You're in business for yourself, so you know *who* you're working for, but *where* are you working? Now it's time to make some decisions about your place of business. This chapter will help you answer the following questions:

- should you work out of your home?
- should you rent or buy business premises?
- should you rent or buy your equipment?

SHOULD YOU WORK OUT OF YOUR HOME?

Running a business from your home is a viable option nowadays if your operation does not require too much space. With voice mail, computer equipment, printers, and fax machines, businesses can project a professional image even if the head office is a basement or spare bedroom. It's not always possible to run a business from home, though; and even when it is, there are advantages and disadvantages to weigh.

Is It Even Possible?

Sometimes a home business is simply not possible. Practically speaking, if your business relies on a walk-in trade, you will want a more high-profile location than your house or apartment can provide. If you're carrying on a business that requires a large facility you won't have the space. If your business requires a lot of equipment, you won't have the necessary infrastructure, reinforced floors, special ventilation, or electrical capacity.

Legally speaking, if you have employees, even if you have the space for them, your home may not meet provincial occupational health and safety requirements. If you live in a condominium or in rented premises, the by-laws or lease may prohibit you from carrying on any type of business in your home. Even if you own your own home, in many municipalities the by-laws prohibit any kind of business in an area that is zoned residential. Most municipalities turn a blind eye to in-home businesses unless someone complains, so you shouldn't run your business out of your home if it's likely to annoy your neighbours because of things like noise, smells, or traffic.

If it's both practical and legal for you to work out of your home, the next question is: should you?

What Are the Advantages?

The main advantage of an in-home business is that it saves money because you don't have to buy or rent premises. A home business saves you money in another important way: you get an income tax deduction for a portion of the costs of running your home—costs that you would have to pay whether you ran your business out of your home or not. (For more on the home business deduction see p. 236 in Chapter 17.)

There are other advantages too. You don't have to commute, so you save time and money and avoid the aggravation of rush-hour traffic. If you get a brilliant business idea in the middle of the night, you can start working on it right away; you don't even have to get out of your pajamas. In fact you can stay in your pajamas all the time if you're not seeing customers or clients. (For your psychological health, we recommend that you get dressed every day, by dinner time at least, but you may still be able to save a fair bit of money by not maintaining an extensive work wardrobe.) If you have children, aging parents, or pets you may not have to pay others to look after them (but beware of the distraction they can cause).

What Are the Disadvantages?

There are some disadvantages to operating out of your home, but most of them can be relatively easily overcome. Your business may need facilities and services that you can't have in your home, but that doesn't mean that you can't have them at all. It's easy to get access to all sorts of business support services like:

- printing and photocopying
- couriers
- product packaging and shipping
- libraries and research materials on CD-ROM or the Internet
- a more impressive business identity: a business mailing address on a major street plus mail forwarding and telephone answering
- office centres that rent out space on a part-time or occasional basis
- freelance secretaries and other assistants who work from their own premises

Probably the biggest disadvantage of working at home is that you may feel too isolated from your business associates and not isolated enough from your family. You'll have to make an extra effort to schedule lunches with colleagues and customers and join community and business associations. Dealing with family distractions may be the single hardest thing to do. You have to make it plain to your family and your pets that you can't be disturbed when you're working. Your family and the dog may be more understanding if you are not working 24 hours a day.

SHOULD YOU RENT (OR BUY) BUSINESS PREMISES?

If your business is bigger than your home, or if the cat is getting on your nerves, you have other options besides working at home.

Temporary Measures

You may think that your only option is to rent or buy an office, store, or space in an industrial building (depending on the nature of your business) and furnish and equip it. But you don't have to go that far right away. You can take an intermediate step. If you need office space you can sub-let a single office from another business or rent an office in a business centre or "packaged office" complex. For a monthly fee you will get your own office (in a business centre or packaged office it will be fully furnished) plus reception services, use of a boardroom and office equipment, and access to support services such as secretarial, word processing, and bookkeeping. If you need retail space, some shopping complexes offer carts or booths. If you need industrial space you may be able to use a self-storage unit for your warehousing needs and maybe even for some assembly of merchandise. All of these options have the same advantages: the premises are smaller and may be cheaper to rent and equip than more permanent space, and they're available on a short-term basis.

Make sure you find a place that really satisfies your needs. Find out:

- what rent will you have to pay? Are utilities included? Do you have to pay a damage deposit? Are there any other extra charges?

- how long is the agreement for? What do you have to do if you want to leave? Can the landlord make you leave before you're ready to go?

- what services are you entitled to? Are they included in the rent? If they're extra, how much do they cost?

- are there any restrictions on the use of the premises that will affect your business?

- can you get access to the premises whenever you need to?

- are the premises secure against break-in?

When you finalize your arrangements, you will be entering into a contract. It should be in writing, and make sure that it includes all of the terms that are important to you.

Permanent Arrangements

Your business may, in fact, need permanent office, retail, or industrial space. You can buy the space or you can rent it. Consider carefully before deciding which to do. Compare the cost of ownership with the cost of renting, and also think about what best suits the needs of your business. Most small businesses can't afford to buy their premises, and may be better off with the shorter-term commitment of renting anyway. There are tax implications as well to the choice between buying and renting (having to do with the deductibility of rent versus mortgage interest), so speak to an accountant before making up your mind.

If it makes business and financial sense for you to buy, you can look for premises with the help of an industrial/commercial real estate agent. You'll find more information about the purchase of property below on p. 134. If you are looking for business space to lease, you can use a commercial leasing agent who will show you various locations that might meet your needs. Once you find space that you like, you will enter into negotiations with the landlord. The process of lease negotiation can be complicated, and it will lead to the signing of a commercial lease, which is even more complicated. In the next section we'll explain to you what is involved in negotiating a lease and go over the essential elements of a commercial lease.

COMMERCIAL LEASES

Whether you are renting office, retail, or industrial space, you are entering into a commercial lease. If you've lived in an apartment any time in your life, you may think you know a thing or two about leases and landlords. Well, you don't—at least not when it comes to commercial leases. Residential tenants have all kinds of legislated protection from their landlords that commercial tenants do not.

An entrepreneurial couple had a retail store selling children's clothing, and they ran it from leased premises, under a commercial lease. Business wasn't great, they were just getting by, and they were regularly late with their rent payments. They had never gone over their lease, either with a lawyer or on their own, and they just assumed that a commercial tenancy was like a residential tenancy and that nothing serious would happen if they paid their rent late. That was their first mistake. One month the landlord got fed up when their payment was late. He locked them out of the store, seized their goods, and disposed of their inventory at fire sale prices. Then the couple made their second mistake. Because they didn't know anything about commercial leases, they didn't realize that the landlord had no right to lock them out *and* sell their inventory for next to nothing. So they didn't bother to consult a lawyer. If they had, they would have been able to get damages from the landlord for his wrongful actions.

What's involved in negotiating a lease? What will you find in a commercial lease? What are the remedies of both the landlord and the tenant under the lease? Read on.

The Negotiation Process

As you look at different premises, and once you start actual negotiations for the ones you've chosen, your main focus will be on the following matters:

- what space will be yours to use in the operation of your business?
- will the landlord pay anything towards the decorating and/or renovating costs (**leasehold improvements**)?
- how much will you pay for the space?
  - what is the flat rent or basic rent?
  - is there anything payable in addition to the basic rent, for example, utilities, or a proportional share of the landlord's taxes, maintenance, or operating costs?
  - is there extra rent payable based on a percentage of your earnings? (this usually only happens in retail leases)
- how long is the term of the lease? Will you have a right to renew?

- what use can you make of the premises?

- in a shopping centre lease will other tenants be prevented from competing with you?

- what services (such as elevators, security, cleaning) will be available to you in the building or shopping centre?

- what rights will you have to transfer (**assign**) your lease to someone else or to sublet the premises?

- can the landlord terminate the lease for demolition or sale purposes?

You may negotiate directly with the landlord or through a leasing agent. Once you arrive at an agreement in principle on these matters, you may be asked to sign one or more legal documents, including a **letter of intent**, an **offer** or **agreement to lease**, and the lease itself.

Letters of intent are not very commonly used in the negotiation of commercial leases, but you may be asked to write or sign one. Its purpose is to get a commitment from the parties at a very early stage in negotiations. The letter is a starting point for the negotiation and contains a very general statement of the parties' intention to negotiate a lease. It is not an agreement, and it usually clearly says that it is not legally binding on the parties.

You are more likely to be asked to make an offer to the landlord setting out the terms on which you are willing to lease the premises. The document may be headed "Offer to Lease" or "Agreement to Lease," but it only becomes an agreement after the landlord signs it too. The agreement is that you will sign a lease on the terms contained in the agreement. The final lease may contain other terms that are not included in the agreement to lease, and they too may have to be negotiated between the parties. To eliminate arguments about the final terms of the lease, many agreements to lease contain a statement that the tenant will sign the landlord's standard form of lease. (The standard form lease may or may not be attached to the agreement to lease.) If the agreement says that you will sign the landlord's standard form lease, you must sign the lease. Therefore do not sign such an agreement unless you have read the lease in full, understand it, and are willing to be bound by its terms.

The lease itself will be prepared by the landlord's lawyers, and will probably be the same document that the landlord uses for all of its tenants. The lease has been drafted to benefit the landlord and to deal with all kinds of situations, many of which will never occur. But unless you're a large tenant, you probably will not be able to convince the landlord to make many, or even any, changes in the lease.

T
I
P

t probably would be a waste of money to hire a lawyer to try to negotiate changes because it's usually a take-it-or-leave-it situation. However, it would still be wise to have a lawyer read the lease and explain it to you so you know whether to take it or leave it. Because commercial leases can be very, very long and complicated documents, you need a lawyer with experience in commercial leasing, who can do this job for you quickly and cheaply.

T I P

The Commercial Lease Itself

Commercial leases are usually categorized according to the way that rent is calculated. In a **gross lease** the landlord sets an amount of rent and that is all the tenant pays. The landlord pays for the building maintenance, all administrative costs, realty taxes, utilities, and insurance on the entire building. In calculating the rent, the landlord estimates what its costs will be and sets the rent at a level that will yield a profit after all of the costs of the building are paid. In a **base year lease** the tenant pays a fixed amount of rent in the first year of the lease. In subsequent years the tenant pays the same fixed amount of rent plus a percentage of any increase in specified costs of the landlord. The percentage that the tenant pays is based on the proportion of the building that the tenant occupies.

In a **net lease** the tenant pays a fixed amount of rent and, in addition, pays a percentage of all of the landlord's costs of the building, including realty taxes, utilities, maintenance, insurance, and administrative costs. The landlord will give an estimate of the tenant's share of those costs for the coming year, and will require the tenant to pay 1/12 of that amount each month as **additional rent**. At least once a year the landlord will give the tenant a statement of the actual costs for the year. If the monthly payments don't fully cover the actual costs, the tenant will have to make up the difference. Net leases are sometimes called "net net" or "net net net" leases. They all mean the same thing—that it is the landlord's intention to pass all possible costs directly on to the tenant. Most commercial leases today are net leases.

Commercial leases tend to be long. A relatively small commercial landlord may use a widely available, pre-printed form of lease of about 10 pages. A big-time commercial landlord will have its own form of lease that can run to 50 or more pages. The six or seven items that are of importance to you in any lease could be dealt with in three or four pages. This means that all the other pages are there to address the landlord's concerns. However long the lease, it will probably cover the following matters:

• a description of the rented premises—the description is often given in terms of square footage. The square footage is important because it may be used to calculate the rent and other payments under the lease. In an office lease, the square footage may be "grossed up" to charge the tenant for a portion of shared space such as corridors, elevators, and stairwells.

• the term of the lease—when it starts and when it ends

• renewal of the lease—the tenant may be given an option to renew the lease for another term. This right is especially important to a retail business, because location affects the goodwill of the business. A renewal clause that either fixes the rent for the renewal period or puts a ceiling on it is the most advantageous for the tenant. It's important to note what steps you have to take to renew the lease and when you have to take them.

• rent—it is usually payable monthly, and it may be a flat amount or it may be an amount calculated on the square footage of the premises. In retail store leases the rent can be calculated on a percentage of the sales or profits of the store, instead of—or in addition to—a fixed minimum rent. If your rent is based on a percentage of your sales or profits, you will be required to give the landlord financial information about your business regularly.

- additional rent—if the lease is a base year lease or a net lease, the tenant will have to make additional payments to the landlord to cover the costs of running the building. Note what kinds of expenses the payments include, how the payments are calculated, and when they must be made. In addition to realty taxes and the usual expenses of running and repairing the building, some landlords try to pass on costs such as personal taxes and capital costs such as improvements and renovations.

- use of the premises—the lease will state what you can (and sometimes what you can't) do on the premises. Make sure that the use is broad enough for you to carry on your business not only as it is now, but as it may be in the future if it grows or changes.

- non-competition by other businesses—in a shopping centre lease, the tenant should ask for a clause stating that the landlord agrees not to permit any other tenant to use space on the premises to provide a service or sell a product that is similar to the tenant's. Landlords are very reluctant to agree to this kind of clause, and if they agree at all, the actual wording of the clause often gives very little real protection to the tenant. If the landlord is willing to put in a non-competition clause, you should have it reviewed by your lawyer.

- insurance—the tenant will be required to get certain kinds of insurance, with an insurer and in a form satisfactory to the landlord. The landlord may require:
  - property (fire) insurance
  - business interruption insurance
  - comprehensive general liability insurance
  - tenant's legal liability insurance
  - automobile insurance
  - broad form boiler and machinery insurance
  - other kinds of insurance depending on the nature of your business

  The landlord wants all of this insurance to make sure that you stay in business after an accident—and keep paying the rent. There is often duplication between the insurance the tenant is required to get and the insurance that the landlord already has.

It's bad enough to have to pay for something you don't really need, but in a net lease, because you, the tenant, are already paying the cost of the landlord's insurance, you're paying twice for something you don't really need! Landlords seem incapable of understanding this, so don't waste your time trying to change the insurance requirements.

- damage to, demolition of, or major renovations to the building—the landlord may have the right to require the tenant to continue paying rent even if the building has suffered major damage or is undergoing extensive repairs or renovation. This can be a real hardship if your business is reduced because of the condition of the building. On the other hand, the landlord may have the right to terminate the lease on fairly short notice if the building is damaged or if the landlord wants to demolish or renovate the building.

- assignment or sub-letting—the lease will probably state that the tenant cannot assign or sub-let without the consent of the landlord and may say that the landlord can unreasonably withhold its consent. Such a clause might make it difficult for you to sell a retail business.

- improvements to the premises—the lease may set out the work that is necessary to make the premises ready for occupation, and specify what the landlord and tenant each is to do and pay for. Most leases say that the tenant must get the consent of the landlord to make any additional improvements during the term of the lease. The lease will also state what will happen to the tenant's trade fixtures at the end of lease—whether they must be left behind or whether the tenant must remove them and repair any damage to the premises.

- hours of operation/access to the premises—in a retail lease there will often be a requirement that the tenant operate the business during specified hours, usually whenever the shopping centre is open. Make sure that the hours suit you. You may be forced to work on a Sunday when you don't really want to, or the shopping centre may be closed on Sundays, but the competition isn't. If you are leasing office space, check whether the landlord agrees to allow you access, electricity, and heat or air-conditioning outside of normal business hours.

As you can see, a tenant is required to pay a lot more than just rent. You will also have to pay whatever amounts are charged to you as additional rent, plus whatever you have to pay personally for your own insurance and business taxes. Be sure that you know what all of your monthly costs add up to.

The Tenant's Remedies Against the Landlord

All of the promises contained in the lease are called **covenants**. There are landlord's covenants and tenant's covenants. A tenant has certain remedies if the landlord breaches one of its covenants, and the landlord has certain remedies if the tenant breaches. Unlike a residential tenant, a commercial tenant has very few options if the landlord fails to fulfill any of its promises under the lease. The tenant can sue for specific performance of the particular promise, for an injunction, or for damages. If the landlord tries to terminate the lease the tenant can ask a court to stop the termination.

The Landlord's Remedies Against the Tenant

Not surprisingly in a document prepared to benefit the landlord, the landlord has quite a lot of remedies if the tenant breaches the lease. The breach that the landlord is most concerned about is the failure to pay rent. Note that "rent" includes not only any base rent but any of the additional charges payable under the lease as additional rent. If the tenant is in **arrears of rent** (has not paid the rent) or has breached the lease in any other way, the landlord has a variety of remedies available:

- the landlord can retake possession of the premises and terminate the lease.
  - if the landlord does only this, it can still sue for arrears of rent or damages but only up to the date the lease was terminated and no later. The tenant will not be required to pay rent that falls due after the date of termination.
  - If the landlord gives the proper notice to the tenant, it will have the right to sue not only for arrears of rent up to the date of termination but also for damages for the future loss of rent under the lease. The tenant may have to pay the difference between

what she would have paid until the end of the lease and what the landlord is likely to get from another tenant.

• the landlord can retake possession without terminating the lease, and relet the premises acting as the tenant's agent. Because the lease continues, the tenant continues to be responsible for the payment of the rent, less anything the landlord collects from the new tenant.

• the landlord can let the lease continue and let the tenant remain in possession, and can sue for arrears of rent or for damages for breach of the lease.

• the landlord can **distrain** to collect arrears of rent—in other words the landlord can seize and sell the goods and chattels of the tenant without having to go to court to get permission.

T I P If your landlord retakes possession of the premises or seizes your goods, you must get legal advice immediately.

T I P

For more about termination and distraint, see below.

The Landlord's Right to Terminate the Lease

The landlord's right to terminate the lease, also called the **right of forfeiture**, arises if the tenant fails to pay rent or breaches almost any covenant in the lease. In most provinces, if the landlord wishes to terminate the lease because of a non-payment of rent, it can only do so after the rent has been unpaid for 15 days or more. If the landlord wishes to terminate the lease because of breach of some other covenant, it must first serve a notice on the tenant that states what the breach is and gives the tenant an opportunity to remedy the breach within a reasonable time. At the end of the 15-day period (for non-payment of rent) or the notice period (for breach of another covenant) the landlord can terminate the lease by either physically retaking possession of the premises or by starting a lawsuit.

If the landlord tries to terminate the lease the tenant can ask a court to grant **relief from forfeiture**, in other words to stop the termination. To get relief, the tenant will have to pay any arrears of rent or correct any breach of the lease.

The Landlord's Right to Distrain

The landlord's right to distrain, also called **distraint** or **distress**, gives the landlord the right to enter the tenant's premises, to seize the tenant's goods and inventory, and to sell them to satisfy the arrears of rent. The landlord must sell the goods for the best possible price. The landlord cannot distrain until the day after the rent was due (and not paid) and must carry out the distress during daylight hours. In most provinces, the landlord can seize all goods and inventory of the tenant on the rented premises except for:

• fixtures

• money

• property on the rented premises belonging to others

• perishable articles

• $2000 worth of tools used in the business

In most provinces, if the tenant removes goods from the premises to avoid distress, the landlord can seize the goods wherever they are found within the next 30 days, and the tenant may also have to pay a penalty to the landlord.

The landlord's right to distrain ends if:

• the landlord has already got a judgment for the arrears of rent

• the landlord terminates the lease or locks out the tenant

• the tenant and landlord agree that the lease is at an end

• the tenant goes bankrupt

BUYING COMMERCIAL REAL ESTATE

If you are thinking of buying your business premises, you must first find out whether the kind of space you are looking for is for sale at all, and if it is, whether you can afford it. A commercial/industrial real estate agent can help you. If you find something you want to buy, you will have to have a lawyer (in Quebec or BC, a notary) act for you to complete the deal. If you make an offer to purchase the property and it is accepted, you will have a binding agreement of purchase and sale with the vendor, so you should have your lawyer (or notary) review the offer before you submit it. Tell your lawyer how you intend to use the property so that he can make sure that the agreement promises that it is zoned to allow the use you have in mind. Before the deal closes, your lawyer will check to make sure that the property *is* zoned as promised. If you're not careful about zoning, you can end up owning property that is useless for your business purposes.

What Is the Cost of Buying?

Whatever you agree to pay the vendor for the property, the actual cost of buying the property will be higher, because it includes:

- the purchase price—what you agree to pay in the agreement of purchase and sale
- sales taxes—land transfer taxes and GST
- lawyer's fees and disbursements
- professional building inspection (optional)
- environmental assessment (optional, but recommended if there may have been chemicals or toxic substances kept or used on the property)
- mortgage costs—the mortgagee may require an appraisal of the property
- adjustments to the purchase price—for such things as rents paid or payable by tenants, property taxes, utilities, and mortgage interest
- relocation costs, moving costs, and installation fees for utilities and the like
- renovation costs

How Will You Pay for the Property?

Unless you have lots and lots of money, you will have to take out a mortgage to finance at least some of the purchase. The maximum you will be able to borrow by way of a **first mortgage** is 60 to 75 per cent of the purchase price. If you don't have cash for the rest, you will have to borrow that money through a business loan. However, they are not as easy to get and have higher interest rates than first mortgages.

What Is the Cost of Carrying the Property?

You should make sure that you can afford the monthly payments associated with ownership. These include:

- mortgage payments
- property taxes—in addition to standard property taxes, there will probably be additional municipal business taxes
- utilities
- insurance
- maintenance and repairs

Business Condominiums

You may be able to buy condominium office, retail, or industrial space. If you do, you become the owner of your commercial unit and also share in ownership of the **common areas** or **common elements** of the condominium complex. These include the exterior structure of the building and all shared mechanical equipment (e.g., heating and cooling systems), and also such things as the hallways, elevators, stairs, lobby, grounds, and parking areas. Owners of a condominium are required to pay a monthly **maintenance fee** that covers the costs of looking after the common area. If there are major or unforeseen problems with these areas, the condominium unit owners can also be required to pay a **special assessment** to cover repairs.

Before you buy a condominium unit you should make sure that the condominium corporation is financially sound and well managed. You should also make sure that the rules and regulations of the condominium do not restrict your ability to carry on your business.

BUSINESS EQUIPMENT

Whatever your business, and whether you run it from your home or from commercial premises, you will need equipment. You can either buy it or lease it. In this section we will tell you briefly some of the advantages and disadvantages of buying and leasing, and the legal implications of each.

Should You Buy or Lease?

If you lease equipment, you don't have to make a down payment, and the lease payments may be spread out over a longer period of time than loan payments would be. A lease usually gives you greater flexibility to upgrade if your current equipment becomes obsolete. On the other hand, unless the lease contains an option to purchase the equipment, you build up no equity no matter how much you pay, and you may pay more over the life of the lease than you would if you borrowed money to buy the equipment. There are also tax implications (concerning the deductibility of lease payments versus the deductibility of interest payments) in the choice between buying and leasing. You should consult your accountant to help you decide which option makes more sense for you.

Buying Equipment

If you buy your equipment you can pay cash or you can finance the purchase. If you borrow money from a third party, the lender will want a chattel mortgage as security for the loan. If you borrow the money from the vendor, the security will usually take the form of a conditional sales agreement. (See p. 114 in Chapter 9.)

In a conditional sales agreement you will be required to make a down payment and pay the balance of the principal and interest on the loan by instalments over a fixed period of time. Until the final payment is made the vendor continues to be the owner of the equipment, but once that final payment is made, you automatically become the owner. Even before ownership passes to you, you are responsible for maintaining and repairing the equipment, and you will be required to keep it insured.

Leasing Equipment

If you lease equipment, it may be a **simple lease** or a **lease with an option to purchase**. If it is a simple lease, no down payment will be required. You will make your payments over the term of the lease, and at the end of it the equipment must be returned to the **lessor** (the owner of the equipment). (You, as the person leasing the equipment, are called the **lessee**.) In a simple lease, the term of the lease is usually the useful life of the equipment, and the payments over the term of the lease are calculated to give the lessor the full value of the equipment plus interest. It is assumed that the property will not be worth anything at the end of the lease.

If it is a lease with an option to purchase, you may or may not make a down payment, but if you do, your monthly lease payments will be less. At the end of the lease you can either return the equipment to the lessor, or exercise your option to buy it by paying the amount specified in the lease. Leasing equipment with an option to purchase is really just another way of financing the purchase. The payments (including the amount to buy the equipment at the end of the lease) are calculated to pay the lessor the full value of the equipment with interest, and the interest rate may be higher than it would be for a loan to buy the same equipment.

The usual terms of an equipment lease include the following:

- a description of the leased equipment
- the term length of the lease
- the payments under the lease—the regular instalments, as well as the amount of any down payment and any buyout at the end of the lease

- that the lessee is responsible for the maintenance and repair of the equipment—sometimes the lessee is required to enter into a separate maintenance contract with the lessor or a third party named by the lessor

- that the lessee is responsible to have insurance against damage to the equipment and damage caused by the equipment

- the consequences of default by the lessee—usually, the lessor can repossess the equipment, and the lessee will have to pay the balance due under the lease to the end of the term, less whatever the lessor gets by selling or re-leasing the equipment. A lease that contains an option to purchase falls under the *Personal Property Security Act*. How assets can be repossessed and sold under the PPSA is discussed on p. 307 in Chapter 22.

Some leases contain a clause making the lessee guarantee that the equipment will be worth a specified amount at the end of the lease term (if there is no option to purchase or if the option is not exercised). The equipment is returned at the end of the lease and is sold by the lessor. If the sale price is less than the guaranteed amount, the lessee will have to pay the difference to the lessor.

If you have problems with your leased equipment, you will have to complain to the manufacturer of the equipment, not to the lessor. And whether the equipment works or not, you'll have to keep making your lease payments.

As with any contract that involves a lot of money or a long-term commitment, think about having your lawyer look at an agreement to lease before you sign it.

CHAPTER ELEVEN

INSURING YOUR BUSINESS

If you're in business, you run risks all the time. A competitor may suddenly appear in your field offering better prices. A big client may delay paying your bill and send your cash flow into a coma. The value of the Canadian dollar may rise and your exports may be shunned in foreign markets, or the dollar may fall and your imports may sit on the shelf. There's no easy way for you to control the damage if something like this happens.

Besides those nightmares, there are many other unpleasant events that can harm your business. For example:

- there may be a fire on your premises
- a consumer may be injured by the product you manufacture
- a client may be injured in your office
- your computer system may fail
- your employees may steal from you
- you may carelessly give a customer or client wrong advice
- you may become disabled, or your partner may become disabled or die

Any one of these things may seem as bad as, or worse than, a tumbling (or skyrocketing) Canadian dollar, but there's a big difference here. These are risks that you can plan against and manage by taking out appropriate insurance. With insurance you can reduce the financial losses your business suffers when certain catastrophes strike.

WHAT KINDS OF INSURANCE ARE AVAILABLE?

You can't insure your business against every possible risk. Even if you were willing to pay the huge premium attached to 100 per cent insurance coverage, you probably wouldn't be able to find insurance companies that offered all the coverage you would need. Although you may be able to arrange to insure against risks that are peculiar to your business, you will most likely start with standard business insurance that offers coverage against risks common to businesses in general. Such insurance covers:

- property
- business interruption
- general liability
- crime or theft
- key persons

PROPERTY INSURANCE

If you have business premises or if you have business assets—in fact, unless your business consists only of you and a pencil—you will need property insurance.

> **T I P**
>
> If you are renting your business premises, be sure to show a copy of your lease to your agent or broker because it will specify what coverage you are required to have. That way your agent or broker can make sure that your policy covers everything that's required by your lease.
>
> T I P

What Property Is Covered?

Generally speaking, property insurance covers:

- the building your business is in, and (if you rent rather than own) any tenant's (leasehold) improvements
- interior and exterior glass and signs
- contents of the premises (such as equipment, furniture, and inventory), property that is off the premises (including portable business tools), and personal property of employees that is on the premises
- accounts receivable and valuable papers

Property insurance usually does *not* cover:

- automobiles, aircraft, and watercraft
- money, cheques over $500, stamps, securities, or documents that are evidence of ownership or of debt
- cellular or mobile phones, or two-way radio sets
- jewels, precious metals, or furs
- property that was illegally acquired or that is being illegally kept or stored
- buildings that are vacant or have been unoccupied for more than 30 days, and their contents

Property insurance does not cover buildings under construction or that are undergoing extensive renovations, but it is possible to get **builders' risk** insurance for them.

What Perils Are Covered?

The troubles you may encounter, or risks to your business, are called **perils**. An insurance company will only agree to insure you against certain risks that are stated in the policy. These risks are called the **insured perils** or **insurable perils**.

Property insurance comes in three forms, **fire, fire and extended coverage**, and **all risks**. If you choose fire coverage, your business is insured against the following:

- fire

- lightning

- explosion of natural, coal, or manufactured gas

and nothing else.

   If you choose fire and extended coverage, usually your business will be insured against the perils in the list above plus the following:

- smoke

- windstorm

- hail

- riot

- leakage from fire protective equipment

- vandalism or malicious acts

- impact by aircraft, spacecraft, or land vehicle

and nothing else.

   If you choose all risks coverage, your business is insured against all perils *except those specifically excluded in the policy*. Typically, with all risks coverage your business will be insured against everything included in fire and extended coverage, and, depending on the wording of the policy, it will also be insured against some or all of the following:

- burglary, theft, or attempted theft

- water damage caused by something other than fire protective equipment

- damage to pipes caused by freezing

- rupture of pipes or breakage of "apparatus" (that's insurance policy lingo—don't ask us what it means. If something breaks, just hope that it was an apparatus.)

and that's it.

Some of the risks usually excluded in an all risks policy are:

- water seepage and leaks
- mechanical or electrical breakdown, or electrical or magnetic disturbances
- changes in temperature and humidity, freezing, heating, leakage of contents, contamination, rust
- "mysterious disappearance" (something is missing but you have no clue what happened to it)
- shrinkage of inventory
- wear and tear, gradual deterioration, and defects in equipment or products
- losses due to suspension or cancellation of any contract, lease, or licence, and losses due to fines or damages for breach of contract
- war and civil war

In practice, all risks coverage doesn't include a whole lot more than fire and extended coverage does. The following are also usually excluded from all risks coverage, but you can pay extra and get coverage against them through a rider:

- flood
- earthquake
- explosion, collapse, bursting, cracking, burning, etc. of boilers and machinery owned, operated, or controlled by your business (this rider is the "boiler and machinery" insurance you heard about when we discussed commercial leases in Chapter 10)
- cost of complying with municipal by-laws passed since the building was originally constructed, if it is rebuilt or repaired after it has been damaged or destroyed
- pollution of your own property by either gradual or sudden and accidental emission

What Coverage Should You Get?

When you take out property insurance, get **replacement cost** coverage. If you don't, when you make a claim you will only be paid the *actual* value of your property at the time it was damaged or destroyed. That is, you'll be paid what it would have been worth if you had tried to sell it on the open market, rather than being paid what it will cost you to replace it.

Replacement cost coverage costs more than **actual value** coverage, so you may decide not to get it. However, be very careful about insuring your property for less than its actual value. If your coverage does not equal a stated percentage of the value of your property (usually 80 to 90 per cent according to the **co-insurance** clause in your policy), and your insurer finds this out when you make a claim, you will not be paid *even the actual value* of your lost property. That's because you become a co-insurer with your insurance company if you don't insure your property adequately, and you bear some of the risk of loss yourself. For example, the co-insurance clause in your policy may require you to insure your business assets for at least 90 per cent of their value. If your assets are worth $100,000, you must insure them for at least $90,000. If you insure them for just $80,000, the insurer is entitled to pay you only eight-ninths of any claim you make, even if you aren't claiming the full amount of the policy.

On the other hand, don't over-insure your property. If you do, you'll still only get paid actual value or replacement cost (whichever you have chosen) when you make a claim. If you make a claim and you are paid either actual or replacement cost value, the insurance company has the right to take the damaged property. This is called the right of **salvage**. If you make a claim for property that was stolen and are paid for it, the insurer has the right to take the property if it is found.

BUSINESS INTERRUPTION INSURANCE

Business interruption insurance is most often an extension of coverage under property insurance. It covers you if you cannot carry on your business because your business premises have been damaged. Whatever form of property insurance you choose, the same risks are covered and the same exclusions apply for your business interruption insurance.

The insurance may cover you (usually for up to 12 months) for:

- actual loss of earnings until your business reopens

- actual loss of profits until your business reopens and returns to normal

- extra expense to retain customers until your business reopens

- reduced profits that result from damage to another business in the building

GENERAL LIABILITY INSURANCE

General liability insurance covers your business if your **negligence** or carelessness (see Chapter 20) causes injury to a customer, client, consumer, or other **third party** not involved in your business, or causes damage to a third party's property or financial interests. There are different kinds of general liability insurance, and some or all of them may be included in the same insurance package. You can get insurance for:

- **commercial general liability**, which covers third-party loss or injury of many kinds (for example, if a customer slips on your wet floor, or if a customer's car is damaged when your store sign falls on it). You may be able to get an extension of coverage for loss or injury caused not by your negligent conduct but by your wrongful acts such as defamation or false imprisonment (see pp. 286-87 in Chapter 20).

**T
I
P**

Any time a third party suffers an injury, contact your insurance company immediately. Your policy may give the insurer the right to deny coverage unless there is immediate notification.

T I P

- **product liability**—which covers third-party loss or injury caused by a defect in a product you manufacture (for example, if you manufacture a boiler that explodes in the user's factory, shutting down operations for several weeks)

- **professional liability** or **errors and omissions**—which covers third-party loss and injury caused by you giving careless advice or doing careless work as a professional (for example, if an architect designs a building with windows that leak every time it rains)

- **tenant's liability**—which covers loss and injury to other tenants of the building (for example, if a fire starts in your coffee room and the smoke spreads into the other tenants' offices)

- **employers' liability**—which covers injury to employees (that is not covered by workers' compensation)

- **limited pollution liability**—which covers loss and injury to third parties caused by an unexpected or unintentional discharge of pollutants from your business

Automobile insurance is a kind of general liability insurance, but it is not normally included in commercial policies. If you have a company car or a fleet of delivery vans, you'll have to arrange separate automobile insurance coverage for them.

Some general liability insurance provides coverage for damage to the insured rather than to a third party, for example:

- **tenant's legal liability**—which covers the insured tenant if its own premises are damaged and the landlord's insurer refuses to pay to repair the premises, on the grounds that the damage was caused by the tenant's negligence

- **contractual liability**—which covers the insured against liability taken on under a contract rather than liability that has been imposed by a statute or common law

- **surety bonds**, **performance bonds**, and **guarantee bonds**—which are not general liability insurance but are a related idea. They are taken out (usually through an insurance company) to protect one party to a contract if the other doesn't perform required obligations. In the event of non-performance by the bonded party, the amount of the bond is paid to the protected party. (For example, if a general contractor building a house wants a subcontractor electrician to start work on a certain date and finish properly by a specified date, the general contractor might require the electrician to put up a performance bond. The company that issued the bond will pay the general contractor if the electrician doesn't finish on time.)

Directors' and Officers' Liability

Directors' and officers' liability (D&O) insurance is another kind of general liability insurance. Directors and officers can be sued by the shareholders, creditors, and employees of the corporation, or by members of the general public for committing a wrongful act such as a tort (see Chapter 20), or a breach of a statutory duty (see Chapter 19). If they are sued, the corporation may pay them back (**indemnify** them) for the cost of defending the lawsuit and for the amount of a money judgment ordered by a court.

A corporation can buy directors' and officers' liability insurance to cover itself if it has to indemnify a director or officer. A corporation can also buy D&O insurance that will pay the director or officer directly if the corporation can't indemnify (for example, if the corporation doesn't have enough money, or if the incorporating documents forbid the corporation to indemnify directors and officers).

CRIME OR THEFT INSURANCE

Crime or theft insurance covers losses to the insured business that are caused by:

- dishonesty of the employees of the business
- breaking and entering, burglary, robbery
- forgery of cheques and counterfeiting of currency or money orders

In addition to getting insurance coverage for crime, you may want to have employees **bonded**, especially if your business involves handling valuable property (such as money or jewellery, yours or anyone else's) or working in other people's homes. A **fidelity bond** can usually be arranged through an insurance company or a bonding company. If a bonded employee steals from the business or from a customer who makes a claim against the business, the bonding company compensates the employer.

KEY PERSON INSURANCE

You can take out some form of income replacement insurance (**disability insurance** or **critical illness** insurance) to help you financially if you can't work. But what happens to your business if you become very sick or your partner does? You may want to take out **overhead expense insurance** to cover the fixed expenses of your business while you are (or your partner is) temporarily out of commission. Disability insurance or overhead expense insurance can be expensive.

You may also want to think about what will happen if a partner dies or must retire because of illness or disability. A business can set aside some of its profits yearly to build up a fund to buy out the interest of someone who dies. Or it can get insurance. A business can take out **key person** life insurance (or, as an alternative, **business continuation** insurance) on someone who's essential to the running of the business. On the death of the person, the business can use the insurance proceeds to buy the deceased's partnership interest or shares from her estate, instead of using the assets of the business for a buyout or folding up the business and distributing the assets. The business may also be able to take out critical illness insurance on an essential person, which would allow the business to buy out the partnership interest or shares if the person's illness prevented a return to work.

Before an insurance policy will be issued, the person being insured will probably have to undergo a medical examination. The cost of insurance increases with age and medical problems, and if the person is over a certain age or has certain kinds of problems it may be impossible to get insurance for him at all.

HOME BUSINESSES

If you run your business out of your home, you probably still need business insurance. Your home insurance policy may not be adequate. It may cover some of your business equipment and books of account (usually up to a value of $1000), but it does not cover goods for sale or samples. Your home insurance policy does not cover you for claims made against you by customers or clients or consumers.

ROLL THE DICE!

When you enter into an insurance contract by taking out a policy, what you're really doing is gambling with the insurance company that there's trouble in your future. The insurance company is gambling that there isn't. If you win the bet (by running into one of the troubles you and the insurance company agreed to gamble about), the insurance company will pay money to fix the trouble. If you lose the bet (by having nothing bad happen to you), you keep on paying premiums to your insurance company.

Just because you're gambling doesn't mean that the only thing that's important is luck. Use your good entrepreneurial sense when insuring your business. Choose an insurance agent or broker who is familiar with the kind of business you're in, and make sure that she has errors and omissions insurance in case you aren't provided with the right coverage. If you're aware of any particular risks involved in your business, tell your agent or broker about them, and go over the terms of any policy with him to make sure it meets your needs before you agree to take it.

An entrepreneur who owned a garage bought a tow truck. He had insured many vehicles over the years, and when he insured the truck he didn't bother to discuss possible options with the agent. He simply told the agent exactly what insurance coverage he wanted: coverage for driving to and from work and for pleasure, but not for commercial towing. The agent knew that the coverage specified did not insure the truck against fire damage if the truck was used to tow anything, but did not mention that. After arranging for the insurance, the entrepreneur occasionally used the truck to tow vehicles that he bought to fix up and resell. A few months later, the truck was destroyed by fire. The insurance company paid the claim for the cab and chassis of the truck, but refused to pay for the towing equipment. The entrepreneur sued the agent for not giving him proper advice about the coverage he needed. He lost because he had not asked for the agent's advice and had instead behaved as though he was very knowledgeable about insurance and did not need advice.

Don't just accept a standard policy if it doesn't meet your needs. See if you can get it amended.

T I P

When you are arranging to take out insurance, answer truthfully any questions that your agent or broker asks you. If you lie, or misrepresent, or fail to mention a fact during the application process, your insurance policy can be voided. That means you'll get *nothing at all* if you try to make a claim and you're found out. Once your coverage takes effect, you must let the insurer know about any substantial changes to your business as they occur (for example, changes in the nature of the business or in the use made of your business premises, and non-occupancy of the premises for more than 30 days).

T I P

Arranging your insurance coverage is not a one-time affair. You should review it yearly because your business, and your insurance requirements, can change.

PROTECTING
YOUR IDEAS

I t's fairly easy to protect most of your business assets. If you have a car you use for business purposes, you never leave the keys in it. If you sell jewellery, you install an alarm system in your store. But if your business consists of inventing better mousetraps, writing books, designing furniture, or creating new computer software, how do you protect your most important asset—your idea? Don't worry. It's all been worked out. There's a whole field of law concerned with protecting ideas and it's known as the law of **intellectual property**.

Intellectual property? Now there's an expression that only a lawyer—or better yet, a team of lawyers charging by the hour—could have thought up. You'll be pleased to know that this area of law is about as annoying as its name. Unfortunately, that doesn't give you an excuse to ignore it. Almost every entrepreneur these days has some valuable form of intellectual property to protect: if not training manuals, designs, or computer programs, then the secret formula for cold fusion, or at least a great business slogan or logo. You have to take as much care of these things as you do of your business premises or your inventory, because they're at least as important to your business's success.

HOW DO YOU PROTECT IDEAS?

One way of protecting an idea is simply to keep it a **trade secret**. As long as you keep it a secret, it's yours and yours alone. The Coca-Cola Company, for example, has kept its formula for Coke a secret since its invention in 1886. The problem with a trade secret is that if someone finds out your secret and uses it, there's usually not much you can do.

There are alternatives to keeping your ideas secret. They involve making them public, in return for a reasonable amount of protection from competitors.

- If you've invented a new technology, you can get **patent** protection under the federal *Patent Act*.

- If you've created a literary, artistic, dramatic, or musical work, or a sound recording, or a computer program, you have **copyright** protection under the federal *Copyright Act*.

- If you've designed a new shape, pattern, or ornamentation for goods that are mass-produced, you can get **industrial design** protection under the federal *Industrial Design Act*.

- If you use a word or words, a symbol, a design, or a combination of the three, to distinguish the goods or services you provide, you can get **trademark** protection under the federal *Trade-marks Act*.

- If you've created an innovative microchip, you can get **integrated circuit topography** protection under the federal *Integrated Circuit Topography Act*.

PATENTS

A patent gives the inventor the exclusive right to make, use, or sell the invention for a maximum of 20 years from the date of the patent application. In return, the inventor makes the details of the invention public. The inventor can sell or licence the patent to other people.

What Can and Can't Be Patented?

You can apply for a patent for a product, a machine for making a product, a chemical composition, or for an improvement on any of these three things. (Ninety per cent of patents are granted for improvements rather than for completely original inventions.) However, getting a patent isn't automatic. There are three criteria for granting a patent: novelty, utility, and ingenuity. In other words, whatever you've invented must be:

• new—the first in the world, and not made public more than one year before you applied for the patent

• useful—it has to have a useful function to begin with, and it has to work

• extremely clever—in fact, so clever that until you invented it, it wasn't obvious to a skilled person in that field

You cannot patent:

• an idea—you have to turn the idea into a physical description of something that works
• a scientific principle
• a medical treatment
• a business method

Do You Really Need a Patent?

If you get a patent and someone else uses your patented product, process, or machine without your permission, you can sue for damages for patent **infringement**. If you don't have a patent, you won't get anything unless the person who is infringing previously signed a non-disclosure or confidentiality agreement with you.

It is expensive to get a patent. Between filing fees and patent agent's and/or patent lawyer's fees, you're looking at a few thousand dollars. Before you make up your mind to spend the time and money involved in a patent application, ask yourself:

• will anyone manufacture this thing, and how much will it cost?

- will anyone buy this thing, and how much will they pay for it?

- can you keep your invention a trade secret and use it without worrying about someone stealing your idea? (If you decide to go this route, don't talk to people about your invention and be sure to get non-disclosure agreements from anyone you employ or work with when you're manufacturing or using your invention.)

How Do You Get a Patent?

Patent applications are not for do-it-yourselfers. You'll need a registered patent agent and/or a patent lawyer to help you from the very beginning. The federal Patent Office keeps a list of registered patent agents. As for the lawyer, you'll want to use the services of a law firm that specializes in intellectual property. The firm will have a patent agent on staff as well.

Applying for a patent is a lengthy process. You must start with a preliminary search of existing patents and patent applications to determine whether your invention (or a similar one) has been patented before. We don't want to discourage you before you even start, but there are more than 1.3 million Canadian patents. The search can be done at the Patent Office in Hull, Quebec, or through the on-line Canadian Patent Database. It may be wise to do a search at the US Patent Office too. Is the patent agent starting to look like a good idea? Then you (or your lawyer or agent) must prepare and file the patent application, which consists of a number of documents including specifications of the invention. The specifications are a complete description of the invention and how it is useful, and your claims about exactly what it is you own with respect to the invention. Eighteen months after the application is filed, it is automatically opened for public inspection. Anyone who wants to can inspect your application and question the patentability of your invention by filing information about existing patents and applications, or about relevant published material, or can file a protest against the granting of the patent.

After your application has been made public, you must formally request to have it examined by the Patent Office. You can request examination up to five years from the date you originally filed your application. The examination process can take up to three years. The patent examiner decides whether your application has been properly made, and then studies your claims, and searches existing patents and literature to see whether your claims are valid.

While you're waiting to see whether a patent will be granted, you can mark articles made with your invention "patent applied for" or "patent pending." A "patent pending" mark doesn't actually provide legal protection in itself (although it may scare off some competitors), but if the patent is eventually granted, you can sue anyone who steals your idea after the application was made public but before the patent was granted.

What with thinking about the 1.3 million patents you have to search, and your brilliant invention being made public by the Patent Office before you have any protection, and the patent examiner moving more slowly than a glacier, you're probably having palpitations by now. Well, you can always open a vacuum-cleaner franchise instead.

If you want to patent your invention outside Canada, you have to apply for a foreign patent, through a single application at the Canadian Patent Office pursuant to the Patent Cooperation treaty, which covers nearly a hundred countries including the US, the European Economic Community, and Japan; or through the patent office of the foreign country or countries. (You'll have to pay all the applicable foreign patent fees however you proceed.) Patent law varies from country to country. In some you cannot patent an invention if it was publicly disclosed anywhere before you filed your application there (and that includes public disclosure through an application to the Canadian Patent Office). In others, you may be required to manufacture your invention in that country within a short time, or to licence someone else to do so.

At Last You Have a Patent!

Once you have the patent, you can go on using the idea yourself, sell it to someone else, or licence someone else to use it in exchange for paying you royalties. In certain situations, you can be *forced* to licence your patent rights. Someone who wants to use your patent can apply to the Commissioner of Patents, three years after your patent is granted, for a **compulsory licence** under your patent. The Commissioner may grant the licence if you've been "abusing your patent rights" by refusing to grant a licence at all, by offering to grant one but only on unreasonable terms, by not producing enough of your invention to meet demand for it in Canada, or by unfairly prejudicing the production of an unpatented product through the use of your patented process.

COPYRIGHT

A copyright is an exclusive right to copy an original work, for example by reproducing, publishing, performing, adapting, or translating it. The person who creates the work is usually the **first owner** of the copyright, but if the creator is hired or commissioned to create the work, the person who hired the creator or who commissioned the work is the first owner of the copyright unless it was agreed otherwise beforehand. Only the owner (whether the first owner or a subsequent one) of the copyright has the right to publish or use the work, although (as with patents), a compulsory licence for someone else to use the work can be granted by the federal Copyright Board. Copyright generally lasts for the life of the creator plus 50 years. In the case of photographs, films, videos, and sound recordings, copyright lasts 50 years from the date of their making. After copyright expires, the work enters the **public domain** and is no longer protected.

A copyright can be transferred (for example, by sale) or licenced to someone else in exchange for royalties. You can join an organization that licences people to use your work and collects royalties on your behalf. SOCAN (The Society of Composers, Authors, and Music Publishers of Canada), for instance, deals with the performance and broadcasting of musical works, while CANCOPY deals with the photocopying of written works.

If you create a work and then transfer your copyright to someone else, you keep "moral rights" in the work. That means that your name has to stay attached to the work. It also means that neither the new copyright owner nor anyone else can modify the original work in a way that damages your reputation, unless you've given permission.

If you are offered a publishing contract for a work you have created, it's a very good idea to have it reviewed by a lawyer familiar with such contracts before you sign. If your work is a book, you can get contract advice, or even help with the negotiations, from the Writers' Union of Canada. After you publish a book or manufacture a sound recording in Canada, under the federal *National Library Act*, you (or your publisher) have to send two copies of any book or one copy of any recording to the National Library in Ottawa within a week of publication.

What Can and Can't Be Copyrighted?

You can copyright an original literary, dramatic, musical, or artistic work such as:

- a book, article, poem, or other literary work
- a play, script, screenplay, or other dramatic work
- a film, video, television, or radio program
- a drawing, photograph, map, or architectural design
- a painting, sculpture, or other artistic work
- a song, score, or other musical work
- a record, tape, CD, or other sound recording
- a computer program
- an adaptation or translation of an existing work

You *cannot* copyright:

- facts
- an idea or plot
- a title
- a name
- a character
- a catchphrase or slogan
- a work that is already in the public domain, such as one of Shakespeare's plays or Mozart's symphonies

An entrepreneur had a brilliant idea for a software program, but he didn't have the know-how to write the program. He enlisted a couple of friends to write it, and the three of them agreed that he would concentrate on the marketing. The three also agreed that they didn't need a formal written agreement to split equally any profit they made, because they'd been good friends for so long. When the program was close to being finished and it was clear that it was potentially worth several million dollars, the entrepreneur began approaching possible buyers. At one company he discovered that his two "friends" had been there before him, trying to sell the program on their own behalf. Furious, he confronted them—and they pointed out that while they had copyright in the program because they had written it, he himself had no legal rights because an idea can't be copyrighted. The three eventually hammered out a deal to share any proceeds; but unfortunately by that time several similar products had reached the marketplace and the program was worth nothing.

Do You Really Need a Copyright?

Actually, you get copyright automatically when you create an original work. Without lifting a finger to do anything, you have copyright not only in Canada but in about 60 foreign countries including the US, most European countries, and Australia and New Zealand. You don't even need to put a copyright notice at the front of your work (the copyright sign ©, the year of first publication, and your name). If you like, you can register your copyright by filling out an application and paying a small fee to the federal Copyright Office. To register, you don't have to send a copy of your work; the Copyright Office (unlike the Patent Office) does not check to see whether the work you're claiming copyright in is really original and really yours before issuing the certificate of registration. Registration is not proof positive of ownership of the copyright, although it can provide useful evidence of validity of the copyright.

Remedies

If someone infringes your copyright—for example by printing and selling without your permission a book that you wrote—you can sue for damages and/or for a court order to stop them. In serious cases, a criminal charge can be laid under the *Copyright Act*.

TRADEMARKS

A trademark is a mark that distinguishes your goods or services from those of other businesses. Registration of a trademark gives you an exclusive right to use the mark throughout Canada for 15 years, and you can renew registration when that period ends. You can also transfer your right to someone else.

What Can and Can't Be Registered as a Trademark?

A trademark can be:

- a word, or words (such as a slogan)
- a symbol
- a design, including the shape of a product or package

or any combination of these things.

If you want to register something as a trademark, generally speaking it cannot be:

- your name or someone else's name
- the picture or signature of a person who is alive now or who has been dead for less than 30 years—unless you have the consent of the living person or of the dead person's estate
- a **trade name** or business name you carry on business under, unless you use it to identify your goods or services
- a geographical name
- the name of your product or service simply translated into another language
- an official symbol (such as a Red Cross or the Canadian flag)

  Nor can it be:

- obscene or immoral
- purely descriptive of your goods or services (for example, "Cold Ice Cream")
- misleading about your goods or services

- confusingly similar to someone else's trademark that is being used for similar goods or services

Do You Really Need to Register Your Trademark?

You can become the owner of a trademark without registering it—all you have to do is be the first person to use it and it's yours. You don't have to show the registration symbols ® (registered) or MD (marque déposée), or the symbols TM (trademark) or SM (service mark) or MC (marque de commerce), although you probably should. (You can use TM, SM, or MC whether you've registered your trademark or not.) However, an unregistered trademark is only protected in the particular geographical area where it is used. A registered trademark is protected across Canada, even if it is not being used in all parts of the country.

How Do You Get Your Trademark Registered?

Registering a trademark isn't quite as complicated as applying for a patent (sighs of relief all round), but you should probably hire a registered trademark agent rather than trying to do it on your own. You can get a list of registered agents from the federal Trade-marks Office. Before you apply to register your trademark you should search the records of the Trade-marks Office in Hull, Quebec, to see if your trademark is confusingly similar to a trademark that is already registered or has been applied for. You should also search existing trade names (business names) in a database such as NUANS (see p. 61 in Chapter 6) to get an idea whether your chosen trademark is confusingly similar to a trade name someone is already using. After you file your application, together with a drawing of any symbol or design, the Trade-marks Office also searches the records for similar trademarks (doesn't anyone trust you?) and publishes your application in the *Trade-marks Journal*. At that point, anyone may challenge your application. However, if the search didn't turn up an existing conflicting trademark and no one objected to your application, your mark will be registered on payment of a fee.

Remedies

If a competitor infringes your trademark by using it for his own goods or services, you can sue for damages and/or a court order forcing him to stop. If your trademark is registered, you can sue a competitor anywhere in Canada (even if you don't do business or have a business reputation in that particular location). If your trademark is not registered, you can only sue a competitor using your trademark in the geographical area where you do business. You can also sue someone who is *not* competing with you but who is reducing the value of your trademark by using it without your permission.

If your product becomes so well known that your trademark starts being used as a synonym for the generic product (as happened to "Aspirin" in the United States), you'll lose your exclusive right to the trademark—unless you come down like a ton of bricks anytime anyone uses it without your permission.

INDUSTRIAL DESIGN

An industrial design is an original artistic shape, pattern, or original ornamentation that is to be applied to a useful article that will be reproduced at least 50 times (mass-produced).

What Can Be Registered as an Industrial Design and What Can't?

The shape, pattern, or ornamentation you've created may have copyright or trademark (or even patent) protection, but if it is going to be used in mass-production it also needs industrial design protection. For example, you could have an industrial design for:

• the shape of or decorative pattern on furniture or tableware

• the design on a poster

• a pattern for clothing

You cannot register the following as industrial designs:

- an idea for a design (rather than the design itself)
- a design for an article that isn't useful
- a design that is intended to be functional rather than attractive
- a design for a part of the object that is not visible
- a method of or materials for manufacturing an object
- a colour

Only the person who is the "proprietor" of the design has the right to register it. That usually means the creator of the design, but if the creator produced the design under a contract (including a contract of employment) with another party, the proprietor is usually the other party. Once you've registered a design, you can prevent anyone else from using it in Canada for up to 10 years, but registration is non-renewable. After the 10 years are up, anyone can use the design.

Do You Really Need to Register Your Industrial Design?

Yes, you do. Although you have automatic trademark and copyright protection without registering, you do *not* have automatic industrial design protection without registering. If your design has not been registered, anyone can imitate it and you have no legal means of stopping them. After you have registered your design, you can licence it to others for use, or transfer your rights in the design to others.

Registering your design in Canada gives you protection only in Canada. If you want to protect it in other countries, you must apply for registration separately in each country. In some countries you will not be able to register your design if has previously been registered elsewhere, for example, in Canada. Because of this problem, the Industrial Design Office allows you make your application in Canada but delay registration here until you have received the foreign registration.

How Do You Register an Industrial Design?

You should probably get some help to register your design, from a registered patent agent. Before you file, you should search the records in the federal Industrial Design Office in Hull, Quebec, to see whether your design really is new and original. Then you have to prepare an application, which includes a description in writing of the design's original artistic features, and drawings or photographs of the design as it appears in the product. You may be asked to provide a sample of the design as well. There is a deadline for filing an application for an industrial design of one year after the design has been made public. After the Industrial Design Office receives your application and fee, it will examine the design and do a search for similar pre-existing designs that have been applied to a similar article. If such a design exists, you will not be able to register yours. (If someone else applies to register the same design as yours at the same time, the application received first will be the one granted.) You have to wait a minimum of six months from the date of filing until registration is granted, and the process may take up to a year.

Remedies

After your design is registered, you can mark it with a Ⓓ followed by your name as proprietor. If you have registered *and* marked your design, you can sue anyone who infringes your design for damages and/or a court order to prevent further infringement. If you have registered your design but are not using the mark, you can only sue for a court order to prevent further infringement. You have only three years from the date of the infringement to start a lawsuit.

INTEGRATED CIRCUIT TOPOGRAPHIES

An integrated circuit is a semiconductor chip, or microchip, and an integrated circuit topography is the series of layers that make up the chip. Random Access Memory (RAM) and Read Only Memory (ROM) are examples of integrated circuits.

To register an IC topography you must fill out an application, provide a description of the nature or function of the topography together with overlay sheets, drawings or photographs of the topography, and pay a fee. No official investigation of the topography's originality will be made. You must file the application no later than two years after the first commercial use of the topography anywhere in the world. If you register your topography, you have the exclusive right for up to 10 years to copy it, incorporate it into a manufactured product, and sell, lease, or distribute it or a product that incorporates it. You can sue anyone who infringes your topography for damages and/or a court order to stop.

There are some limitations on your right to protect your topography. You cannot prevent anyone from copying your registered topography for the purpose of analysis, research, or teaching. You also cannot prevent someone from reverse engineering your topography and registering the resulting new topography.

AND IN CONCLUSION

We haven't told you about the intellectual property rights you can acquire in new varieties of certain plant species under the *Plant Breeders' Rights Act* because we fear you may be losing interest in the whole field of intellectual property by now. For further information about plant breeders' rights or any form of intellectual property, you can contact the Canadian Intellectual Property Office (CIPO), which is part of Industry Canada.

CHAPTER THIRTEEN

CONTRACTS FOR GOODS AND SERVICES

In the course of business you will enter into many contracts to buy and sell goods and services. Theres just no escape from contracts! Generally speaking, it's up to you and the other party to decide what goes into a contract, and this chapter addresses the essential matters you need to consider. However, there may be legislation governing the particular business you are in that requires you as a provider of goods or services to include certain matters or terms in your contract, or that will imply certain terms. Speak to your lawyer or your professional or trade association, or contact the government to find out if you are in such a business.

WHAT SHOULD CONTRACTS FOR SERVICES DEAL WITH?

Whatever kind of services you are giving or getting, your contract should always deal with the following things:

The Parties to the Contract

This may sound too obvious to mention, but you have to know exactly who is involved in the contract.

Who is providing the services?

Is it an individual, a partnership, or a corporation? If a specific person is supposed to do the work, the contract must say so. The actual named party to the contract (even if the party is an individual and not a corporation) doesn't necessarily have to do the work—unless it's a contract for personal services—although the party to the contract is responsible for making sure that the work is done and done properly.

Who is paying for the services?

Is it an individual, a partnership, or a corporation? An individual or each partner in a partnership is responsible for paying for the services, but no individual associated with a corporation is automatically on the hook to pay if the corporation doesn't.

> **T I P**
> f you're signing a contract as an officer of a corporation, make sure that's clear in the contract if you don't want to be held personally liable to pay for the services.
>
>

The Services

It's not enough to know who's doing the job and who's paying for it—you also have to be clear about the job itself.

What services are to be performed?

The contract should describe in detail the nature of the services and may describe what standard of quality they must meet so that both parties know what's expected. A trade contract may say that the work must be done "in a good and workmanlike manner;" a professional contract may say nothing, but even so the work must be done competently.

What is the timing of the contract?

The contract should set a starting date and maybe a finishing date too. Some contracts are for the provision of regular services over a period of time, and such contracts may provide for early termination (in case one party is not happy) and renewal (in case everyone is happy).

> **TIP**
>
> If you are providing the services, you want to define clearly the other party's right to terminate the contract and limit it to some sort of wrongdoing on your part. Termination by the other party for any other reason should only be allowed after you are given reasonable notice. You might also want to include a provision that would give *you* the right to terminate the contract, for instance, if the other party is uncooperative, or if the cost of materials rises sharply. If a renewal clause is included in the contract, make sure that it takes into account the possibility that your cost of providing the services will rise.
>
> TIP

Is a licence or permit required to provide the service?

If the supplier of the services is required by law to be properly qualified or licenced, she should state in the contract that she has the necessary qualifications or licence. If a permit is required for the particular job, the contract should state who will get and pay for it.

Payment for the Services

Payment is not the only important part of a contract, but it's often the one that parties think about most.

What will the services cost?

Is the cost fixed or is it based on time spent? Is the cost reasonable? In some provinces consumer protection legislation gives a consumer (but not a customer that is a business) the right to have the contract set aside if the service provider grossly overcharges, and the service provider can also be prosecuted and fined.

How is payment to be made?

Is the whole amount to be paid at the beginning, or at the end, or is payment to be made in installments as the work is done? If there's a discount for payment in cash or for payment by a cer-tain date, the contract should say so. If the business providing the service is extending credit, the terms should be set out, includ-ing the amount and date of the payments, and the annual rate of interest being charged. See below on p.181 for more about extending credit.

What taxes have to be paid?

Goods and Services Tax (GST) of 7 per cent is payable on services throughout Canada. In addition, every province except Alberta has a provincial sales tax (ranging from 7 to 10 per cent), and some services are subject to sales tax. In Newfoundland, Nova Scotia, and New Brunswick, GST is combined with provincial sales tax into Harmonized Sales Tax (HST) of 15 per cent. The person who provides the services is responsible for collecting these taxes and then paying them to the government. It is illegal for a supplier of services to avoid paying GST/HST, and it is also illegal to conspire with the supplier to allow him to avoid paying the tax. See p. 247 in Chapter 17 for more about the GST.

Breach of Contract

You enter into a contract assuming that it will be performed, but although you're hoping for the best, you must prepare for the worst.

What happens if the party getting the services doesn't pay?

Any party that has to sue for payment after the service has been provided is at a tremendous disadvantage, but some service providers are entitled by law to claim a **lien** against property if the customer doesn't pay. This improves their chances of collecting the debt. For example, a mechanic who repairs a vehicle may be able to keep and sell it if payment isn't forthcoming; a storage facility can keep and sell the stored goods; an electrician who rewires premises can register a construction lien against the property. Find out if the other party has any lien rights if you are buying the service. If you are providing the service, mention your lien rights in the contract. It may make your customer think twice before stiffing you.

What happens if the service is not properly performed?

The party paying for the service will want the contract to say what rights she has if the quality of the work is unsatisfactory. The supplier may offer a **warranty** that it will remedy any problems for a fixed period of time after the service has been performed.

> **TIP**
>
> If you are providing the service, the contract should be drafted so that you are only liable to the customer or client if you do not meet objective reasonable standards of performance, as opposed to failing to meet every whim. In addition, the contract should limit what you have to do if you fail to meet that objective standard, for example, correct the mistake or reduce the contract price by a fixed maximum amount.
>
> T I P

The cautious customer or client may insist that the service provider get a **performance bond** (see p. 150 in Chapter 11) especially if the work being done is part of a larger project. If the work isn't started or finished on time, the client will be compensated through the bond.

What happens if the person performing the services causes injury to someone, or causes damage to property?

Many people who supply services will try to limit or avoid liability for injury or damage that they cause. Clauses in a written contract (often deeply buried) that limit responsibility in this way are called **exculpatory**, **exclusion**, or **exemption clauses**. The buyer of the services does not want an exclusion clause in the contract, but may have trouble getting the provider of the services to take it out.

> **TIP**
>
> The provider of the services should have insurance in case he causes damage or injury, but may also want the customer to have insurance in case the customer causes any damage or injury to the provider. Whether you're the provider or customer, you may already have the necessary insurance. See Chapter 11, and check your insurance policy, or contact your insurance agent or broker.
>
>

WHAT SHOULD CONTRACTS FOR GOODS DEAL WITH?

Just as with contracts for services, it's up to you and the other party to decide what goes into a contract for goods. However, if you happen to leave certain things out of a contract to buy and sell goods, almost every province has a *Sale of Goods Act* that may fill in the blanks for you. We can almost hear you saying, "What fresh hell is this?" You'll know soon enough if you keep reading.

Your contract for the purchase of goods should deal with the matters discussed below.

The Parties to the Contract

As with services, the actual parties to the contract are the ones who must provide the goods (and who will be responsible if there's anything wrong with them) and who must pay for the goods.

> **TIP**
>
> If you're extending credit to a corporation that is buying your goods, consider taking security and/or asking for a personal guarantee from an individual behind the corporation.
>
> T I P

The Goods

Now the complications start. Take a deep breath (or, better yet, have a stiff drink) before reading further.

What are the goods in the transaction?

The contract should describe the goods in detail, specifying a brand name and/or model number if that's important, and should state the quantity of goods.

Who is the owner of the goods that are being bought?

Only the owner of the goods, or a person who has the authority of the owner, can legally sell the goods. The contract may contain a promise that the seller of the goods is the true owner. Even if the contract is silent on this point, according to the *Sale of Goods Act* there is an implied promise that the person selling the goods actually owns them. If the promise turns out to be false, and the seller is not, in fact, the owner of the goods, the general rule is that the buyer cannot become owner of the goods, even by paying for them and taking delivery. The true owner still has the right to take the goods back. The seller's promise does not give ownership if the seller isn't the owner; it merely gives the buyer a right to sue the seller to get back the money paid. For example, if you buy a stolen computer from the thief or a middleman, the computer's owner can take it without paying you anything, and *you* have the right to sue the thief or middleman to get your money back. (In ordinary retail contracts there is unlikely to be an ownership problem.)

Are there any liens or claims against the goods?

If there are, the contract should say so, and should say whether the claims or liens are to be paid off or whether the buyer is taking the goods subject to them. If there are prior claims against the goods, even if they have been registered under the *Personal Property Security Act*, the buyer is protected from those claims as long as the goods are being sold by the seller in the ordinary course of the seller's business. (That means it's safe to buy a car from a car dealership.) If the goods are being sold outside of the seller's ordinary course of business, the buyer is not protected. (That means it's *not* so safe to buy a car from a car rental agency that's getting rid of some of its older cars.)

> **T**
> **I**
> **P**
>
> You should do a search under the *Personal Property Security Act* before you buy any costly goods for your business from sellers who are selling outside the ordinary course of their business.
>
> T I P

The contract may contain a promise that there are no prior claims against the goods, but even if it says nothing, the *Sale of Goods Act* implies a promise that there are no prior claims. This promise does not give the buyer ownership that is free from existing claims; it only gives the buyer the right to get some of the money back if there is a claim.

What is the quality of the goods?

Most contracts for the sale of goods deal with the quality of the goods by stating what the seller's or manufacturer's responsibility is if there's something wrong with the goods. For example, a seller may agree to repair the goods free of charge if something goes wrong with them within 90 days after the sale because of a defect in materials or workmanship. The contract usually goes on to say something like "any other representations, warranties, or conditions are excluded," which means that defects that appear after 90 days, or defects that cause injury to people or damage to other equipment, are the buyer's problem, not the seller's.

> **T I P**
>
> As a seller of goods to other businesses, you are responsible for their quality unless the contract says you're not. So if you intend to exclude or limit your responsibility (for example, if you only want to repair and not replace goods, or if you only want to repair goods for a limited period of time) you must say so in your contract.
>
> T I P

If the contract says nothing about the quality of the goods or the seller's responsibility for problems with the goods and does not exclude any other representations, warranties, or conditions, the *Sale of Goods Act* implies certain promises about the quality of the goods, as follows:

• if the buyer buys goods based on a description, the goods received must match the description. If on delivery it turns out that the goods don't match the description, the buyer doesn't have to accept them or pay for them. If the buyer only finds out that the goods don't match the description after taking delivery and paying, the goods can be returned for a refund. Even if the goods match the description, they must not have any defect that would have stopped the buyer from buying them at the price paid if the buyer had known about the defect. A buyer can return defective goods for a refund.

A seed company supplied a farmer with cabbage seeds that it described in its catalogue as "the most popular and versatile" variety that it sold. In its contract for sale, the company included an exclusion clause limiting its liability to the cost of the seeds. The farmer used the seeds and harvested a disappointing crop, so he sued the seed company for breach of contract. The trial judge awarded the farmer damages, but the company appealed and the court of appeal decided in its favour. The court found that while it was true that other *varieties* of seed grew better, the seeds in question were as good as those of the same variety sold by other seed dealers, that the company had no obligation to point out the weaknesses in its product, and that even if the company had been careless in not supplying seed that matched the catalogue description it was protected by the exclusion clause.

- if the buyer buys goods after inspecting a sample provided by the seller, the goods must be of the same quality as the sample. The buyer has a reasonable amount of time after delivery of the goods to inspect them. If the vast majority of the goods are not of the same quality as the sample, the buyer has the right to reject the goods and get back the money.

- if the buyer asks the seller for a recommendation about what product to buy for a particular purpose, and if the product is one that the seller ordinarily sells, the goods recommended must be reasonably fit for that purpose.

In Quebec, under the *Civil Code*, there is an implied promise that goods sold are free of hidden defects and will not fall apart or malfunction earlier than expected, and that the seller will notify the buyer in writing on learning that a product is defective.

Provincial consumer protection legislation won't allow a seller of goods to limit responsibility for the quality of the goods in a sale to a consumer (rather than to another business). Also, certain promises about the quality of the goods are automatically included in the contract and the seller *cannot* exclude them. Check out your provincial legislation. Depending on the province, these promises include:

- that the goods are of the quality implied under the *Sale of Goods Act*
- that the goods are new and unused, unless it's clearly indicated that they're used
- that the goods are reasonably durable
- that the goods meet all statutory standards for health, safety, and quality
- that repair services and parts will be reasonably available

When and where are the goods to be delivered?

The contract may or may not fix a time and place for delivery of the goods. If nothing is said, the *Sale of Goods Act* comes into play again. If no place for delivery is fixed, the buyer must pick up the goods at the seller's place of business. If a place of delivery is named but no time is fixed, the goods are to be delivered within a reasonable period of time. If a delivery time is fixed the buyer cannot necessarily reject the goods if they are not delivered at the fixed time. The buyer can only do that if the contract fixes a delivery date and states that "time of delivery is of the essence."

When does the buyer become the owner of the goods and bear the loss if the goods are damaged, destroyed, or stolen?

Owning goods, possessing goods, and bearing the risk of loss if the goods are damaged, destroyed, or stolen are three separate matters. The buyer can become the owner of goods before they come into the buyer's possession. The owner generally bears the risk of damage or loss, but it's possible to be saddled with the risk before becoming the owner, or be the owner and bear no risk at all. For example, in a conditional sales contract, the seller remains the owner of the goods until the final payment has been made. However, the buyer usually bears the risk of any loss from the time possession is taken.

All businesspeople are concerned about damage to goods during shipping. Some contracts state who bears the risk of loss if goods are damaged before delivery to the buyer. If *you* bear the risk, don't just ask yourself if you feel lucky, insure the goods to their full value before they are shipped. There are shipping terms commonly used in contracts to indicate who bears the risk of loss or damage. A more complete set of these terms can be found on pp. 266-268 in Chapter 18, but here are some that you may have heard of:

- **CIF** (Cost, Insurance, and Freight)—The seller bears the risk of loss until the goods are handed over for shipping. Once the goods are handed over, the buyer bears the risk of loss. The cost of the goods includes both shipping and *minimum* insurance, which the seller arranges.

- **COD** (Cash on Delivery)—In a COD contract, the buyer pays for the goods on delivery. If they are damaged or destroyed any time before they are delivered and paid for, the loss is the seller's.

- **F.O.B.** (Free on Board)—The seller bears the cost of shipping and the risk of loss to a designated place such as the buyer's premises. (FOB has a more restricted meaning in international shipping: see p. 268 in Chapter 18.)

If the seller ships the goods under a **bill of lading**, which is a contract between the seller of the goods and the shipping company, the bill of lading will state the name of a **consignee**, who is the person who has the right to take delivery of the goods at their destination. If the buyer of the goods is named as the consignee, the buyer bears the risk of any loss or damage to the goods during shipping. If the seller of the goods is named as the consignee, the seller bears the risk until the goods reach their destination.

If the contract does not state who bears the loss, the general rule is that the owner of the goods bears the loss if the goods are damaged, destroyed, or lost. Once again the *Sale of Goods Act* rears its ugly head, and gives five rules that determine who is the owner of the goods at any given time. You may be surprised by the haste—we might even say the unseemly haste—with which ownership gets transferred from the seller to the buyer:

- Where there is a contract to buy specific goods that are immediately ready for pick-up or delivery, the buyer becomes the owner as soon as there is a contract, even if payment and/or delivery take place later.

- Where there is a contract to buy specific goods but the seller has to do something to them (for example, modify or assemble them) before they are ready for pick-up or delivery, the buyer becomes the owner once that thing, whatever it is, has been done and the buyer has been notified.

- Where there is a contract to buy specific goods that are ready for pick-up or delivery, but the goods have to be weighed, measured, counted, or tested in order to determine the price, the buyer becomes the owner as soon as the goods have been weighed, measured, counted, or tested and the buyer has been notified.

- Where there is a contract to buy specific goods on approval, the buyer becomes the owner by either notifying the seller of his approval, or by keeping or using the goods.

- Where there is a contract to buy goods that can't be distinguished from other identical goods (for example, a contract to buy 200 dozen tins of soup from a soup manufacturer), the buyer becomes the owner when the goods are separated from the identical goods and set aside for the buyer. If the goods are yet to be grown or manufactured the buyer becomes the owner when the goods have been grown or manufactured, separated out, and set aside for the buyer.

Whether a seller would hold you to the *Sale of Goods Act* if goods were damaged while still in the seller's possession would probably depend on whether the seller was properly insured and on how much the seller valued your business.

T
I
P

D o you really need a tip about this? If you don't want the *Sale of Goods Act* running your business, make sure your contract covers which party bears the risk of loss of the goods, and when. Then insure the goods to their full value if you bear the risk of loss. Insure the goods to their full value, as well, if the other party bears the risk of loss but is not required to insure them fully.

T I P

Payment for the Goods

The price to be paid must be agreed to by the parties; but there are other considerations too.

When must the buyer pay for the goods?

Most contracts for the sale of goods state when payment must be made—either before delivery, at the time of delivery, or after delivery of the goods—and whether a deposit is required. If the contract doesn't say anything, the *Sale of Goods Act* (Aggh! there it is again! Somebody hit it with a shoe and kill it!) says the buyer must pay at the time of delivery. Before agreeing to accept payment after the date of delivery, many sellers will require a credit check and credit references. If credit is extended, the contract should set out the terms for payment, including the amount and date of the payments, and the interest rate being charged. (For more about extending credit, see below on p. 181.) Unless credit arrangements have been made, no sane seller delivers goods until they're paid for.

What taxes have to be paid?

As with contracts for services, GST, provincial sales tax, and/or HST must be collected and paid by the person who provides the goods. It is illegal for a supplier of goods to avoid paying GST, PST, or HST, and it is also illegal for a buyer to conspire with the supplier not to pay taxes.

GETTING PAID

We've already said a number of things about getting paid for the work that you do or the goods that you provide, but we haven't run out of steam—or law—yet, so we'll say a few more things.

Extending Credit

If you are extending credit to a corporate customer or client and the corporation does not appear to have significant assets, you may want to get personal guarantees from the people associated with the corporation. If the corporation doesn't pay you, you can collect what you're owed from the guarantors.

If you are selling goods on credit, you may want to take a security interest in the goods until they are fully paid for by selling the goods under a conditional sales contract or by putting a provision in the contract for a purchase money security interest in the goods. (See p. 113 in Chapter 9 for more about security interests.) In either case, you will have to register notice of your security interest under your province's *Personal Property Security Act*. (Your lawyer can complete and register the necessary forms. If you want to do it yourself, contact the provincial government for information about the registration requirements.) If you have taken security on any of your clients' or customers' property, you can realize on the security by taking and selling the property if the debt owed to you is not paid. There are procedures that have to be followed that we discuss on p. 307 in Chapter 22. You may want to contact your lawyer for advice and/or assistance, or use a **bailiff** (a person who is licenced by the provincial government to seize goods) to actually go out and get the property.

Charging Interest

If you are extending credit to a buyer and charging interest, you want to comply with the provisions of the federal *Interest Act*. Your documents should state the applicable interest rate in annual terms instead of (or in addition to) daily, weekly, monthly, quarterly, or semi-annual terms. If they don't, the *Interest Act* says that you will only be entitled to charge 5 per cent interest per year. (See p. 110 in Chapter 9.)

If you are extending credit and charging interest in a transaction with a consumer rather than a business client, provincial consumer protection legislation requires you to disclose the cost of borrowing to the consumer. You must disclose the total dollar amount that the consumer will have to pay to borrow, including all interest charged and any other bonuses, fees, or amounts that you are charging. In addition to disclosing what these costs will total over the life of the loan, you must state the cost of borrowing as an annual percentage rate. The penalty for failing to disclose the cost of borrowing varies from province to province. You will either be prevented from collecting any interest at all or you will be limited to collecting a specific amount of interest.

T
I   t is probably a wise idea not to extend credit to consumer customers
P   but to ask them to use credit cards instead.

                                                              T I P

What If a Business (or Person) That Owes You Money Goes Bankrupt?

If you are a secured creditor of a business that goes bankrupt, you can still realize on your security by seizing and selling the property covered by your security (see p. 307 in Chapter 22) because property that is secured is excluded from the bankruptcy. If you realize on your security but the money you get doesn't cover the whole debt, you must try to recover the shortfall as an unsecured creditor in the bankruptcy proceedings.

If you supplied goods to the bankrupt business and they were not fully paid for, you may be able to get them back if the bankrupt business still has them and they can be positively identified. You must make a demand in writing, within 30 days of delivering the goods.

If you are not a secured creditor or a supplier, you must file a **proof of claim** with the bankrupt's trustee in bankruptcy. The **trustee in bankruptcy** will sell the bankrupt's unsecured assets and use the proceeds to pay off the bankrupt's debts. Keep in mind that there will be more debts than proceeds. **Preferred** creditors' claims are paid in full first and they include (in the order that the claims will be paid):

- bankruptcy administration costs
- employees' wages prior to the bankruptcy to a maximum of $2000 per employee
- municipal property taxes
- three months' arrears of rent plus three months' accelerated rent
- workers' compensation premiums

If there is anything left, **unsecured** creditors' claims will be paid on a **pro rata** (proportional) basis. For example, if a particular creditor is owed 20 per cent of the business's debts, that creditor will receive 20 per cent of whatever amount is available for all of the unsecured creditors.

Instead of going bankrupt, the business that owes you money may file a **notice of intention to file a proposal** under the bankruptcy legislation. A proposal is the business's suggested plan for reorganizing its debts, and it may deal with both secured and unsecured debts or just with the business's unsecured debts. After filing the notice, the business has 30 days to file the proposal. A meeting of the creditors must be held within 21 days after the proposal is filed so that the creditors can vote on the proposal. From the time the notice of intention is filed until the proposal is filed, no creditor, secured or unsecured, can take any action to collect from the business. From the time the proposal is filed until the meeting of the creditors, all unsecured creditors are still prevented from taking any action, although secured creditors are only prevented from taking action if they are included in the proposal.

At the meeting of the creditors, all unsecured creditors get to vote on the proposal. Secured creditors only vote if they were included in the proposal. If you are an unsecured creditor and the proposal is accepted, even if *you* didn't vote for it you are bound to accept payment in accordance with the proposal. If you are a secured creditor, you are only bound by the proposal if the secured creditors also voted to accept the proposal. If they did not, you are then free to realize on your security by seizing it and selling it.

If the unsecured creditors vote against the proposal, the business is bankrupt. If you are an unsecured creditor, you will have to try to recover your claim through the bankruptcy. If you are a secured creditor you can realize on your security by seizing it and selling it.

AVOIDING PROBLEMS

It's better to try to anticipate and avoid contract problems (such as not getting paid or even getting sued if you're providing the goods or services, or ending up dissatisfied if you're the buyer) than to have to solve them. Here are some pointers:

•   Choose the parties you deal with wisely—Your best protection against contract problems is to do business with someone with a good track record.

Even if you're providing services, choose your customers or clients with a little care. It's every business person's dream to be so successful that you have to turn customers away, but even if you're not that busy, there will be times when you should decline to work for someone.

T
I
P

I f you don't have the time or ability to do a job well, it is better for your business reputation in the long run to refer a prospective client or customer elsewhere. If you find that you are dealing with a client who has unrealistic expectations, you might be better off not dealing with her than running the risk of not being paid, being bad-mouthed, or getting sued. If your client really can't afford to pay for your services there is a good chance that he won't, so unless you're willing to risk doing the job for free don't agree to do the job at all.   T I P

- If you're the buyer, choose the product carefully—Compare the price and quality of different brands. Check the warranty that comes with it and the reputation of the manufacturer for dealing with customer problems and complaints.

- If you're the seller, don't misrepresent yourself or your product, and don't make promises you can't keep—If you do, the other party may be able to get out of the contract or sue you for damages for breach of contract. A consumer may complain to the authorities, and then you'll have the government to deal with. Just as important, you'll have a dissatisfied customer who won't recommend you to others or give you repeat business.

- Don't automatically accept the other party's terms—In theory, the terms of your agreement with the other party should be arrived at by a process of bargaining to make sure that the needs of both sides are being met. In actual fact, your ability to insist on what you want will depend on the parties' relative size, power, and need of each other. If you are presented with a pre-printed, standard form contract, you may not be able to change anything (for example, if you are dealing with Bloated Mega-Global Multi-national Inc.) or you may be able to change lots of things (if you're dealing with a Joe's Print Shop & Fishing Tackle and you're giving Joe a big contract).

T
I
P

I f you're given a pre-printed contract, pay special attention to exclusion clauses that attempt to limit the seller's responsibility to you in any way.

T I P

T
I
P
If you place an order for inventory or supplies by telephone and don't set terms for your contract with the seller, the terms will be governed by the wording on the invoice that the seller includes with the shipment. Have a copy of the invoice or standard contract faxed to you before you place an order with a supplier you haven't dealt with before.

T I P

If you're the one presenting the standard form contract, you want to be flexible about making changes in it so you don't lose the deal, but may want to consult with your lawyer about the effect of the changes so that you don't end up shooting yourself in the foot.

- Try to arrive at an agreement that's fair to both sides—Even if you do have the bargaining power to crush the other party in your fist, you shouldn't enter into a deal that is totally one-sided in your favour. If you drive too hard a bargain, the other party may simply walk away from the contract, figuring it's no worse financially to be sued than to perform. Or the other party may go through with this contract, but never want to deal with you again. If you are the seller and your client or customer is a consumer rather than another business, there are further concerns under provincial consumer protection legislation; if you take advantage of a consumer, the contract can be set aside.

- Get something in writing—Even if it's only a contract to paint a wall, the key terms of your agreement should be in writing. And the more complicated the deal, the more detail you will want in the contract. Putting the agreement into writing forces the parties to define the details, and that's how you'll find out if there really *is* an agreement. In addition, a detailed written contract serves as evidence of what was agreed to in case there's a dispute later on.

T
I
P
Provincial legislation requires contracts for the purchase of goods worth more than $30 to $50 (depending on the province) to be in writing unless the purchaser takes at least some of the goods with him or pays part of the purchase price.

T I P

- Consider having a lawyer draft the contract or review it before you sign it—You don't have to have every single contract you enter into drafted or reviewed by a lawyer, but if the contract involves a lot of money or a long-term commitment, you should ask your lawyer to take a look at it. At times like this you'll realize that having a monthly retainer agreement with your lawyer can save you money (see p. 17 in Chapter 2).

T
I
P

If you repeatedly enter into the same kinds of contracts for goods, you should have your lawyer prepare or approve a standard form contract for you to use.

T I P

WHAT HAPPENS IF THERE'S A PROBLEM?

No matter how hard you try to anticipate every situation, unforeseen problems may arise. Here are some of the problems that can arise with contracts for services, and some solutions:

• A service provider who doesn't finish the work can be sued.

T
I
P

If you're the customer, you will have to find someone else to finish the work. As long as you haven't paid more than the value of the work done, you won't lose too much money. Before you hire someone else, notify the first provider in writing that you consider your contract to be at an end. If you overpaid for the value of the work that was done, you'll probably have to sue to get the overpayment back.

T I P

• A service provider who does the work badly can be thrown off the job and can be sued.

T
I
P

If you're the customer and you realize as the services are being provided that the work isn't satisfactory, you should ask for the problems to be corrected. If they are not, you may be able to end the contract because it has been breached. Then you can refuse to pay (but check it out with your lawyer first). If you have already paid something, you'll probably have to sue to get it back. You may also want to sue for additional damages, if the supplier screwed up royally. The supplier may have a different view of the matter and may sue you for the unpaid balance.

T I P

- A service provider who injures someone or damages someone's property can be sued, but if the service provider has third-party liability insurance, the insurance should cover compensation.

- A service provider who doesn't get paid can sue, or can exercise any available lien rights.

Here are some problems and solutions involving contracts for the sale of goods:

- A seller who doesn't deliver the goods doesn't get paid.

T I P	If you're the buyer, in order to protect yourself in the event of non-delivery, try to keep the amount you pay before delivery as low as possible. If the goods don't show up and you haven't already paid for them, don't make any payment. If you have paid some or all of the purchase price, you will probably have to sue to get it back.

T I P

- In addition to not getting paid, the seller can be sued for damages for any loss the buyer suffers because of the non-delivery. These damages can be higher for a business customer than for a consumer if the seller is held responsible for the business buyer's lost profits.

T I P	If you're the seller, an exculpatory or exclusion clause in your contract of sale may offer you some protection against business customers. It could, for example, limit your responsibility to the amount the buyer paid for the goods, or it could state that you are not responsible for any injury, loss, or damage, however caused.

T I P

- A seller who delivers the goods late may still be able to insist on full payment. Unless it was a term of the contract that time is of the essence, the buyer has to accept late delivery. However, the buyer may be able to sue the seller for damages for any loss caused by failure to deliver on time. If you're the seller, consider protecting yourself with an exculpatory clause.

- A seller who delivers the wrong or damaged goods cannot insist that the buyer take delivery and pay for them, and may be sued for damages as well. If the buyer notices a problem with the goods at the time of delivery, she doesn't have to accept or pay for them. Whether the buyer notices the damage at the time of delivery or later, she may be able sue for damages, although if the seller has offered a warranty, the buyer may only be able to get the defective goods repaired or replaced. (The buyer can sue if the seller refuses to fulfill the warranty.) A contract that contains an exculpatory clause may protect the seller from claims for damages brought by business customers, but it probably won't offer full protection from claims by consumers.

> **T I P** If you're the buyer, even if you have no contractual rights against the seller that you can enforce you may have rights against the manufacturer of defective goods in tort law (see Chapter 20 on p. 283 for a discussion under the heading "Product Liability").
>
> T I P

AND ANOTHER THING...

Actually, there isn't another thing. We've said it all, and we find it hard to believe that there's anyone left reading (or even breathing) at this point. But if you're still with us, congratulations. As a reward, we're going to give you an executive summary of this chapter.

When you enter into a contract to buy or sell goods or services, you're looking for certainty. You want a written contract that says exactly what the goods or services are and who's providing them; who's paying for them, how much, how payment is to be calculated and how it's to be made, and what happens if payment isn't forthcoming; and who pays and how much if the services are substandard or the goods are defective, or damaged or lost, so that you know whether you need insurance. You're also looking for a peaceful business life, so you want to deal with suppliers who are reliable. If you can manage it, you'd also like to deal with customers who are reliable, at least about paying you; but since that isn't always guaranteed, be careful about extending credit, and make sure you take some form of security if you're selling goods and not getting cash on the nail head. Remember that knowing how to make and how to fulfill contracts is key to succeeding and prospering in your business.

CHAPTER FOURTEEN

BECOMING AN EMPLOYER

With good management and a little luck, your business will grow to the point where you can't do all of the work yourself. When you reach that point you have several options, depending on the kind of help you need:

- you can take in a partner or shareholder who will share not only the work but also the management and profits of your business.

- you can enter into a contract with an individual, partnership, or corporation to provide services to you for a limited period of time or on a non-exclusive basis. For example you can have a contract with a bookkeeper to come to your office once a week, or with a writer to produce your business's monthly newsletter.

- you can hire employees.

In this chapter we are going to take you through the steps you must take to become an employer. In the next two chapters we will discuss the rights and duties of both employers and employees, and what you must do to fire an employee.

INDEPENDENT CONTRACTORS

Independent contractors, such as the bookkeeper or the writer we mentioned above, usually work only for a fixed (short) term or on a particular project, supply their own tools or equipment, perform their work without training or direct supervision by the person they are working for, can work for other people as well (even for competitors), and run a risk of making a profit or suffering a loss. The person for whom an independent contractor works does not provide the contractor with benefits or with pay for overtime, vacations or statutory holidays, and does not take statutory deductions (for income tax, Employment Insurance, Canada Pension Plan, and workers' compensation) from the money paid to the contractor. When the term of the contract is up or when the project ends, the independent contractor has no rights, such as the right to notice or to pay in lieu of notice, against the person he is working for. (See Chapter 16.)

If you hire an employee you take on many legal responsibilities, from paying special taxes and levies, to providing a safe workplace, to giving notice if you want to end the employment. In an attempt to avoid these responsibilities some employers try to categorize workers who are really their employees as independent contractors. Instead of paying the workers a salary, they have the workers bill them. Instead of withholding tax from the workers and remitting it to the government, they leave it to the workers to pay taxes as sole proprietors. They don't provide vacation or holiday pay, or any benefits. Some workers will go along with this just to get a job, or to get the advantages of certain tax deductions that self-employed people are allowed. But the bad news is that you can't call someone an independent contractor just to avoid your responsibilities as an employer. If you have an employee that you're calling an independent contractor, the employee may sue you for wrongful dismissal after being terminated, or the federal and provincial tax departments and your provincial labour department may come after you, and if any of them do, you'll end up paying a lot of money.

GOVERNMENT REQUIREMENTS

Many of your responsibilities as an employer are dictated by federal and provincial law, and some of them are going to cost you money. Before you place your first Help Wanted ad you should know the cost of employing someone and the demands the government will make of you. This information will help you decide whether or not you really want to be an employer, and will also help you set your employee's hours, pay, and benefits. For information about your statutory duties as an employer, and to get any necessary forms including registration forms, you should contact:

- the provincial ministry of labour to find out about employment standards in your province. These standards govern such things as minimum wages, maximum work hours, vacation entitlement, statutory holidays, and termination of employment. The ministry of labour can also provide you with information about the occupational health and safety standards you'll have to meet in your workplace.

- the provincial workers' compensation board to find out if you are required to pay for coverage of your employees under your provincial workers' compensation legislation.

- the provincial ministry of finance, revenue, or taxation to find out if you are required to pay any employment-related provincial taxes, such as a payroll tax or health insurance tax.

- the provincial or federal human rights commission for information about human rights legislation that prohibits employers from refusing to employ people on certain grounds such as race and sex. (See below for a discussion of human rights legislation.)

- Revenue Canada to get information about your obligations to make employers' Employment Insurance and Canada Pension Plan contributions, and about your obligations to withhold from your employees' salary their EI and CPP contributions and income tax and to remit these amounts directly to Revenue Canada.

HUMAN RIGHTS LEGISLATION

Federal and provincial human rights legislation prohibit employers from refusing to hire people on a number of grounds that are considered discriminatory. Employers are also prohibited from asking questions in application forms or interviews about any of these matters. The grounds may differ slightly from province to province, but they usually include the following:

- race, colour, ancestry, ethnic origin, place of origin, or citizenship
- religion
- sex or sexual orientation
- age (although in some provinces it's permitted to refuse employment to a person on the basis that she is under 18 or over 65)
- marital status and family status (whether a person is married, has children, is pregnant, or is planning to have children)
- physical or mental disability (unless the disability actually prevents the person from performing the work)
- political beliefs
- criminal record for a provincial offence or for a *Criminal Code* offence for which the person has been pardoned (*Criminal Code* offences are more serious matters like theft and assault, while provincial offences are less serious matters like driving over the speed limit or hunting out of season)

However, there are some exceptions. If a person's age, sex, marital status, disability, or criminal record would make them unqualified for a particular job, an employer may be able to refuse to hire the person on that basis. For example, an exercise club could refuse to hire a man who applies for a job as an attendant in the women's locker room, or a sales company could decline to hire a profoundly deaf person to take telephone sales orders, or a trucking company could refuse to hire a driver who had a history of convictions under the provincial highway traffic act.

On the other hand, someone with a disability (for example, someone who uses a wheelchair) may be able to perform the job if certain accommodations are made. You can't refuse to hire a person with a disability if that person can perform the job with reasonable accommodations. You are only required to make *reasonable* accommodations, although an accommodation may be considered reasonable even though it causes hardship to your business (but not if it causes great hardship). A small employer is not required to make as many accommodations as a large employer. For example, any size business might be required to provide a special chair and/or frequent breaks for someone with back problems, or flexible working hours to an employee with young children. On the other hand, while a large business might have to install a ramp, wide doorways, and special washroom facilities to make the premises wheelchair accessible, a very small business might not.

If an employer wrongfully refuses to hire an applicant, that person can complain of discrimination to the human rights commission. The commission will investigate the complaint and, if it believes that there is some truth in it, will try to work out a settlement between the employer and the rejected applicant. If a settlement can't be reached, the matter may be referred to a board of inquiry or an adjudication panel. In the most extreme case, the employer could be ordered to hire the applicant, pay back wages from the original date of rejection and also pay damages to the applicant.

THE HIRING PROCESS

Hiring an employee involves a lot more than interviewing applicants. You'll have to draft a description of the job and list the qualifications needed to do the job. You'll have to find prospective employees and invite applications, screen out applicants you're not interested in, interview the ones you are interested in, and finally choose one person to fill the position.

Draft a Job Description and Qualifications

Before you take any steps towards hiring an employee, you must figure out what you want the employee to do. Write this down in a job description. The job description should be quite detailed, including such matters as:

- duties to be performed
- days of the week to be worked
- starting and finishing time
- whether overtime is required
- whether overnight travel is required
- special physical demands, such as heavy lifting, sitting for prolonged periods, keyboarding for long periods
- whether the employee needs to be bonded to hold the position

Having a detailed job description can do more than simply help you find a properly qualified employee. It can also protect you from accusations of discriminatory hiring practices, because you will be able to show that you refused to hire an applicant strictly because of his failure to satisfy a legitimate job requirement. And you'll be using the job description not only to hire the employee in the first place, but also to train that person, do performance reviews, decide on whether or not a raise in pay is deserved, and (if necessary) to fire the employee.

After you draft a job description, you must decide what qualifications a person needs to handle the job properly. Write this down as well. It will help you to draft an ad or instruct an employment agency, and to screen job applicants. Then find out how much a job like the one you're looking to fill ordinarily pays, and calculate how much you can afford to pay.

Where to Find Prospective Employees

You can find prospective employees through:

- newspaper ads
- a sign in your window
- employment agencies
- schools, colleges, or universities
- your local Human Resources Development Canada office
- friends and business associates

Any ad or employment notice must be drafted so as not to exclude prospective applicants on the basis of any of the prohibited grounds of discrimination mentioned in the "Human Rights Legislation" section above. For example, your ad or employment notice *should not* indicate that you are looking for "a male salesperson" or a "single white female receptionist." Your ad or employment notice *should* clearly set out the legitimate qualifications for the job. If it does, it will be harder for a rejected applicant to claim that she was denied the job for one of the prohibited reasons. If you prepare an application form for people to fill out, make sure that it does not ask for information about any of the grounds prohibited by human rights legislation. For example, it should not ask applicants when or where they were born, or whether they are single, married, widowed, or divorced.

Screening Applicants

You may be flooded with applications. If that happens you won't possibly be able to interview everyone, so you'll have to screen the applicants to decide which ones to interview. The screening process should be based on the job description and qualifications list you prepared for the job, and not on any of the grounds prohibited by human rights legislation.

It is good policy and common courtesy to send a polite letter to all applicants whom you do not plan to interview, simply telling them that you cannot offer them an interview at this time. That way the applicant knows that the application was at least received and considered.

The Interview

When you interview a prospective employee you are trying to find out if that person:

• has the skill and ability to do the job

• will be honest and reliable

• can take direction and/or work independently as needed

• is likeable and easy to work with

Your interview questions should be designed to bring out that information from the prospective employee. But remember that you cannot ask questions about any of the matters prohibited under human rights legislation. You might think that someone's age, health, or family status will affect their ability to do the job or their reliability. While one man of 55 may not be able to lift heavy boxes, another may be able to do it with ease. On the other hand there may be a strapping lad of 22 who can't lift a thing. While one woman with one child might miss one day of work a week, another woman with eight children might never miss even part of a day's work in a full year, and a man with no children might sleep in and be late for work every day. The point is that you can't make assumptions about how capable or reliable an employee will be based solely on things like race, sex, age, disability, religion, or membership in a political party. That's why human rights legislation across the country says that you can't ask questions about those things. You can, however, ask questions about whether the employee can actually do the job and work the hours required.

For example,

YOU CAN'T ASK:	YOU CAN ASK:
Where were you born? What is your nationality?	You can ask: Are you legally entitled to work in Canada?
Are you married?	Are you available to travel out of town/overnight? Would you be willing to relocate?
Can I see your driver's licence? (because it contains information about age and disability)	Are you licenced to drive a car?
Do you have children? What are your day care arrangements?	Is there anything that would prevent you from being at work from 8 AM to 4 PM? Is there anything that would prevent you from working overtime?

YOU CAN'T ASK:	YOU CAN ASK:
Do you have back problems?	Is there anything that would prevent you from lifting 25 pounds frequently over the course of a day? Is there anything that would prevent you from sitting for long periods of time?
Have you ever been convicted of an offence?	Is there anything that would prevent you from being bonded? (if that is a reasonable and genuine requirement for the job)

Check References

A prospective employee can write anything on a resume or job application and say anything (quite convincingly) in a job interview—and turn out to be a liar. So check references to confirm an applicant's qualifications and employment history. Contact educational institutions and licencing bodies to confirm that the applicant has the credentials claimed. Telephone past employers to confirm the period of employment, position held, duties performed, and compensation received. You should also ask past employers about:

- the quality of the applicant's work
- the applicant's attendance and punctuality
- the applicant's ability to get along well with others
- whether the applicant had a good attitude and was motivated
- the applicant's honesty
- the reason the applicant left that job
- whether they would hire the applicant again (a key question)

Most Canadians are polite and reluctant to say anything bad about someone. They're also afraid of getting sued for **defamation**—saying or writing something false that would harm a person's reputation. (For more about defamation, see p. 289 in Chapter 20.) So you may only get answers to the questions "Was the person employed?" "Why did the employee leave?" and "Would you rehire the person?" You can try asking other questions anyway. People are not afraid to say nice things about their former employees, but will probably clam up instead of saying something nasty. Listen to what's not being said as well as to what is being said.

Because of the nature of your business you may want to be sure that anyone you hire does not have a criminal record. You can normally only refuse to employ someone on the basis of a *Criminal Code* conviction for which that person has not been pardoned. It's not that easy to find out about criminal convictions. To begin with, no one but the individual has the right to request information about his record. Another obstacle is that only the RCMP has information about convictions made anywhere in Canada, rather than about local convictions (which the local police might be able to help you with), and they only work from fingerprints. What you'll have to do is ask the applicant to go to a private company that specializes in taking fingerprints for non-criminal purposes (look in the Yellow Pages or contact the RCMP), give her fingerprints, and request a certificate from the RCMP. The certificate and cover letter will be returned to the applicant, not to you. If the person you hire will be handling money or valuables, you may want the employee to be bonded. Contact your insurance agent or broker for information about bonding.

If your thoughts are now turning to a private investigator to find out something about a prospective employee, you should know that the information they can get is also limited—and they can be expensive. They can get general information about a person's background and habits. They can only get more information than you could about past employment from fellow employees on an informal basis, and they can't get any more information about a criminal record than you can.

HOW DO YOU AVOID HIRING THE WRONG PERSON?

No employer can afford to hire the wrong person for the job. Even though you can fire a dishonest, disobedient, or incompetent employee, untold harm can be done to your business before you get rid of the person. And it's not that easy to fire employees, either. (See Chapter 16 for more information.) Unfortunately you can't always get the necessary information about an applicant's past to determine whether he will do the job well—and even an employee with great qualifications and glowing recommendations can turn out to be wrong for you. So what can you do? The best solution we can offer is to hire on probation or on a contract basis to begin with. If an employee is hired for a probationary period of a few weeks or months, you can decide at the end of the period whether to hire the employee permanently or direct her to the door. Similarly, if you hire an employee on short-term contract you can decide when the contract period is up whether or not to renew the contract, either temporarily or permanently.

A growing medical partnership needed a new secretary. The partners interviewed a woman who was very pleasant and who came highly recommended by one partner's wife who knew her socially. She came poorly recommended by her last employer, but she explained he'd been impossible to work for and none of his secretaries ever lasted more than six months. This sounded like a reasonable explanation, so the partners accepted it and hired her. The secretary turned out to be a nightmare. She was disorganized and slow, she couldn't spell, she misfiled papers, and she made documents disappear like a magician. But even though they had the legal right to dismiss her, none of the partners could bring themselves to do it—because she was so nice, because she really needed the work, and because she was a friend of one partner's wife.

HIRING FAMILY MEMBERS

One of the advantages of having your own business is that you can hire a family member. Your business may be ready to take on an employee, and your spouse or child may legitimately be the best person for the job. Or your business may be in a position where some help would be nice but isn't desperately needed, or where help is desperately needed but your business can't afford it yet. The good thing about hiring a close relative is that the money you pay in salary stays in the family. In fact, if you pay your spouse or child a salary, you may end up with more money in the household than if you brought all the salary home yourself. When the income is split between two people so that your tax bracket is lowered, the tax that the two of you pay will be less than you would pay alone if the salary were all yours. But you can't pay a salary to a family member just to split income—the family member actually has to do some work. If Revenue Canada doesn't believe that the family member is really working, it will tax your business as if there were no employee and no salary expense.

To avoid getting into trouble with Revenue Canada you must treat your family member as you would any other employee by:

- having the family member actually do work for the business

- making sure that the amount you pay for the work is reasonable and more or less what you would pay to any other employee for that kind of work

- withholding tax, Employment Insurance, and Canada Pension Plan contributions, and making remittances to Revenue Canada

- issuing a T-4 slip at the end of each year

CHAPTER FIFTEEN

BEING AN EMPLOYER

Once you say to a job applicant "You're hired," you and your employee have a contract, with both rights and duties toward each other. Some of these are imposed by law and can't be changed; other rights and duties *will* be imposed by law unless the two of you agree otherwise, and still others don't exist at all unless they are specifically agreed on by the two of you in an oral or written contract.

Most employers and employees do not have a written contract. They have an oral one instead, and the vast majority of those expressly address only a few of the terms of employment, most commonly the job title, wages, hours of work, and amount of vacation. The other rights and duties of the parties (and trust us, there are lots) are never mentioned and are therefore all imposed by law.

Some of the law that governs the employer/employee relationship has developed over many years as the result of court decisions. The law contained in these court decisions is called **common law**. In Quebec, where there is no common law, many of the same duties are created by the *Civil Code*. In addition, both the federal and provincial governments have passed statutes that affect the rights and duties of employers and employees.

In this chapter we will examine the rights and duties of employers and of employees. We will also discuss written employment contracts and employee records.

THE RIGHTS AND DUTIES OF AN EMPLOYER

T I P

THE RIGHTS AND DUTIES OF THE EMPLOYER

Your duties as an employer are to:
- pay the employee
- provide a safe workplace
- provide a workplace that is free from discrimination or harassment
- provide necessary tools
- direct what work is to be done and how it is to be done
- repay the employee any money spent in the course of employment
- honour any contracts that the employee properly entered into on behalf of your business

Your rights as an employer are to:
- direct what work is to be done and how it is to be done
- receive any profits made by a worker in the course of your business
- monitor the activities of your workers
- terminate the employment (see the next chapter)

You have no right as an employer to:
- discipline an employee for misconduct (for example by docking wages or suspending the employee from work) unless you and the employee have specifically agreed that you have that right

T I P

The Duty to Pay

According to the common law, an employer must pay an employee a "reasonable" wage for the work done. What's a reasonable wage? At the top end of the scale, it's whatever you and your employee agree on. At the bottom end, it's minimum wage. You can agree to pay an employee more than the minimum wage, but you usually can't pay less. All provinces have employment standards legislation that sets a minimum wage for most workers in the province. The minimum wage is different in each province, but it's generally in the range of $5 to $7 dollars an hour. There are specific classes of employees to whom the minimum wage does not apply. These vary from province to province, but may include commissioned salespeople, farm workers, and professional employees such as accountants, doctors, or lawyers (but try getting a doctor or a lawyer to work for you for less than minimum wage). Unless you are paying all of your employees exactly the same amount, you may have to be concerned about provincial pay equity legislation that requires employers to pay equal wages for work of equal value regardless of the sex of the employee.

Provincial employment standards legislation also requires you to pay your employees overtime (almost always at the rate of one and a half times their usual pay) if they work over a fixed number of hours in a week (generally 40, 44, or 48 hours depending on the province). In most provinces, you have to give your employees a half-hour meal break if they work for five hours in a row. However in most provinces you do not have to pay them for that break, and the time it lasts is not considered work time for the purposes of calculating the number of hours worked. You are not required to give your employees a coffee break, but if you do, it is usually considered work time and you must pay them for it.

Under the common law, if you pay your employees other than a salary or hourly wage (for example, if you pay them on a commission basis) you must give them enough information about how you calculate their pay to allow them to verify the amount by calculating it themselves.

Employment standards legislation in every province gives employees the right to take a two-week vacation (in Saskatchewan, three weeks) after the completion of one full year of employment. In some provinces employees are entitled to a three-week vacation (in Saskatchewan, four weeks) after working for you for five or six years. You have to continue to pay regular wages while your employees are on vacation. Employment standards legislation may also give employees specific public holidays off (totalling from five to nine days depending on the province), although some employees can be required to work on statutory holidays and may be entitled to overtime pay for doing so. Employees who meet certain conditions (such as length of employment with you and number of days worked in the preceding weeks) are entitled to take statutory holidays off *and* be paid.

Employment standards legislation in every province requires you to let pregnant employees take a specified number of weeks off work before delivery. The same legislation requires you to let new parents take a specified number of weeks off work after a child is born (or, in some provinces, after a child is adopted). You cannot terminate employment on the grounds that an employee is pregnant or wants time off for parental leave. You do not have to pay an employee who is on pregnancy or parental leave, but you do have to take the employee back in the same or a comparable position when the leave ends. In most provinces, the employee must have worked for you for a minimum period of time (it varies considerably by province, from a few weeks to a year) to be eligible for pregnancy or maternal leave, and may also be required to ask for the leave in writing and provide a medical certificate. If the employee is not eligible for pregnancy or maternity leave, you do not have to take the employee back.

The government has a number of ways to make sure that you comply with the requirements of employment standards legislation. If an employee complains, the government will investigate the complaint, and has the power to order you to pay the employee back wages at the legislated rate. The government can also prosecute employers who do not comply with the legislation. An employer who is convicted can be fined tens of thousands of dollars, and even sentenced to a term of imprisonment.

No provincial law requires you to pay your employees while they are off sick, although you may agree to allow them a certain number of sick days with pay. Nor does any law require you to provide other benefits such as supplementary health coverage, prescription drug plans, dental insurance plans, disability insurance, life insurance, death benefits, retirement benefits, or pension plans.

Remitting Taxes on Behalf of Employees

As an employer you are required to make deductions from employees' earned wages and remit them to Revenue Canada as follows:

- income taxes—including taxes on salary and on any taxable benefits you provide (such as personal living expenses, discounts on merchandise or services, disability benefits and medical expenses, professional dues and club memberships, among many other things)
- Canada Pension Plan contributions
- Employment Insurance contributions

There are nasty financial penalties if you do not make these remittances.

Duty to Provide a Safe Workplace

Under the common law, an employer must provide employees with safe tools and equipment, work procedures that are safe, and co-workers who are not likely to endanger anyone.

On a very hot day when the employees in the warehouse were doing physically demanding work, the general manager of a manufacturing company provided them with beer to cool off. One of the employees drank eight beers over a four-hour period and then left work in his car. He went to a bar and had another couple of beers, and on his way home he drove off the road into a ditch and suffered serious injuries. He sued the company and won. The court held the company 75 per cent responsible for the employee's injuries (and the employee 25 per cent responsible) because it hadn't taken reasonable care for the safety of its employees. An employer that provides alcohol in the workplace has to monitor how much the employees consume, and make sure that no employee drives while impaired.

An employer also has statutory duties to make the workplace safe, and we'll now discuss those in more detail.

Occupational Health and Safety Legislation

In all provinces there is occupational health and safety or other labour legislation that requires employers to take reasonable steps to provide a safe and healthy workplace. The legislation may dictate such things as the amount of space each employee is entitled to and the kind of washrooms that must be provided. Employers are required to establish specific safety procedures or programs, depending on the nature of the work, for example, to insist that workers wear protective equipment. They may also be required to let workers know about any hazardous materials used in the workplace, including such ordinary things as photo-copier chemicals and cleaning fluids. Employers are required to post a copy of the health and safety legislation and provide workers with information necessary for them to protect themselves. Workers have the right to refuse to work in conditions that they reasonably believe are unsafe. Work premises can be visited by government inspectors, and employers who do not comply with the legislation can be charged with an offence.

Workers' Compensation Legislation

Workers' compensation is an insurance program that provides benefits to workers who have been injured on the job. Not all businesses are covered by workers' compensation, so you'll have to check with your provincial workers' compensation board. If your business is covered, you must pay premiums to the workers' compensation board. The amount of the premium is based on a combination of the level of danger in the industry as a whole and on the employer's individual safety record. In a business that is covered by workers' compensation, an employee who is injured at work cannot sue the employer, but can make a claim to the workers' compensation board. Workers are entitled to compensation even if the employer wasn't at fault. If an employee makes a successful claim your premiums may go up. You will be notified if an employee makes a claim and will be given an opportunity to object (for example, on the grounds that the employee was injured outside your workplace).

If your provincial workers' compensation legislation applies to your business, you may also be required to follow specific procedures and meet specific standards to keep your workplace safe.

Duty to Provide a Workplace Free from Discrimination or Harassment

Human rights legislation requires employers to provide a workplace that is free from discrimination, or from harassment on any of the prohibited grounds of discrimination. (See the previous chapter for details about prohibited discrimination.) This means that you can't discriminate against or harass any employee and you also can't allow your employees to harass or discriminate. An employee who feels he has been discriminated against or harassed can make a complaint to the human rights commission. Any complaint will be investigated by the commission, and if there is a basis to it, the commission will first try to help the parties settle the matter. If it can't be settled, the commission will conduct a hearing, and if it finds there has been harassment or discrimination you can be ordered to compensate the employee financially. You could be held responsible for the actions of an employee even if you weren't aware of the conduct, unless you had taken reasonable precautions to prevent harassment or discrimination. For that reason it is wise to have a policy in place to prevent harassment or discrimination in the first place, to educate your employees about harassment and discrimination, and to deal with either by investigating any complaint and disciplining those responsible.

Duty to Provide Necessary Tools

Under the common law, an employer must provide employees with whatever tools are necessary to do their work, unless it's customary in the particular trade for workers to provide their own. So you would definitely have to have a computer, keyboard, and printer for your secretary, but you might not have to provide a woodworker with hand tools. Employers must properly maintain any tools or equipment they provide, and make sure they are used properly.

Your provincial occupational health and safety legislation may require your business to use specific equipment to carry out certain kinds of work. Contact your ministry of labour to find out if this is the case. Occupational health and safety legislation reinforces the common law duty to keep equipment in good condition and make sure that it is used properly. It also requires you to tell workers about any dangers involved in the use of the equipment. Government inspectors have the right to inspect your business premises and order you to comply with health and safety standards. If you don't, you can be fined or your business can be shut down until you do comply.

Duty (and Right) to Direct What Work Is to Be Done

Under common law, you have the right to tell your employees what to do and how you want it done, and you also have a duty to tell them. The duty to tell them how you want work done may include training a long-term employee to do new and unfamiliar work.

Provincial occupational health and safety legislation may require you to direct your employees to carry out certain activities in a specified manner. Again, contact the ministry of labour to find out if your business is affected in this way by the legislation. If your business does have to carry out specific procedures in a way set out by legislation, you may also be required to provide workers with written instructions and/or training in the procedures.

Duty to Repay the Employee

Under common law, if you ask employees to do something as part of the job and it costs them money, you have to pay them back. For example, if you ask an employee to drive to the next town to deliver a package, you'll have to reimburse the cost of gas and parking, although you have the right to ask for receipts before you pay.

Duty to Honour Contracts Made by an Employee on Behalf of Your Business

Under common law, if part of an employee's job is to enter into contracts on behalf of your business (either to have your business provide goods or services for customers or clients, or to get goods and services for your business), then your business has to perform the contracts your employee makes.

Right to Receive Profits Made by Employees

Under common law, if your employees make a profit doing your work, that profit has to be turned over to you. If your employees make a profit doing work for their own benefit when they should be doing work for your benefit, *that* profit has to be turned over to you as well. (For example, if one of your workers plays the stock market on company time instead of taking sales orders, and makes a killing, the money she makes is yours. You'll have to sue to get it, of course.) If you hire an employee to invent devices or to write something, you are the owner of the invention or the written material unless you and the employee have an agreement otherwise (see also Chapter 12). If an employee competes with your business without your consent you may be able to sue the employee for the profits made or for your lost profits. (An employer's chances of recovering anything in such a case are much greater if the person is a full-time, high-level employee.)

Right to Monitor Workers' Activities

An employer has a right to keep an eye on employees as they perform their jobs mainly because no Canadian legislation presently prevents an employer from doing it. The Canadian Constitution does not protect an individual's privacy, and there are no Canadian statutes that govern the collection or use of information about individuals in private business (the federal government says such a statute is coming soon). Some businesses are worried that employees might steal, others that they aren't devoting their full time to the work they're paid to do, still others that employees are committing wrongful acts (such as displaying pornography on a computer monitor, which might be considered sexual harassment under human rights legislation) for which the employer may be held legally responsible.

You can ask employees to open handbags and parcels for searching before they leave the business premises. You can listen in on customer service telephone calls to make sure that your employees are handling them properly. You can monitor your employees' e-mail and their use of the Internet. You can install video surveillance cameras. There is no law to prevent you from doing any of these things (although video cameras in washrooms or change rooms may leave you open to charges of sexual harassment or discrimination). But you should carefully weigh the benefits you are likely to achieve by doing any of these things against the hostility that will almost certainly be aroused among your employees. If you do intend to monitor your employees, draw up a clear policy about what activities will be monitored, why and how, and make sure that all of your employees know about it.

There is nothing to stop an employer from asking that employees submit to drug tests, but there's not much to be gained from such testing. If an employee who tests positive has a substance-abuse problem, then he is considered to have a disability that, under human rights legislation, the employer must accommodate (for example, by allowing the employee a leave for drug rehabilitation).

THE RIGHTS AND DUTIES OF AN EMPLOYEE

T **I** **P**	**THE RIGHTS AND DUTIES OF AN EMPLOYEE** The duties of an employee are: • to work • to act in the employer's best interest while working • to be competent

- to obey the employer's reasonable orders that relate to the employee's job
- to use the employer's property carefully
- not to reveal information that belongs to the employer

The employer may have the right to fire an employee who breaches any of these duties. (See the next chapter.)

The rights of an employee are for the most part the flip side of the employer's duties. An employee has the right:

- to be paid a reasonable wage for the work done (see "Duty to Pay" above)
- to be safe in the workplace (see "Duty to Provide a Safe Workplace" above)
- not to be discriminated against or harassed in the workplace (see "Duty to Provide a Workplace Free from Discrimination or Harassment" above)
- to be provided with necessary tools (see "Duty to Provide Necessary Tools" above)
- to be told what work to do and how to do it (see "Duty (and Right) to Direct Work" above)
- to be reimbursed for money spent in the course of carrying out her duties (see "Duty to Repay the Employee" above)
- to quit (see the next chapter)

TIP

Duty to Work

This may seem obvious, but an employee has to show up at the workplace and has to work. If employees miss work without permission, you don't have to pay them for the time missed and you have the right to fire them, although brief absences for legitimate reasons such as illness are allowed. If an employee is absent for a long time because of illness, you can't fire him without running afoul of human rights legislation, unless you have taken reasonable steps to accommodate the employee's disability (chronic or frequent illness is a disability). If an employee is often late for work, again you have the right to fire the person (unless the lateness is caused by a disability, in which case you have to try to accommodate by setting different work hours, although you may not have to if the original work hours were critical to the job). If the employee shows up on time and stays the required hours but either does no work or does it badly, you can fire her, unless (here it comes again) the employee's incompetence or failure to do his or her job is caused by a disability. If it is, you have to accommodate. Alcoholism, drug abuse, and mental disturbance are all considered disabilities. Accommodation would involve getting professional help for the employee. (Yes, it's a nightmare.)

Duty to Act in Employer's Best Interest

During work hours, an employee must devote his full time and attention to the employer's work, serve the employer honestly and faithfully and act in the employer's best interest in carrying out his duties. These are common law duties. An employee who steals from the employer, conceals or falsifies information that the employer is entitled to, or acts abusively towards other employees, customers, or suppliers, is not acting honestly and faithfully and can be fired.

Duty to Be Competent

Whatever an employee does, the common law says that she must do it competently. You have the right to fire an employee for incompetence if the employee's performance falls below the standard of others. (This means that if all of your employees are incompetent, you're in big trouble. You may never be able to get rid of any of them!) An employee who is hired as a professional or as a skilled tradesperson must perform his work to the standard of a reasonable person in that field. Keep in mind (as always) that you may have to accommodate an employee whose incompetence is caused by a disability.

There is no general duty on an employer to train employees, but rather than hiring and firing until you find someone who isn't incompetent, you might do well to have a training program.

Duty to Obey Reasonable Orders

According to the common law, an employee has to obey the employer's orders if:

• they are reasonable

• they are understandable

• they are related to the employee's job description or usual work duties

• the employee is capable of doing the work ordered

• the work is not likely to endanger the employee's health

Duty to Use the Employer's Property Carefully

An employee has a common law duty not to damage the employer's property either deliberately or carelessly. In addition, under occupational health and safety legislation workers have a duty to tell the employer about problems with specified equipment, and a duty not to remove or cripple protective devices on such equipment.

Duty Not to Reveal Information

Under common law, employees must not reveal confidential information that belongs to the employer. For example, they cannot reveal the employer's trade secrets (such as devices, formulas, processes, or plans—see Chapter 12), or information about customers or clients or about the employer's financial affairs.

WRITTEN EMPLOYMENT CONTRACTS

All of the things we've discussed above under Employer's Rights and Duties and Employees' Rights and Duties are part of the employment contract *without your having to do anything other than hire the employee.* The duties and rights implied by law are quite complete but some employers and employees choose to have written employment contracts. Employers and employees enter into written employment contracts for many different reasons:

- There are some matters implied by law that can be changed by an express contract between the employer and the employee (although many can't).
- There are other matters that the parties may want in their employment contract that are not implied by law.
- The employee's duties may be wide-ranging and complicated and/or the method of calculating the employee's compensation may be complex.
- The employer (and occasionally the employee) may want the right to end the employment relationship without having to give a reason or pay compensation to the other party.
- If the contract of employment is for a stated period of time longer than one year, in most provinces it is required by legislation to be in writing.
- Finally, the parties may simply want a written record of everything that was agreed to.

If you decide to have a written employment contract, it should address the matters in the list below. Not all of them are automatically covered by the law discussed in this chapter or the next (on termination of employment); those matters that aren't are italicized. Matters that are covered by law may not be covered adequately from your point of view. Your contract should include:

- *a job description*
- any employee representations about his qualifications
- *when the job starts* and how long it is to last, whether for a fixed period or an indefinite period
- a period of probation during which employment can be terminated by either party without having to give a reason and without

either party having to compensate the other for having terminated the contract

- employee's *duties* and hours of work

- anything the employer must do to enable the employee to perform the work properly (such as provide a vehicle or information of certain kinds)

- remuneration including salary, *commission, bonuses,* overtime, holidays, vacations, and *sick days,* and *the method for determining any raises in pay*

- reimbursement for business expenses

- *any employee benefits*

- *methods to be used to evaluate the employee's performance*

- *any employer rights to discipline the employee, for example, by docking pay, temporarily suspending from work, or demoting*

- employee's promise to devote her full time and attention to the employer's business

- employee's promise not to reveal trade secrets or other confidential information obtained during the course of employment

- employer's right to ownership of anything invented or created by the employee in the course of his employment

- the reasons for which either the employer or the employee can terminate the employment relationship, and any requirements to give notice or pay compensation to the other party

- any agreement by the employee not to compete with the employer after termination of his or her employment

If you want to have a written employment contract, it should be prepared by your lawyer, or at least reviewed by your lawyer before you sign it. If you have prepared an employee manual that sets out the terms of employment and benefits an employee is entitled to, you should state in the contract that the manual forms part of the contract, and you should give the new employee a copy of the manual.

COLLECTIVE AGREEMENTS

Until now we've been assuming that you are dealing with each of your employees on an individual basis. If your employees become unionized then you must negotiate with them as a group (**collective bargaining**) and enter into a contract with them as a group (a **collective agreement**). While a business employing as few as two employees can be unionized, most private businesses are not. The law as it relates to unionized workers is very complex and is beyond the scope of this book, but the right of employees to unionize is protected by law, and if your employees try to unionize, you should consult a lawyer who specializes in labour law.

KEEPING RECORDS ABOUT YOUR EMPLOYEES

There are some records concerning your employees that you are required to keep, and there are others that you should keep for your own convenience and/or protection. All employee records should be kept confidential.

Records Required by Law

Revenue Canada and provincial employment standards legislation require you to keep records for each employee. Generally speaking, an employer may be required to keep a record of:

- employee's name
- employee's occupation
- employee's address
- employee's date of birth
- employee's sex
- employee's social insurance number
- employee's dependants
- date employment commenced
- number of hours worked per day and per week, including overtime

- rate of pay
- actual wages paid
- deductions from wages
- vacations and statutory holidays taken, and vacation pay
- information on pregnancy or parental leave, and on sick leave
- date of termination

Revenue Canada requires records to be kept for six years after the end of the taxation year in which they were made. Depending on the province, you may be required to keep employee records for a year from the time the record is made all the way up to seven years after the termination of employment.

Other Records

You should set up a file for each employee that contains a chronological record of the employee's history on the job, starting when you begin the hiring process. The file should contain:

- the job description and qualifications you prepared before hiring the employee
- any ad or job notice
- any resume from or application form filled out by the employee, including any letters of reference
- any notes of the job interview with the employee
- any notes or documents related to your reference checks on the employee
- a record of the employee's attendance and punctuality, and reasons for absence or lateness
- any changes made to the initial job description
- copies of periodic performance evaluations (see below)
- a record of any merit bonuses and/or increases in pay
- a record of anything noteworthy in the employee's performance of his duties (whether good or bad)

T
I   If there's a problem with the employee's performance, make a detailed
P   note of it at the time—don't wait until you're thinking of firing the
         employee to start documenting performance problems.

                                                                    T I P

• copies of any correspondence with or about the employee

You will be able to use this personnel record to decide whether to (and to justify any decision to):

• give the employee a raise or bonus

• give or withhold a promotion

• terminate employment

Performance Review

It is a good idea to review the performance of your employees on a regular basis and to document the results of the review. It helps to establish an atmosphere of fairness in the workplace if you let your employees know what they've done right and what they've done wrong, and if you give them an opportunity to correct any shortcomings. If employees believe they are being treated fairly they are less likely to complain about being passed over for a raise or promotion. And, if it becomes necessary to fire an employee, you will have the documentation to prove what the individual did wrong, and, where appropriate, that the employee had been made aware of the problem and been given an opportunity to remedy the situation.

CHAPTER SIXTEEN

TERMINATION OF EMPLOYMENT

Your business needs may change. The employee who was perfect for you two years ago may not have the skills that you need today, and you may want to replace her with someone who has not only her skills but others as well. Or your business may not have done as well as you hoped and you can no longer afford to keep on the employee(s) you hired. Or your business may be just fine but your employee gives you a pain.

Employees can get up to all kinds of annoying things, but when can you fire them? And how do you do it? You may not be able to fire them without paying them off. In fact you may not be able to fire certain employees without getting yourself into big trouble. WARNING: Before you fire an employee, consult a lawyer with experience in employment law.

WHAT'S INVOLVED IN FIRING AN EMPLOYEE?

You almost always have the right to fire an employee, but firing one is not simply a matter of saying "You're fired!" and watching

him vanish in a puff of smoke. You may have to give him notice
or pay a lot of money to get rid of him. You can fire an employee on the spot for **just cause**, however, if you don't have just
cause, you must either give the employee **reasonable notice** that
his employment will end or else give the employee **pay in lieu of
notice**. Firing an employee without just cause, or without reasonable notice, or pay in lieu of notice, is **wrongful dismissal**.

Firing for Just Cause

There are certain reasons for firing an employee that the law rec-
ognizes as good ones. If such reasons exist, you have just cause
for firing the employee and you don't have to give her any
advance notice or pay any money in lieu of notice. You just tell
the employee to leave right away. The following are commonly
considered just cause for firing an employee:

- dishonesty toward the employer, including theft or embezzlement

- other criminal activity of a serious nature, on or off the job,
  whether or not the employee is convicted of or charged with the
  crime

- insubordination or disobedience, including refusal to obey reasonable orders or talking back to superiors

- disruption of corporate culture by continued bad behaviour
  toward other employees, customers, or suppliers, including rude-
  ness, shouting, or sexual or racial harassment

- drunkenness or drug abuse that the employee has been warned
  about and that affects the employee's work (but human rights
  legislation requires an employer to accommodate first)

- repeated absences or lateness without a reasonable medical or
  personal excuse

- incompetence or carelessness in the performance of the job that
  continues in spite of warnings

- long-term physical or mental illness that prevents the employee
  from carrying out the job notwithstanding the fact that reasonable accommodation has been made ("reasonable" accomoda-
  tion may go further than an employee would like)

An office assistant was employed by a talent agent specializing in child actors. The assistant made all appointments and supervised the reception area, which was always filled with children. One day the assistant told the agent that he needed time off—he didn't know how long—to recover from the stress of the job. The talent agent was required by law to hire temporary help until the office assistant was ready to return to work several months later.

- conflict of interest with the employer, for example, competing with you, taking business away from you, or using your property for personal benefit

In most of these situations (excluding dishonesty and other criminal activity), you cannot fire the employee the very first time she does something wrong. You have to give the employee a warning about the behaviour first and an opportunity to improve it.

The following reasons do *not* amount to just cause:

- personality conflict between the employee and you or other employees (short of insubordination or disruption of corporate culture)
- filing of a complaint against you with the government
- short-term illness, pregnancy, childbirth, or parental leave
- in Ontario, refusal of a retail employee to work on Sunday
- the employee's attempts to unionize the workplace
- financial problems of the business
- reorganization or restructuring of the business

If you have hired an employee on probation, you cannot fire him without acting fairly and reasonably, and having sufficient reason. The purpose of an initial period of probation is to train and evaluate the employee, and you can't evaluate him until after the training is finished. Then you can fire him without notice if he can't do the work.

If the employer and employee have a written contract of employment, it may limit the circumstances that amount to just cause. If this is the case, those circumstances are the only reasons for which the employer may fire the employee without notice. On the other hand, the contract may give the employer greater rights to fire the employee without notice. In that case, the employer's right to fire is governed by the contract unless the provisions are very unfair to the employee or they contravene human rights legislation.

Firing Without Just Cause

If you wish to fire an employee without just cause, you must give her reasonable notice of the termination of employment. In other words, you can't just say, "You're fired. Get out." You must say something like, "You're fired. Get out in x weeks." The $65,000 question is what does x equal? What is reasonable notice?

Employment standards legislation in every province states the minimum notice that you must give an employee, and although it varies from province to province, generally speaking:

- an employee who has worked for you for less than a minimum period of time (depending on the province, a period between one and six months) is not entitled to any notice.

- an employee who has worked for you for more than one to six months (depending on the province) is entitled to one week's (in some provinces, two weeks') notice in the first year and then one week's notice for each subsequent year he worked for you, up to a maximum of eight weeks (in a few provinces the maximum notice period is only two or four weeks). The notice must be in writing.

The notice periods set out in employment standards legislation are just minimums. If the employee sues you, a court may rule that the employee is entitled to a longer notice period depending on such factors as position, salary, and responsibilities, the number of years she has worked for you, the employee's age, and likelihood of finding another job easily. Based on common law decisions, the rule of thumb is that an employee is entitled to one month's notice for each year he worked for you. Remember this is only a rule of thumb. For example, an employee with a great deal of work experience and a position of responsibility may be entitled to considerably more than one month's notice if you fire her after one year.

You may not want an employee hanging around for weeks or months after you've said "you're fired." Just think of all of the mail that can get dropped into the storm sewer instead of the mailbox and all of the computer files that can be wiped out. The good news is that you can make the employee leave your place of business immediately. The bad news is that it will cost you. If you don't want to give the employee the full or any amount of notice, you can pay him instead of giving notice. This payment is called pay in lieu of notice or termination pay. You must pay him the full wages and benefits he would have earned during the notice period. In other words, if you would be required to give an employee two months' notice, you can instead pay two months' salary and benefits and show her straight to the door.

If the employer and employee have a written contract of employment, it may state how much notice or pay in lieu of notice the employer must give if the employee is fired without just cause. If that is the case, the contract will govern unless the notice period is less than the minimum set out in provincial employment standards legislation.

If an employee is hired for a specific project, the employment ends with the project. If an employee is hired for a fixed period of time, the employment ends when that time has passed. In either case the employer does not have to give the employee notice that the employment is ending. If, however, the employer allows the employee to continue working after the end of the project or after the fixed termination date, the general rules discussed above about notice apply. Similarly, if you hire someone for seasonal employment, the employment ends without notice at the end of the season. If you have a mandatory retirement age that you apply across the board to all employees and your employees are made aware of it, employment ends without notice when the employee reaches that age.

Wrongful Dismissal

Any time an employer fires an employee without just cause, or without reasonable notice, or pay in lieu of notice, the firing is called a wrongful dismissal. An employee who has been wrongfully dismissed can sue the employer for damages. For the employee to win, the court must conclude that the employer did not have just cause for firing the employee, and did not give reasonable notice. The court will decide what period of notice should have been given and will order the employer to pay damages that may include:

- an amount equal to the wages and benefits the employee would have earned during the reasonable notice period
- compensation for mental distress if the firing was carried out in a humiliating or embarrassing way
- compensation for damage to the employee's reputation caused by the employer making untrue statements about him or her to other employees, customers, or business associates

An employee who has been fired has to **mitigate damages** (take all reasonable steps to reduce her damages) by looking for other work and accepting any reasonable offer of employment, even if it's a somewhat lower position. A court will reduce the amount of damages it awards the employee by any amount of money earned or that could reasonably have been earned during the notice period.

An employer fired a sales clerk without just cause and without notice. The sales clerk sued for wrongful dismissal. The court found that he was entitled to four weeks' notice and therefore payment in lieu of notice of $250 per week for four weeks ($1000). However, because he found a $200 per week job one week after he was fired, his damages were reduced by $600, and the employer only had to pay $400.

If an employee who was hired for a fixed term or project is fired before the end of the term, the employee may be entitled to damages for breach of contract amounting to the wages that she would have earned during the remainder of the contract. Those damages probably won't be reduced by a court if the employee manages to find another job before the finish date of the contract.

Constructive Dismissal

Sometimes an employee who quits is treated in law as if he had been fired. Quitting when you've really been fired is called **constructive dismissal**. It is considered constructive dismissal if an employee quits after the employer:

- says "Either quit or you're fired."
- puts a long-time employee on probation without good reason (such as poor performance)
- repeatedly criticizes the employee without good reason
- demotes the employee without good reason
- reduces the employee's pay or benefits
- significantly changes the employee's job description or responsibilities
- fails to promote the employee as promised

Constructive dismissal is a form of wrongful dismissal.

Human Rights

Remember how we told you that you almost always have the right to fire an employee? We told you that if your reason wasn't good enough it might cost you money, but that you could get rid of an unwanted employee. Well, the situation is a little more complicated than that. Under human rights legislation there are certain grounds on which you are not allowed to fire an employee. These may differ slightly from province to province, but they usually include all those on the list on p. 194 in Chapter 14.

You may not think you're firing someone on one of those prohibited grounds. You may think you're firing the person for persistent lateness or absenteeism or for an inability to perform the required work. However, if the underlying reason for the lateness, absenteeism, or inability to do the job is, in fact, one of the prohibited grounds of discrimination, you must first take steps to accommodate the person. For example, an employee with young children may not be able to start work at 9:00 but can easily get to work by 9:30. Unless it's essential to the job that the employee be at work by 9:00, the employer must attempt to accommodate the employee, by allowing her to start work later and make up the half hour later in the day. If an employee develops a drug or alcohol addiction, the employer may have to accommodate by allowing the employee time off work to attend a rehab program.

You are not required to make accommodations that cause "*undue* hardship," but you would have to prove that a particular accommodation causes you more hardship than you should have to put up with by pointing to such factors as the size of your business, the cost of the accommodation to your business, any safety risks involved, and the effect of the accommodation on the morale of other employees.

If an employee believes that he was fired on one of the prohibited grounds of discrimination, the employee can complain of discrimination to the human rights commission, which will investigate and may try to work out a settlement. If that's not possible, the matter may be referred to a board of inquiry or an adjudication panel. Human rights cases are different from other cases of wrongful dismissal in that giving adequate notice or pay in lieu of notice is not enough. In the most extreme case, the employer might be ordered to rehire the employee, pay back wages from the original date of firing, and also pay damages to the employee.

Preparing for Potential Wrongful Dismissal Lawsuits

As we said in the last chapter, you should keep a file on every employee to document the employee's performance, and you should review and evaluate your employees' performance on a regular basis. If you start to have problems with an employee, make detailed notes in the file about every incident when it occurs. If you decide to fire an employee, this file will help you prove that you had just cause. Remember not to fire an employee until you have first warned her about problems in her job performance and given her a reasonable chance to correct the problems. Be sure to warn the employee in writing and to keep a copy of the warning letter in her file.

When enough is too much and you've made up your mind to fire the employee, it is essential that you first speak to a lawyer with experience in employment matters for advice about:

• whether you actually have just cause

• whether you have any human rights concerns

• how much notice you are required to give

• whether it makes sense to give notice or pay in lieu of notice

• how much you may be required to pay in wages and benefits

• whether to offer payment to the employee at the time of termination in return for the employee's **release** (a promise not to sue)

• whether to offer the employee nothing at all at the time of termination and hope that he gets a new job within the notice period

• how to handle the employee's physical departure from the business premises

• how to handle the topic of the dismissal with other employees
  and with people outside the business

• how to deal with a reference for the employee

It's important to have good legal advice before you fire the employee. You may be able to prevent a lawsuit altogether, and if you are faced with a lawsuit you'll be in a better position to fight it.

WHAT IF AN EMPLOYEE QUITS?

An employer's rights to fire an employee are limited. You may think that an employee's right to quit are *unlimited*, but they're not. An employee must give notice to the employer before quitting unless he has a valid reason (cause) to quit immediately. In some provinces, employment standards legislation sets out the exact notice that employees have to give employers—usually no more than two weeks. If there is no statutory notice period, reasonable notice by the employee is required. That is ordinarily the length of time it would take the employer to find and train a replacement.

An employee can quit without notice and leave right away if she has cause. That includes:

- dangerous working conditions that the employer refuses to do anything about
- an employer's order that is unreasonable or dangerous
- employer's activities that are illegal or immoral
- serious mistreatment of the employee by the employer

If an employee gives notice, decide whether to allow him to continue to work through the notice period. If you want him to leave immediately, you will have to pay wages and benefits he would have earned during the notice period. If you tell the employee to leave immediately but do not pay those wages and benefits, it amounts to wrongful dismissal.

Preparing (Once Again) for Potential Wrongful Dismissal Lawsuits

When an employee quits, you want to make sure that he can't later say that he was fired. So do the following:

- send a letter accepting the employee's resignation
- if the employee left immediately or worked to the end of the notice period, pay only wages and vacation pay owing to the last date worked (if you want to give the employee some kind of payment, make it clear that it's in recognition of service and that it is not termination pay or pay in lieu of notice)
- when you fill out the Record of Employment (see below), indicate that the employee has quit

---

T I P — An employee who quits in a temper may not have quit at all. Look for supporting evidence that the employee has quit, such as comments to co-workers or the return of property belonging to the business (keys or supplies). If the employee hasn't really quit but you don't allow the employee to come back to work, you could be sued for wrongful dismissal. Sometimes an employee who quits has really been dismissed, and then again you could be facing a wrongful dismissal lawsuit. See "Constructive Dismissal," above.

T I P

Suing the Employee

If an employee you really liked or needed quits, there's not much you can do about it. You can beg her to come back and offer more money or a corner office with a view, but you can't get a court order forcing her to return. However, you *can* sue her for damages for **wrongful resignation** or **wrongful termination** if she leaves without cause and without giving you reasonable notice. You'd have to show that you suffered harm because the employee left and you couldn't find a replacement in time to avoid the harm. It's not usually worth the employer's time and money to sue an employee.

WHEN THE EMPLOYEE IS GONE

Whenever an employee leaves, whether he quit, was fired, or has reached the end of the term of a contract for employment, there are a number of loose ends that have to be tied up:

- You must complete a **Record of Employment Form** (ROE) required under the Employment Insurance system and mail one copy to the employee and one to Human Resources Development Canada within five days after the last day the employee worked for you. The purpose of the ROE is to allow the employee to apply for Employment Insurance benefits. The form involves a lot of math, but you can get information and a guide book on how to complete it from Human Resources Development Canada.

> **T**
> **I**
> **P**
> When filling in the reason for issuing the ROE, state that the employee quit if that is the case (don't concern yourself about her entitlement to Employment Insurance). Otherwise the employee may be able to use the ROE against you in a wrongful dismissal lawsuit as evidence that she was fired.
> T I P

- You must pay any outstanding wages and vacation pay within a short time after termination (it varies from province to province, from "immediately" to 21 days), as set out in your provincial employment standards legislation. Remember to withhold income tax, CPP, and EI from this final payment.

- If you agreed to provide benefits like insurance after the employee leaves, contact the benefit provider to make sure that coverage continues.

You may well be contacted for a reference about the employee. Many employers are nervous about giving a negative reference. Some are so concerned that they say nothing at all, even though they may have some good things to tell, because they are worried about being sued for defamation. As an employer giving a reference you probably can't be successfully sued for defamation as long as:

- you honestly believe that what you are saying about the employee is true

- you have reasonable grounds for believing what you say

- you're not saying something negative for an improper motive, such as to take revenge on the employee or to prevent the employee from getting another job

If this doesn't give you enough comfort and you want extra protection:

- try to reach an agreement with the employee about what you will say or write to anybody who asks for a reference

- ask the employee to sign a release giving up any right to sue you over any reference you give

CHAPTER SEVENTEEN

TAXES

We are lawyers, not accountants, so this chapter is not an exhaustive tax guide. It is intended to give you just enough information to help you understand the legal requirements to pay taxes—and perhaps every third word your accountant says to you. Your business should have an accountant for proper tax advice and planning.

Every level of government—federal, provincial, and municipal—levies taxes on businesses. These fall into four main categories:

- income taxes—levied by the federal and provincial governments
- sales taxes—levied by the federal and provincial governments
- payroll taxes—levied by the federal and provincial governments
- business taxes—levied by the federal, provincial, and municipal governments

It's amazing that there's anything left for your business when all of the government hands are finally out of your pockets!

INCOME TAXES

Even if you have gone into business as a sole proprietor, you, in fact, have a partner—Revenue Canada. Revenue Canada has a stake in your business, to say nothing of in your heart. Revenue Canada collects both federal and provincial income tax from individuals in all provinces and from corporations in all provinces except Alberta, Ontario, and Quebec, where the federal and provincial governments collect corporate income taxes separately.

You want to organize your business affairs so that you pay as little tax as is legally possible. This is called tax **avoidance**, and is perfectly legal. Tax **evasion** is not. To make sure that you avoid as much tax as is legally possible without crossing the line into evasion, your business must have expert tax advice from an accountant and/or tax lawyer, because income tax laws and regulations are very complicated and change constantly.

If your business is a sole proprietorship or partnership, the income of the business is taxed as part of your personal income. The business does not have to pay taxes separately from you. If your business is a corporation, the income of the business is taxed in the hands of the business. Any salary or dividends that you receive from the corporation will be taxed as part of your personal income.

What Are You Taxed On?

You're not taxed on every penny your business takes in. You are only taxed on the profit your business makes during the taxation year. Profit is the business's revenue or income (the money that your business takes in) minus its legitimate expenses. In tax law it is key to understand what is considered to be income and what is considered a legitimate expense.

What is Business Income?

Business income is money earned (or commercially valuable property received) from any activity you carry on for profit or with a reasonable expectation of profit. Money earned as payment for the provision of services or goods sold regularly in your business, rental payments, or interest payments are all considered to be income. As far as the tax department is concerned, most of the time you don't have to wait to actually receive the money or property to earn it. The income is earned as soon as you send out a bill for your goods or services.

In addition to earning regular income, on occasion a business may make a capital gain by selling **capital property** at a profit. The distinction between income and capital gain is important, because income is fully taxed, while only three quarters of a capital gain is. Capital property is usually property with long-term value, such as land, a building or equipment used to run the business. It does not normally include property that the business is ordinarily in the business of selling.

Your antique business owns, and is run out of, a small historic building in a scenic village. You buy and sell antiques throughout the year, selling each item at a profit. The profits that you make on the sale of the antiques are taxed as income. If your business sells the building to move into a larger shop, the profit your business makes on the sale of the property is taxed as a capital gain.

What Are Legitimate Business Expenses?

It's not difficult to figure out what your business income is. It's far more challenging, and for tax purposes far more important to you, to figure out your legitimate business expenses. The more of those you claim, the lower your profits will be for tax purposes, and therefore the lower your taxes.

Revenue Canada says that you can deduct any reasonable expense you incur to earn business income. For example, you can deduct:

• rent for business premises, or mortgage interest if you own the premises

• salaries, wages, and benefits paid to employees

• office expenses and supplies

• telephone and utilities

• cost of leasing equipment used for business purposes

- cost of buying or producing the goods you sold during the year
- delivery, freight, and transportation expenses
- the cost of minor maintenance and repairs to property used to earn income
- some of the expenses incurred to run a motor vehicle to earn business income
- business insurance premiums
- some advertising and promotion expenses
- licence or permit fees, and municipal business and property taxes
- membership fees and dues for professional, trade, or commercial organizations
- interest paid on money you borrowed to run the business
- bank charges
- 50 per cent of business meals and entertainment
- legal, accounting, and other professional fees
- travel expenses incurred to earn business income

Whenever you have an expense for an item that is used for both business and personal purposes (such as your car), you can only deduct the portion of the expense that relates to the business use of the item. If you operate your business out of your home, there are certain expenses that you won't have, such as rent for commercial space. However, you are allowed to deduct expenses for the business use of your home. You can deduct a percentage of the following costs, based on how much of your home your business occupies:

- mortgage interest or rent
- realty taxes
- heat
- electricity
- water
- maintenance and repairs
- home insurance

Add up all of these expenses and then calculate what percentage of your home you use for your business, either how many rooms of the total in your home, or how many square feet out of the total area you use in your home. You can deduct that percentage of your total costs to run your home as a business expense.

If you buy buildings, vehicles, or equipment for use in your business, you are not allowed to deduct their full cost as a business expense. These items are capital property. Because they will continue to be useful to your business for more than one taxation year, you can only claim a portion of the cost as an expense. You continue to claim a portion of the cost over a number of years until the entire cost has been claimed. Revenue Canada establishes different percentages for different kinds of capital property. These are designed to allow taxpayers to claim the full cost of capital property over the anticipated useful life of the property because it loses its value gradually over a period of time (**depreciates**). The amount you are allowed to claim each year as an expense is called **capital cost allowance**. By the way, although land is also capital property, you can't claim capital cost allowance for it because it doesn't depreciate in value.

If you buy a franchise, a licence to manufacture or distribute a product, goodwill, or other property that does not physically exist but still gives you a lasting economic benefit, you are not allowed to deduct its full cost as an expense either. These things are usually considered to be **eligible capital property**, and you may only claim part of their cost each year. Revenue Canada establishes the percentage.

What Happens When You Dispose of Capital Property?

Generally when you sell capital property for more than it cost you, you have a capital gain. If you sell it for less than it cost you, you have a capital loss. The purchase price of a piece of capital property is not the only thing that determines what the cost of the piece of property is for capital gains purposes. A capital gain or loss is calculated on the basis of the property's **adjusted cost base**, which includes not only the purchase price of the property, but also other costs of acquiring the property such as legal fees, commissions, licencing fees, the cost of the financing, and the cost of any additions or improvements to the property.

Likewise, the money paid to you on the sale is not the only thing that determines what the sale price of the property is for capital gains purposes. A capital gain or loss is calculated on the basis of the property's **adjusted sale price**, which is the sale price of the property, less the expenses you incur when selling it, such as advertising costs, fixing-up expenses, legal fees, and commissions. The capital gain (or loss) is the difference between the adjusted sale price and the adjusted cost base.

Your business buys a small building for $100,000 for use as a warehouse. You pay lawyer's fees of $5000. After a year, you build on an addition at a cost of $25,000. Five years later you sell the building for $200,000. At that time you pay a real estate commission of $7000 and legal fees of $3000.

Your adjusted sale price is:

sale price	$200,000
less real estate commission	7,000
less legal fees	3,000
adjusted sale price	$190,000

Your adjusted cost base is:

purchase price	$100,000
plus legal fees	5,000
plus cost of addition	25,000
adjusted cost base	$130,000

The capital gain is:

adjusted sale price	$190,000
minus adjusted cost base	130,000
capital gain	$ 60,000

If you have a capital gain in any year, three quarters of it is added to your income and taxed. If you have a capital loss in any year, it can be used to reduce capital gains, but it can't be used to reduce your other income. If you don't have any capital gains in the taxation year that you have a capital loss, you can carry the loss back to be applied against capital gains in the past three years, or forward to be applied against capital gains you may have in the future.

Capital gains and losses get a bit more complicated when you have claimed capital cost allowance against the property. If you sell the property for more than its **undepreciated capital cost** (its value after claiming capital cost allowance), it means that you claimed too much capital cost allowance over the time the business owned the property, and you have to pay back that excess capital cost allowance. This excess is called a **recapture** and is added to the business's income. If you sell the property for less than its undepreciated capital cost, it means that you did not claim enough capital cost allowance over the time the business owned the property, and you may be able to deduct the loss, called a **terminal loss**, from the income of the business.

HOW IS A BUSINESS TAXED?

How your business is taxed depends on the form of your business. Whether it is a sole proprietorship or a partnership or a corporation will make a difference.

How Are You Taxed as a Sole Proprietorship or a Partnership?

If you carry on business as a sole proprietor, the business's income is your personal income. You need to file only one income tax return, your personal one. The business does not file a separate return. You detail the business's income and expenses, and calculate its net profit or loss in a schedule that is attached to the return. Any net profit is included as part of your income on your personal tax return. Any net loss is subtracted from your other income for the year. If you have no other income for the year, or if the net loss from your business is greater than your other income, you may carry the loss back and apply it against income you earned in the past three years, or you may carry it forward and apply it against income you earn in the next seven years.

If you carry on business in a partnership, your share of the business's income is also your personal income. Again, you have to file only one income tax return, your personal one. The partnership does not file a separate return. If the partnership has fewer than six partners, you detail the partnership's income and expenses and calculate its net profit or loss in a schedule attached to the return. If the partnership has six or more partners, the partnership must file a partnership information return with Revenue Canada, and must give each partner a statement of partnership income. You must attach a copy of the statement of partnership income to your tax return. As a partner, your share of the partnership's net profit is included as part of your income on your personal tax return.

You can reduce your share of the net profit by claiming expenses that you incurred personally (and which the partnership did not pay back to you) that were not included in the partnership's statement of income and expenses. Your share of any net loss of the partnership is subtracted from your other income for the year. As with a sole proprietorship, if you have no other income for the year, or if your share of the partnership's net loss is greater than your other income, you may carry the loss back or forward to apply it against income you earned in the past three years, or the next seven.

You must pay federal and provincial income tax on your personal income. The percentage rate of tax you pay depends on your total income—as your income increases so does the percentage rate at which it is taxed. The combined rate of federal and provincial tax varies from province to province, but on average taxpayers earning:

- less than approximately $6500 pay no tax at all
- between approximately $6500 and approximately $29,500 pay about 27 per cent
- between approximately $29,500 and approximately $59,000 pay about 42 per cent on the amount between $29,500 and $59,000
- over approximately $59,000 pay about 50 per cent to 55 per cent on the amount over $59,000

How Are You Taxed as a Corporation?

If your business is incorporated, it has to file a corporate income tax return. In Alberta, Ontario, and Quebec the corporation must file a federal income tax return as well as a provincial one. In the other provinces the corporation only has to file a federal return (it includes provincial tax, though).

The corporation's tax return will detail its income and expenses and calculate its net profit or loss. The corporation will pay federal and provincial income tax on its net profit. If the corporation suffers a net loss, it can be carried back or forward, and applied against income the corporation earned in the past three years or may earn in the next seven. A corporation's loss cannot be applied to reduce your personal income for tax purposes.

Unlike individuals, whose tax rate increases in stages with the amount of income earned, corporations are taxed at a flat rate. As we discussed in Chapter 4, the actual combined federal and provincial flat tax rate will depend on a number of factors. The highest combined tax rate is about 45 per cent, but the federal Small Business Deduction reduces the tax rate to between approximately 18 and 23 per cent (depending on the province) on the first $200,000 of taxable income of Canadian Controlled Private Corporations. For taxable income of the corporation over $200,000 the combined tax rate rises back up to the mid-40 per cent range on the income in excess of $200,000, although corporations in a manufacturing business still get a tax break to keep them in the 30 to 40 per cent range. The Small Business Deduction does not apply to income from a **specified invest-ment business**—if most of the corporation's income is from interest, dividends, rents, or royalties (and the corporation does not have more than five full-time employees); or to income from a personal service business (see p. 51 in Chapter 4).

If your business corporation pays you a salary, benefits (such as travel benefits or personal use of the corporation's car), a bonus, or dividends, you will have to file a personal tax return and pay tax on what you receive from the corporation. You pay tax on your salary, bonus, or benefits at your personal tax rate. Dividends are also taxed at your personal tax rate, but to a maximum of about 35 per cent (depending on what province you live in) to recognize the fact that the profit has already been taxed once in the hands of the corporation before the dividend is paid.

What Are Your Filing and Payment Requirements?

Every taxpayer is required to file an annual income tax return by a certain date and pay taxes owing.

Sole Proprietors and Partners

Sole proprietors and partners are self-employed and must file personal income tax returns. Most sole proprietorships and partnerships have to have a **fiscal period** or taxation year that runs from January 1st to December 31st (December 31st being the year end), and must file their income tax returns on or before June 15th of the year immediately following the year end. Note that your income tax return may not be due until June 15th, but your taxes must be paid on or before April 30th. Go figure.

Taxpayers who are employed by a business have income tax deducted from every pay cheque. Self-employed taxpayers don't get a pay cheque that can be gnawed away by the tax authorities, so they must pay their tax by quarterly instalments. (Taxpayers who have both employment and self-employment income must make quarterly payments once they owe $2000 more in taxes than has been withheld and remitted by the employer during the current year plus one year out of the last two years.) Revenue Canada calculates your instalment payments based on your income for the current year and the past two years, and sends you instalment billing notices.

You don't have to pay the instalment amounts calculated by Revenue Canada. You can make your own instalment calculation by dividing the tax payable on your last return by four and you can pay that amount each quarter. Or, if you think your income will be down in the current year and you get Revenue Canada's permission, you can estimate your income for the year, divide it by four, and pay that amount each quarter. In either of these cases, if you underestimate the total tax you owe for the whole year, you will have to pay interest, which is compounded daily. If you make your instalment payments in the exact amount requested by Revenue Canada, you will not have to pay interest or penalties if it turns out that you owe more tax for the whole year than you have pre-paid quarterly.

Corporations

A corporation's income tax return must be filed within six months after the end of the corporation's fiscal period or taxation year. Unlike a sole proprietorship or partnership, a corporation can choose any date for its year end.

Except during its first taxation year, when no instalment payments have to be made, a corporation must pay income tax in monthly instalments unless the tax payable for the year or the preceding taxation year is $1000 or less. The corporation is responsible for calculating the amount of the instalments, which may be calculated in one of three ways: based on an estimate of tax payable in the current year, based on the tax paid in the preceding year, or based on a combination of the tax paid in the preceding year and the year before that. If the corporation owes more income tax than it paid in monthly instalments, the balance must be paid within two months after the end of the corporation's fiscal year. If the corporation is a Canadian Controlled Private Corporation eligible for the Small Business Deduction and with income of less than $200,000, the balance must be paid within three months after the end of the corporation's fiscal year. Notice that the due date to pay the balance of tax is earlier than the due date to file the income tax return.

If your corporation employs you and pays you a regular salary, it has to deduct income tax from each of your pay cheques and remit it to the government. (If you owe more than your corporation has remitted during the year, you'll have to pay the extra when you file your personal income tax return by April 30th of the following year.)

When Do You Have to Pay Interest or Penalties?

Whether your business is a sole proprietorship, partnership, or corporation, you will have to pay interest if your instalment payments are late or insufficient. You also have to pay interest if you do not pay any balance of tax owing by the due date—which is April 30th for individuals and two or three months after the fiscal year end for a corporation. The interest charged is compounded daily.

You will have to pay a penalty if your instalment interest charges for any year are more than $1000. You may also have to pay a penalty if you file any income tax return late, fail to report income, or knowingly or negligently make false statements or omissions. Penalties start at 5 per cent of unpaid taxes, and rise rapidly.

What Records Must You Keep?

Any person who carries on a business, or is required to pay or collect taxes, must keep books and records that allow the amount of taxes payable by that person to be calculated and verified. These books and records must be kept for at least six years after the taxation year they relate to. Corporations also have to keep all information used to calculate their taxes, and all books and records (including any related accounts and vouchers) must be kept for at least six years from the end of the fiscal year they relate to. Permanent records of the corporation such as general ledgers, minutes of directors' and shareholders' meetings, share registers, and special contracts must be kept until two years after the corporation is dissolved.

If a taxpayer is involved in an objection or an appeal, all records relating to the appeal should be kept until the process is finished.

WHAT IF YOU'RE AUDITED?

Nobody is really keen to pay taxes, and people in business for themselves have opportunities for tax evasion that employees don't. The federal government likes to keep an eye on entrepreneurs for that reason, and has hundreds of auditors to help it. So you may be unlucky enough to get audited at some point.

When an income tax return is filed, it is reviewed by Revenue Canada. When the review is completed a notice of assessment is issued, setting out the amount of tax payable for the year. Even if the return is initially accepted as filed, Revenue Canada has the right to reassess it later, and can also reassess your current return and your returns for the last three years (longer if they suspect fraud) and ask you for more money.

A tax audit is different from an assessment or reassessment. It involves going over all your records, including the ones you weren't required to send in with your tax return, to see whether you've declared all your income and deducted only your legitimate and provable expenses. Just in case you're ever audited, you should carefully keep receipts for all your income and expenses. Make sure expense receipts are dated and show what business activity they related to.

If Revenue Canada decides to audit any of your returns, you will be notified by letter that your tax return for a stated year (or years) has been selected for review, and you will be asked to provide specified information within 30 days. You can respond to the request for information on your own, hire an accountant or tax lawyer, and you can ask for an extension if you need more time. The auditor may ask you to justify some of your claims. When you meet the auditor, be cooperative and polite. Have your records organized—don't just fling a shoebox of unsorted bills and receipts at him. When the auditor is finished, he will send you a letter setting out proposals for changes to your income tax return, and will give you time either to accept the changes or dispute them by providing additional information. Then Revenue Canada will send you a notice of reassessment setting out any balance you owe and the date by which it's due.

If you accept the auditor's conclusion, you will have to pay the balance due. If you can't pay by the due date, you should contact the Collections Department at Revenue Canada to make other arrangements. If you have been charged penalties and/or interest, under certain circumstances you may be able to have them set aside by the Fairness Committee at Revenue Canada.

If you disagree with the reassessment, you may file a Notice of Objection at your local tax office within 90 days from the date of the reassessment. If you disagree with the outcome, you may appeal the decision to the Tax Court of Canada. If you are still unhappy, you can appeal to the Federal Court of Appeal, and again to the Supreme Court of Canada. You may be able to represent yourself at the local level and even at the Tax Court of Canada, but you should have a lawyer to represent you if you take your appeal to the Federal Court of Appeal or the Supreme Court of Canada.

SALES TAXES

Sales taxes are charged when goods are sold and/or services are provided. Every province except Alberta has a sales tax, and the federal government has the Goods and Services Tax (GST). In Nova Scotia, New Brunswick, and Newfoundland, the provincial sales tax and federal GST are combined into a Harmonized Sales Tax (HST). Provincial sales taxes range from 7 to 10 per cent, depending on the province; the GST is 7 per cent and the HST is 15 per cent.

Provincial Sales Taxes

Provincial sales taxes are charged on the sale of most goods and on some services. Businesses that sell taxable goods or provide taxable services are responsible for collecting the tax from the buyer and remitting it to the provincial government on a regular basis. The tax is collectible from the final consumer only. Businesses do not have to pay sales tax on goods that will be resold. They must, however, pay tax on goods bought for their own use. The sales tax in Quebec (QST) works differently—it's more like the GST (see below).

Businesses that will be selling taxable goods or providing taxable services must register with the provincial government's ministry of finance and get a registration certificate with a provincial tax number. The certificate must be shown in order to buy goods for resale without having to pay sales tax. All registered businesses must file periodic (usually monthly) returns with the ministry of finance and remit the tax collected (some provinces pay businesses a small commission on the tax collected). Businesses must keep proper books and records to document the amount of tax collected and may be audited by the provincial government. If a business fails to file returns, collect taxes when required, or remit the taxes collected, the government may charge an interest penalty or may even prosecute.

Goods and Services Tax

The federal Goods and Services Tax applies to almost all goods sold and services supplied. Unlike retail sales tax, GST is charged to everyone along the production and sale chain from the supplier of materials, through the manufacturer, wholesaler, and retailer to the consumer. But the government only keeps the tax paid by the ultimate consumer. Everyone else in the chain is allowed to claim a refund on the GST they paid (called an **input tax credit**). (The HST and QST work in the same way.)

GST Is Charged on "Supplies"

The GST legislation refers to goods and services as "supplies," and the GST is imposed when goods or services are "supplied." A good or service can be supplied in many ways, including by sale, rental, barter, or gift. There are three categories of supplies. The first category of supplies are taxable at 7 per cent and includes:

- real property—land, buildings, fixtures, options to purchase land, leases of real property
- personal property that has a physical existence, such as equipment and supplies
- personal property that has no physical existence such as a patent, trade secret, trademark, right, option, or share

The second category are taxable at 0 per cent (yes, that's zero) and includes:

- prescription drugs and medical devices
- basic groceries
- travel services to places outside of Canada
- international transportation services
- services and property that are exported
- sales of precious metals
- farm and fishing products and equipment designed for use by farmers and fishers

The third category includes:

- residential housing resales or rentals
- health care, personal care, child care, or educational services
- legal aid services

These supplies are tax-exempt.

We're sure that you're wondering what the difference is between supplies that are taxed at 0 per cent and supplies that are tax-exempt. No GST is payable on either, and to the ultimate consumer there is no difference at all. There is a big difference, however, to the business that is doing the supplying. If your business supplies zero-rated supplies, you don't have to charge GST to your customers, but you can still claim input tax credits on the GST you pay to get goods and services. However, if your business supplies tax-exempt supplies, you cannot claim input tax credits for any of the GST you pay to get goods and services.

Who Has to Register and Collect GST?

Many, but not all, businesses are required to register with Revenue Canada for a **business number** and to collect and remit the GST. Any person, partnership, corporation, trust, association, business, or organization engaged in commercial activities with annual sales and revenues of GST-taxable goods or services of more than $30,000 must register and charge the GST. If your business's annual sales and revenues are less than $30,000, you do not have to register, but you may still do so voluntarily. If you do not register, you do not charge GST, but you cannot claim input tax credits. Many businesses with sales of under $30,000 register not only for the input tax credits, but also because they don't want their customers to know that their business income is so low.

GST is usually calculated on the price paid by the consumer, including any customs or excise duties and transportation taxes, but excluding provincial sales taxes. GST is calculated on the price charged before any discounts for early payment or penalties for late payment are taken into consideration.

A business must report the amount of tax collected and remit it to the government on a regular basis. A business with annual sales of more than $6,000,000 must report and remit GST every month. A business with sales of less than $6,000,000 but more than $500,000 must report and remit GST quarterly, but may choose to report and remit monthly. A business with sales of less than $500,000 must file a GST form annually, and remit GST quarterly but may choose to report and remit monthly. In any filing period, you must account for the GST your business charged and paid. The difference between what you charged and what you paid is the amount you must remit to the government. If you paid more than you were charged, you are entitled to a GST refund. Most businesses with annual sales of under $200,000 may use a "quick method" of accounting for GST that calculates the amount of GST to be remitted at a predetermined percentage of the business's total sales. The percentage is different for different types of businesses.

If your business does not report or pay GST as required, you will be charged interest and penalties. Anyone who wilfully fails to pay, collect, or remit the GST can also be convicted of an offence and be fined or imprisoned. GST registrants are required to keep books and records, including invoices to support all input tax credits claimed and GST collected, for six years.

Harmonized Sales Tax

In Nova Scotia, New Brunswick, and Newfoundland, the Harmonized Sales Tax combines the GST and provincial sales tax at a rate of 15 per cent. Businesses anywhere in Canada that supply goods or services in these provinces are required to collect and remit the HST to Revenue Canada. Any business that is registered for the GST is also registered for the HST, which has the same basic operating rules as the GST. Vendors who provide goods or services in the HST provinces have to include HST in the retail price of goods and services, and clearly identify that the price includes HST, but businesses that provide 100 per cent of their services to other businesses do not have to use HST-inclusive pricing.

The federal government is trying to persuade the remaining provincial governments to harmonize their provincial sales taxes with the GST.

PAYROLL TAXES

Payroll taxes are levied by the federal government and some provincial governments on businesses that have employees. The federal government collects payroll taxes for Employment Insurance and the Canada Pension Plan. Employers must make contributions to EI and CPP on behalf of their employees, and must also withhold and remit contributions made by their employees. (If the employer is a corporation and the employee a majority shareholder in it, the employer does not have to contribute.) The employer's contribution for each program is a percentage of the employee's gross wages up to a maximum annual wage. Remittances must generally be made to the government, generally on a monthly basis.

Some provincial governments collect payroll taxes to fund their provincial health insurance programs. The contribution of the employer is calculated as a percentage of the business's payroll, and the employer must file returns and make remittances on a regular basis. Most provinces require employers in insured industries to pay workers' compensation premiums; these are also calculated as a percentage of the business's payroll.

BUSINESS TAXES

In addition to income taxes, sales taxes, and payroll taxes, federal, provincial, and municipal governments levy certain other taxes on businesses:

- the federal government levies a Large Corporations Tax on corporations with taxable capital in Canada of over $10 million.

- some provinces levy a tax on the paid-up capital of corporations. Paid-up capital may include not only the amount the corporation has received for the stock it issued, but also debt incurred to buy capital property, bank loans, and reserve funds. In most provinces, businesses with paid-up capital of under $1 million (under $10 million in some provinces) are exempt from this tax.

- many municipalities levy business taxes, usually based on real property assessment, annual rental value of property, stock-in-trade, square footage, or storage capacity. In some municipalities (notably in the Toronto area) there is a commercial concentration tax levied on large commercial structures such as shopping centres and office buildings.

T
I
P

You can't run away from most taxes. You'll have to pay them wherever you go. But you may be able to run away from municipal taxes because each municipality sets its own. If you have flexibility in locating your business, check for the lowest municipal taxes.

T I P

DEATH AND TAXES

So now you know exactly what we meant when we said that Revenue Canada has a stake in your heart. You've heard of the underground economy? It means that taxes have driven some businesses to hide their activities from the various taxing authorities. But after reading this chapter you may think it means that taxes have driven businesses six feet under.

CHAPTER EIGHTEEN

IMPORTING AND EXPORTING

In Chapter 13 we talked about buying and selling goods. We assumed in that chapter that you, the businesses you are buying from, and the customers you are selling to are all located in Canada. Now we're going to look at what happens if you're buying or selling outside Canada. There are special considerations if your business is importing or exporting products.

IMPORTING

The goods you need for resale or for manufacturing may not be available in Canada, or may not be available cheaply enough. That means you'll have to import them. Be prepared: commercial importing is nothing like bringing home souvenirs from a vacation abroad.

Preliminary Steps

As a commercial importer your business has to have a Revenue Canada Business Number to show on customs documents, or the goods will not be released to you when they arrive. Contact Revenue Canada to register for a business number if you don't already have one as a GST registrant.

Some goods cannot be imported without a permit (for example, restricted or controlled drugs, textiles and clothing, footwear, steel, beef, poultry, eggs, dairy products, wheat, and wheat products). Contact the Export and Import Controls Bureau of the federal Department of Foreign Affairs to find out if you need a permit. A permit costs a small fee.

You may want to use a **customs broker** to help you get your goods through customs. These brokers are federally licenced to deal with customs matters on behalf of importers, and can prepare and present the required documents and information to Canada Customs, pay the applicable duties, and get the imported goods released. However, the importer remains legally liable to pay any duties owing, even after giving the money owing for duties to a customs broker.

The Contract to Buy the Goods

Before entering into a contract to buy goods from a supplier outside Canada, do some investigating. Make sure that the product is a good one, that the seller can produce it and ship it to you in the required quality and quantities and within the required time, and that the seller will stand behind the product if you have problems with it.

The contract with the seller should cover the following:

- the full names and business addresses of the parties
- a detailed description of the goods—you may also want to include the tariff classification of the goods (see below on p. 259)—and quantity of the goods, quality of the goods, and warranties offered by the seller
- the price and the currency of payment
- the terms of shipment (see below on p. 266)
- how payment is to be made, including the terms and conditions of any letter of credit (see below on p. 256)

- inspection of the goods by an independent third party before shipping

- how the goods are to be packed for shipping

- when and from where the goods are to be shipped and by what carrier(s)

- when and where the goods are to be delivered

- what insurance will cover the goods

- the procedure for making a claim against the seller—what country's law will apply if there is a dispute about the goods, whether the parties should have the dispute arbitrated instead of (or before) starting a lawsuit, and in what country a lawsuit may be started

You may want to have the contract reviewed by a lawyer familiar with private international law before you sign it. If you are paying by a letter of credit, you may want to have that reviewed by your lawyer too (as well as by your freight forwarder and bank manager) to make sure that it is consistent with the sales contract and that you can comply with all of its terms.

Paying for the Goods

There are several methods of paying for goods you are importing, and you and the seller will have to agree on one. Starting with the method that is safest for you as importer, they are:

- **open account**—the importer pays after receiving and inspecting the goods. The importer can refuse to pay if the goods are not satisfactory (the seller may sue, of course).

- **documentary collections (documents on payment** and **documents on acceptance)**—the importer makes payment to a bank in her country that is acting as the seller's agent (the "collecting/presenting bank"), after the seller has shipped the goods and sent the bank the shipping documents and a demand for payment (a **draft**). The importer won't be able to get the documents that will allow possession of the goods, and won't be able to inspect them, until they have been paid for (documents on payment) or the demand for payment has been accepted (documents on acceptance).

- **letter of credit** (also known as a **documentary letter of credit** or a **documentary credit**)—the importer's bank (the "issuing bank") pays the seller on the importer's behalf (through an "advising bank" in the seller's country) after the terms and conditions of the letter of credit are met. You must have a line of credit with your bank before it will issue a letter of credit. The terms and conditions contained in the letter of credit may include:

  - the amount to be paid and the currency it is to be paid in
  - whether payment is to be immediate (sight payment) or is put off to a specified date or dates (term payment)
  - the names of the banks used by each party
  - the documents required to be presented by the seller before payment will be made (for example, proof of shipping, certificates of inspection, commercial invoices, insurance certificates)
  - whether the letter of credit is revocable (meaning that the issuing bank can make changes to, or withdraw, the letter before the seller presents it for payment). Letters of credit are irrevocable (meaning that the bank can't change or withdraw them) unless they are stated to be revocable
  - the shipping date, method of shipment, and carrier or forwarder
  - the terms of shipment (see below on p. 266)
  - the seller's promise that the goods meet the specifications set out in the contract for the sale of the goods
  - payment in advance—the importer pays in full partially or before the seller ships the goods

Documents You Need from the Seller

You will need an invoice from the seller that describes the goods in detail. If you are importing from a country that has a **free trade agreement** with Canada you will need a free trade **certificate of origin** of the goods from the seller so that you can claim the lower customs duty rates. If you are importing goods that are covered by a **preferential tariff**, you will again need a certificate of origin, issued by an authorized agency in the country where the goods originated, in order to claim the lower customs duty rate.

Wresting Your Goods Out of the Hands of Canada Customs

As we said, commercial importing isn't like coming home from a vacation in Florida and filling out the customs declaration as your plane lands.

Presenting Your Documents

In order to get your goods released when they arrive in Canada, you or your customs broker will have to **report** them and **account** for them by presenting (in paper form or electronically) at the customs office where the goods have arrived the following:

- the cargo control document—if you are using a carrier, the cargo control document must be in a standard approved form. If you are transporting the goods personally, you do not need to use an approved cargo control document if you account for the goods and pay duties at the customs office where the goods are

- the invoice—which must contain your business name and business number, the exporter's name, the country of origin, the price, quantity, and a detailed description of the goods

- a Canada Customs Coding Form—which contains a description of the goods, the country of origin, the goods' value for duty, the tariff classification, the tariff treatment, the applicable duty rate, and a calculation of the duties owing

- any required import permit or other federal government form

- a certificate of origin, if applicable

Customs has the right to verify your documents, or to ask you to provide proof of their accuracy, before releasing the goods to you.

**T
I
P**

If you are importing goods valued at under $1600, you can easily import them by mail. Canada Post will report them and offer them for inspection to Revenue Canada, and will also collect from you the duties owing and remit them to Revenue Canada. You can also import goods with a value under $1600 fairly easily by courier as long as you're not importing anything that is prohibited, controlled, or regulated, and you have posted security with Revenue Canada. You can import goods valued over $1600 by mail or courier, too, but you have to go through the normal rigmarole of accounting and payment at the customs office.   T I P

Inspection of Your Goods

Your goods may or may not be examined by customs officers before they are released. If you are importing goods that by law have to be inspected (for example, some food products) they will be, otherwise inspections are only carried out randomly—to see whether you are importing prohibited or restricted goods (like firearms, drugs, or pornography), whether the goods match the description, value, and quantity on the invoice, whether the goods are properly marked with their country of origin, and whether you are engaging in the traditional Canadian pastime of smuggling. How often your goods are "randomly" inspected will depend on your good behaviour (**compliance**) record with Revenue Canada and the kind of goods you are importing. If your merchandise is inspected, you may have to pay your carrier extra for unloading and re-loading the goods.

Some imported goods have to be marked with their country of origin. These include household goods, clothing, footwear, certain personal goods, hardware, toys, sporting goods, and paper products, among other things. The importer is responsible for making sure that such goods are marked. If they aren't, they may not be released to you by customs, and you may be fined. Contact Canada Customs for more information.

Paying Duties

You must pay duties to Revenue Canada on any goods imported

into Canada, even if they were only imported temporarily and are going to be exported right away, or if they were only out of Canada temporarily for work or repair. The amount you pay in duties is based on:

• the value of the goods—the price of the goods converted into Canadian funds, with possible additions (such as royalty payments, licence fees, and sales commissions) and possible deductions (such as the seller's brokerage fees, freight costs, and any volume discount you received)

• the **tariff classification**—which you find out by comparing a detailed description of the goods with the goods listed in the 99-chapter *Customs Tariff* (used by countries around the world and known commonly as the Harmonized System of Tariffs or HS Tariff), available at any customs office

• the **tariff treatment**—there are a number of separate tariff treatments, and which one applies to your goods depends on their country of origin. Goods that originate in countries that have a trade or free trade agreement with Canada, or that are covered by a preferential tariff agreement, receive a lower customs duty rate. Tariff treatment information is also available at any customs office.

From the value, tariff classification, and tariff treatment, the applicable customs duty rate can be determined. You have the right to appeal a customs decision about the value for duty of the goods, the tariff classification, or the origin of the goods. Besides customs duties, you will be required to pay GST on all imported goods. You may also be required to pay additional duty and tax (called **excise duty** and **excise tax**) on things like alcohol, tobacco, and jewellery.

You must pay the duties owing by cash or certified cheque (uncertified cheque may be acceptable for amounts up to $2500). Your customs broker can pay on your behalf. If you import goods frequently, you can post security with Revenue Canada, and account fully and pay for each shipment after it is released rather than before.

You May Not Have to Pay Duties

You may be able to get **duties relief** that will reduce or eliminate customs duties. For example, there are duties relief programs that apply to:

- goods imported and later exported in the same condition

- materials imported to manufacture goods that are later exported

- goods that are unused and undamaged but are obsolete or surplus, and have been destroyed under a customs officer's direction

- goods that were defective or were returned to the manufacturer for credit

- goods temporarily imported for a trade show

- goods temporarily exported to the United States for repairs under a warranty and then imported back to Canada

---

T
I
P
You can **defer** (put off) paying duties owed by placing imported goods in a bonded warehouse. They can usually be left there for up to four years and as long as they are in the warehouse you don't have to pay customs duties, excise duties, or GST. If the goods are removed from the warehouse for use or sale in Canada, then you have to pay the duties and GST. But if the goods are exported directly from the bonded warehouse, you never have to pay. While the goods are in a bonded warehouse, you can do various things to them such as mark, label, display, assemble, ticket, package, repackage, test, dilute, or cut them.

Record Keeping

You are required to keep records that show:

- what goods you imported and in what quantities

- the price paid

- the country where the goods originated

You have to keep these records for six years after the end of the calendar year in which the goods were imported. You are responsible for keeping your own records, so even if you use a customs broker, make sure you keep copies of all documents.

Penalties

If you smuggle, or falsify accounting documents, or misdescribe, or undervalue the goods you are importing, moderately bad things will happen to you. Revenue Canada can seize the goods (and the vehicle they're being transported in) and can charge you a penalty of up to twice the amount of duties owing (three times the amount if you're a repeat smuggler). Revenue Canada may even prosecute you criminally.

EXPORTING GOODS

If your business grows so much that the Canadian market isn't big enough for you, or if you're manufacturing or selling a product that isn't intended for the Canadian domestic market, or if you just think that you can make big bucks by selling your goods in some other country, you'll become an exporter.

Before you enter into a contract to export goods, think about the following matters:

• what laws of the target foreign country apply to you? what requirements (for example, labelling) do you have to comply with?

• what will your export price include?—marking or labelling if required, freight forwarder's fees, transportation, insurance, necessary documentation, inspection and certification, duties, taxes, warehousing and storage, customs brokerage fees, fluctuations in the exchange rate? You don't have to charge GST on exported goods.

• is the buyer a good credit risk?—check the buyer's credit rating, inquire about the buyer from other exporters who have dealt with him or with other people in your industry, and contact your trade commissioner.

Preliminary Steps

Your business is a commercial exporter and therefore must have a Revenue Canada Business Number. Contact Revenue Canada to register for a business number if you aren't already registered for the GST.

You may require an export permit if you are exporting to a country that is on the Area Control List (such as Libya) or if you are exporting goods that are on the Export Control List (such as forest, agricultural, and medical products, endangered species, nuclear materials, and certain industrial chemicals). You can get information about the relevant countries and goods, and apply for the export permit, by contacting the Export and Import Controls Bureau of the federal Department of Foreign Affairs. You can also get a permit through any federal International Trade Centre and some customs brokers.

You should make inquiries about labelling your goods to comply with the law of the target country. For example, your goods may have to be labelled:

- in the local language

- with the name of the country where the product originated, and/or with the name of the producer or shipper

- with details about the product such as ingredients or weight (food), fibre content (clothing), technical specifications (machinery), or standards certification (appliances)

You may want to use a **freight forwarder** to look after the shipment of your goods. A freight forwarder will make all your shipping arrangements, including choosing the carrier(s) and negotiating the shipping contract, getting cargo insurance, preparing documents (such as customs invoices, packing list, certificate of insurance, and bill of lading), packing or giving advice on it, giving advice on labelling requirements in the foreign country, organizing transportation of the cargo to the port of embarkation (the place from which the cargo leaves Canada), and lining up warehouse storage. Freight forwarders may specialize in air or ocean freight, in shipping to certain countries, or in shipping certain kinds of products. You may want to get recommendations from a trade or business association before you choose a freight forwarder.

The Contract to Sell Your Goods

Your contract should cover the following:

- the full names and business addresses of the parties
- a detailed description of the goods, including quantity of the goods, quality of the goods, and warranties offered on the goods
- the price of the goods (remember that you don't have to charge GST on exported products) and the currency in which payment is to be made
- how payment is to be made, including the terms and conditions of any letter of credit (see above on p. 256). As an exporter, you prefer to have a confirmed irrevocable letter of credit.
- the terms of shipment (see below on p. 266)
- whether you are required to get a **consular invoice** (a document describing the goods) from the target country's consulate in Canada—some foreign governments require Canadian exporters to have a consular invoice (and to pay a fee for it)
- how the goods are to be packed for shipping
- when and from where the goods are to be shipped, and by what carrier(s)
- when and where the goods are to be delivered
- what insurance will cover the goods
- whether you have to provide the buyer with a certificate of origin (so the buyer can pay reduced customs duties on the goods)
- limitations on (or exclusion of) your liability if you are unable to produce or deliver the goods, or if the goods are defective, lost, or damaged
- which country's law will apply if there is a dispute between the parties, whether the dispute should be arbitrated instead of (or before) legal proceedings are started, and in which country a lawsuit may be started

You should have the contract reviewed by a lawyer familiar with private international law before you sign it, and you may want to have the letter of credit reviewed too.

Insuring Your Financial Risk

The Export Development Corporation, and some private commercial insurance companies, can provide **export credit insurance**, which covers losses suffered because the buyer can't or doesn't pay or cancels the contract, or because export permits are cancelled in Canada, or because war breaks out in the foreign country.

Getting Paid

The same four methods of payment that we discussed under "Importing" are available, except that as an exporter you have a slightly different attitude towards them. (Refer back to p. 255 for more detail.) Starting with the method that is safest for you as exporter, you can negotiate payment as follows:

- **payment in advance**
- **letter of credit**—note that if you have a **confirmed letter of credit**, your bank guarantees to pay you even if the issuing bank does not send the funds, as long as all the terms and conditions in the letter of credit have been met
- **documentary collections**
- **open account**

What Is Required of the Exporter

When you export goods from Canada, you may have to make a written export declaration to Revenue Canada before or at the time of export. In case you're wondering why, it's so the federal government can keep export trade statistics and control the export of dangerous or embargoed goods. You do *not* have to report:

- goods valued at less than $2000 Canadian (unless they include goods of U.S. origin)
- goods you export to the United States for domestic consumption
- goods you export from a bonded warehouse after importing them strictly for export

You can report each individual shipment of goods by filling out an export declaration, or (if you do a lot of exporting) you can provide Revenue Canada with a monthly summary of exports, but to use the summary reporting method you have to have Revenue Canada's approval. Exporters must keep records of their exports for six years after the end of the calendar year in which the goods were exported.

EXPORTING SERVICES

If you are exporting your services instead of goods, find out whether you need a visa to work in the foreign country. It may be very difficult to get one. The contract for your services should include all of the matters discussed in Chapter 13 on pp. 167-172, plus provisions about

- the currency of payment
- who pays for your transportation to and from the foreign country and your living expenses while you are there
- the law that will apply in the event of a dispute, and what country a lawsuit may be brought in

You may be required to file income tax returns and pay taxes in the foreign country as well as in Canada.

Insuring Your Financial Risk

The Export Development Corporation, and some private commercial insurance companies, can provide insurance for the exporter of services, and guarantees to your client that you will perform the services.

TRANSPORTATION OF GOODS

You may be shipping goods by truck, rail, air, or ocean. However you do it, and whether you are importing or exporting, choose a carrier that is knowledgeable about and experienced with customs procedures in the destination country, and that has a reputation for not losing or damaging goods. Unfortunately, even if your carrier has a great reputation, goods do get lost, stolen, or damaged in transit. If they do, someone has to pay. It will usually be the seller, the buyer, or an insurance company (it won't usually be the carrier, because they make a point of limiting their liability), but which one of the three? How do you know, as a buyer or seller, whether you'll be the one who has to pay if something happens to the goods, and therefore whether you're the one that should arrange for insurance? Well, it's all in the shipping terms.

Shipping Terms

The shipping terms specify what is included in the seller's quoted price besides the cost of the goods (such as shipping, insurance, and payment of customs duties), state where the goods are shipped from or to, or both, and indicate when risk of loss or damage is transferred from seller to buyer. That means it's important to understand shipping terms. The International Chamber of Commerce has developed the following standard terms and definitions (called **Incoterms**) that are used around the world.

- **Carriage and Insurance Paid To (CIP)**—the price includes the cost of the goods plus all transportation charges plus *minimum* insurance to the destination agreed between the parties. The seller makes the arrangements for transportation and insurance, and bears the risk of loss until the goods are handed over for transport (from then on the buyer bears the risk of loss).

- **Carriage Paid To (CPT)**—the price includes the cost of the goods plus transportation to the destination agreed between the parties. The seller makes the arrangements for transportation and bears the risk of loss until the goods are handed over for transport.

- **Cost and Freight (C&F or CFR)**—(sea transport only) the price includes the cost of the goods plus shipping to an agreed destination. The seller bears the risk of loss until the goods are handed over for shipping.

- **Cost, Insurance, and Freight (CIF)**—(sea transport only) the price includes the cost of the goods plus all transportation charges plus *minimum* insurance to the destination agreed between the parties. The seller makes the arrangements for shipping and insurance. The seller bears the risk of loss until the goods are handed over for shipping.

- **Delivered at Frontier (DAF)**—usually used for shipments by rail, the price includes cost of the goods plus transportation to a named frontier. The risk of loss is the seller's until the goods arrive at the frontier. The frontier and the "customs border" (wherever the customs office is) of the buyer's country may be some distance apart, but the seller's obligations and risk of loss end at the frontier.

- **Delivered Duty Paid (DDP)**—the price includes cost of the goods plus transportation to the buyer's place of business. The seller must arrange import clearance and pay import duties. The risk of loss is the seller's until the goods are delivered to the buyer.

- **Delivered Duty Unpaid (DDU)**—the price includes the cost of the goods plus transportation to the buyer's place of business. The risk of loss is the seller's until the goods are delivered to the buyer. The buyer must arrange import clearance and pay import duties.

- **Delivered Ex Quay (DEQ)**—(sea transport only) the price includes the cost of the goods plus transportation to a named destination. The risk of loss is the seller's until the goods are made available to the buyer on the quay or wharf at the destination. The seller has to clear the goods for import.

- **Delivered Ex Ship (DES)**—(sea transport only) the price includes the cost of goods plus transportation to an agreed location (the seller charters the ship). The risk of loss is the seller's until the goods are made available to the buyer on board the ship at the agreed location. The buyer has to clear the goods for import.

- **Delivered Ex Works (EXW)**—the price only includes the cost of the goods, made available at the seller's factory or warehouse. The risk of loss is the buyer's once the goods leave the warehouse. The buyer is responsible for loading and transporting the the goods, clearing the goods for import, and paying duties.

- **Free Alongside Ship (FAS)**—(sea transport only) the price includes the cost of the goods plus transportation to the main carrier. The buyer has the obligation to arrange and pay for the main carriage (in practice the seller often makes the arrangements). The buyer is also responsible for clearing the goods for export. The risk of loss is the buyer's from the time the goods reach the main carrier.

- **Free Carrier (FCA)**—the price includes the cost of the goods plus delivery of the goods into the custody of the carrier at an agreed place. The buyer has the obligation to arrange and pay for the main carriage (as in FAS, in practice the seller often makes the arrangements). The risk of loss is the buyer's once the goods are delivered to the carrier.

- **Free on Board (FOB)**—(sea transport only) the price includes the cost of the goods plus the cost of loading them onto the agreed carrier. The seller is responsible for clearing the goods for export. The risk of loss is transferred to the buyer when the goods "pass the ship's rail" at the beginning of the voyage.

Insurance

Carriers limit their liability for damage to goods, usually to an amount based on the weight of the goods shipped. Depending on the form of transportation, this amount may vary from US$5 to US$20 per kilo. For ocean transport, liability may be limited to US$500 per container. Carriers also refuse to accept liability for damage caused in many different ways. Therefore it's essential for you to have adequate insurance whenever you bear the risk of loss of or damage to the goods being shipped, even if the other party is supposed to insure. To be safe, you may want to insure the goods *even when you're not the party with the risk of loss*, because the party with the obligation to insure may only have to provide minimum insurance. You can arrange for insurance coverage through the carrier, your freight forwarder, or an insurance broker.

<table>
<tr>
<td>

T

I

P
</td>
<td>

Don't be alarmed to discover that you have **marine cargo insurance** even though the goods are not travelling by boat or even over water. Marine insurance covers shipment of goods by any means.

</td>
</tr>
</table>

CHAPTER NINETEEN

UNLAWFUL BUSINESS PRACTICES

You're probably already aware that the law will frown on you if you strangle your partner (no matter how much she annoys you), blow up a competitor's store, or put rat poison in a difficult customer's coffee. There are many other things that you can't do without getting into serious trouble, and some of them aren't as obvious as these.

Every law that requires you to do something also has a means of punishing you if you don't do it. Although we've drawn your attention to a lot of federal and provincial laws and municipal by-laws that require you to do things, we're not going to discuss all of them because those that apply to one business may have nothing to do with another. In this chapter we'll be looking at the laws that apply to activities that any business might carry on, and telling you what those laws say you can't do in the course of business.

CRIME AND PUNISHMENT

Some unlawful business activities are crimes under the federal *Criminal Code* or criminal offences under the federal *Competition Act*, some are offences under federal or provincial statutes, and some are **reviewable practices** under the federal *Competition Act*. Crimes are punishable by a fine and/or imprisonment, and the maximum amount of the fine and length of imprisonment vary according to the crime. When a judge sentences someone who has been convicted of a crime, the sentence could be anything from an absolute discharge (no punishment at all) to the maximum fine or term of imprisonment. Offences are often punishable by fine and/or imprisonment just like crimes, but there may be other options too, such as an order that your business stop doing something, or that it be shut down. Reviewable practices can be investigated by the Competition Tribunal, which can order a business to do something or stop doing something.

If your business is a sole proprietorship or partnership, you personally can be fined, imprisoned, ordered (or forbidden) to do something, or your business can be closed down. If your business is a corporation, it can be fined, ordered or forbidden to do something, or closed down, but it can't be imprisoned. The directors and officers of the corporation may be liable to fines or imprisonment if they were the "directing minds" of an offence (if they ordered the action to be taken), or if the corporation breached a statute whose purpose was public protection (such as an environmental protection statute) and the directors cannot prove that they took reasonable care (exercised **due diligence**) to be aware of problems and to correct them. If you are charged with an offence of any kind, consult a lawyer with experience in criminal law.

In this chapter we do not set out the specific range of penalties for each crime or offence. For more tailored information about what can happen to you as you run your particular business and don't obey every requirement of law, contact the usual suspects—specific government departments, trade and professional associations, or a lawyer.

BUSINESS ACTIVITIES THAT MAY TURN OUT TO BE UNLAWFUL

In the ordinary course of business you may carry on an activity that will put you at risk of prosecution for a crime or offence, or that is liable to be reviewed by the federal Competition Tribunal. Below is a list of business activities with suggestions about how *not* to carry out each activity.

Manufacturing and Storage

If your business involves the manufacture of goods, or the storage of any substance that might contaminate the environment, you must not release any harmful substances into the environment, and you must not conceal spills of harmful substances. To do so is an offence under both federal and provincial environmental protection acts.

Getting Goods and Services

When you're getting goods or services:

- you must not get them by false pretences, fraud, deceit, or false-hood—for example, by paying with a cheque that you *know* is going to bounce. If you do, you are committing the crime of **false pretences** or of **fraud** under the *Criminal Code*.

- you must not get the goods or services by means of threats or violence against the seller or owner. This is the crime of **extortion** under the *Criminal Code*.

- you must not hide your property or transfer ownership of it to someone else in order to keep your creditors from getting their hands on it. This is the crime of **disposing of property to defraud creditors** under the *Criminal Code*.

Providing Goods and Services

When you are providing goods or services to others:

- you must not breach a contract, if you know that doing so may endanger human life, cause serious bodily harm, or damage valuable property. This is the crime of **criminal breach of contract** under the *Criminal Code*. (For example, if you've contracted to construct a building with reinforced concrete, it may be a criminal breach of contract to use ordinary concrete.)

- if you run a lawful **multi-level marketing** scheme—an arrangement in which people earn money by supplying products to other people in the scheme, who then earn money by supplying products to still other people in the scheme—don't recruit salespeople by telling them about one spectacularly successful person instead of telling them what the average salesperson makes and how much time and effort is needed to make that amount. And don't turn a multi-level marketing scheme into an illegal **pyramid selling** scheme (a criminal offence under the *Competition Act* unless it's permitted by provincial law) by:
  - forcing your salespeople to buy large amounts of products from you, that they may not be able to sell, before you allow them to join your business
  - refusing to allow your salespeople to return products on reasonable terms
  - asking salespeople to pay for the right to be paid for bringing in new recruits

- don't ask your customers to give you the names of other potential customers in exchange for a reduction of the purchase price of goods the original customers buy, or for a commission on sales to the people they name. This is the criminal offence of **referral selling** under the federal *Competition Act*, unless the practice is permitted under a provincial statute.

- you must not sell your goods or services at a price higher than the price you have advertised. To do so is a criminal offence under the *Competition Act*.

- you must not put two or more prices on a product and then charge the higher one. This is the criminal offence of **double-ticketing** under the *Competition Act*. You must, by law, charge the lower price.

- do not try by means of agreements, threats, promises, or refusals to deal with certain customers, to control the price others charge for a product. This is the criminal offence of **price maintenance** under the *Competition Act*. If you have a "suggested retail price" for a product you supply, you must make it clear that the buyer can resell at a lower price.

- do not discriminate among business customers who compete with each other: when you are selling them similar goods in similar quantities, you must not give just some of your customers lower prices, discounts, rebates, grants, or allowances for promotion or advertising. Doing so constitutes the criminal offence of **price discrimination** under the *Competition Act*.

When you are supplying goods to business customers, there are certain practices that are reviewable by the federal Competition Tribunal, usually on a complaint. You may be engaging in a reviewable practice and you may be ordered to stop if what you're doing substantially lessens competition. Keep this in mind if you:

- require anyone to whom you sell products for resale to sell only within a certain geographical area (or only to certain people). This is the reviewable practice of **market restriction**.

- require anyone to whom you sell products for resale to stock only (or mainly) your products. This is the reviewable practice of **exclusive dealing**. (It may be permissible for a short time to get a new product or supplier into the market.)

- require a customer to take (for example, to buy or lease) a second product from you in order to get one particular product that you supply, or not to distribute someone else's product together with the product you supply. This is the reviewable practice of **tied selling**.

- supply products to a dealer and allow the dealer not to pay for what is not sold and to return the unsold products to you without any penalty. This is the reviewable practice of **consignment selling** if you're doing this to control the price of the product or to favour certain dealers.

- sell your amply available product to certain customers and refuse to sell it to others, if a lack of competition in your market means that your refusal is affecting their ability to carry on business. This is the reviewable practice of **refusal to deal**.

- refuse to sell your product to one customer on the same terms that you offer to other customers. This is the reviewable practice of **delivered pricing**.

- use your position as holder of a large market share of any business to reduce competition (for example, by buying up products to keep prices high, selling products for less than the purchase price, hogging facilities or resources, or buying up rival businesses). This is the reviewable practice of **abuse of dominant market position**.

Advertising and Promotion

When you are advertising, promoting, or selling your goods or services, you must not mislead customers:

- you must not make any representation or statement that is false or misleading about your product or service (for example, about its price, durability, performance, or about its warranty). **Misleading advertising** is a criminal offence under the *Competition Act* and also under provincial consumer protection legislation.

T
I
P

You can be convicted of misleading advertising even if you never intended to mislead anyone. All that has to be proven against you is that the *effect* of the advertising was misleading.

T I P

A grocery store had an in-store advertising campaign about its prices for various goods. Signs said "why pay up to" a stated price and showed a saving that was the difference between the "why pay up to" price and the store's price. An investigation showed that other grocery stores did not charge the "why pay up to" price, although some convenience stores did. The store was convicted of the offence of misleading advertising because, the court said, a reasonable shopper would get the impression that other grocery stores (and not just convenience stores) were charging the "why pay up to" price.

- do not pass your goods or services off as someone else's in order to get people to deal with you. If you pretend they are someone else's, you are committing the crime of **passing off** under the *Criminal Code*. Get rid of the knock-off "Goochi" handbags and the "Roloid" wristwatches, and don't put up yellow arches in front of your hamburger joint.

- don't use a container that has anyone else's trademark on it; don't sell reconditioned goods that have someone else's trademark on them without telling the customer that the goods are reconditioned, and don't forge anyone else's trademark on your products. And on the other hand, don't remove anyone else's trademark from a product. These are **trademark offences** under the *Criminal Code*.

When it comes to persuading people to buy from you:

- you must not advertise a product (or service) at a special low price if it's not available in reasonable quantities. **Bait and switch selling** is a criminal offence under the *Competition Act*. If there is unexpected demand and you run out of whatever you advertised, you have to offer a "rain check" to anyone who asks and you have to provide the product (or service) to those people within a reasonable time.

- if you hold a contest to promote your goods or services, you must clearly state the chances of winning and the number and value of the prizes. You must choose the contestants or distribute the prizes either on the basis of skill (that's where the famous "skill-testing question" comes in) or on a random basis in the geographical area where the prizes are going to be awarded. You must not wait too long to distribute prizes that have been won. If you don't observe these rules you are committing a criminal offence under the *Competition Act*.

- if you're going to have someone who has used your product or service give a testimonial about it, that person has to approve the content and give permission for you to use it. If the testimonial is about how a product performs or how long it lasts, scientific performance testing must have been done. If you make performance claims that you cannot prove, you are committing a criminal offence under the *Competition Act*.

In addition, legislation in your province may govern specific forms of advertising, such as signs, or advertising of specific products or services, such as automobiles or credit.

Getting Paid

When you are arranging payment from customers or clients:

- do not charge an interest rate over 60 per cent. If you do, you are committing the crime of charging a **criminal rate of interest** under the *Criminal Code*.

- do not threaten criminal prosecution in order to get someone who owes you money to pay up. This is the crime of **extortion** under the *Criminal Code*.

- if you are holding money or property that belongs to a client or customer in trust for them, do not use it for your own benefit, even if you think you can replace it before anyone notices. This can be the crime of **theft by a person required to account, misappropriation of money held under direction**, or **criminal breach of trust** under the *Criminal Code*.

Dealing With Unionized Employees

When hiring employees, don't reject a job applicant solely because he is a member of a trade union, and don't dismiss an employee solely because of that. Similarly, don't intimidate or threaten employees to prevent them from belonging to a trade union. Any one of these actions is the crime of **intimidating trade unions** under the *Criminal Code*.

Competing With Other Businesses

The *Competition Act* makes criminal offences of activities that restrict competition. Therefore:

- do not sell your product or service at a loss or an unreasonably low price, or at a lower price in some particular area of Canada than you charge elsewhere, in order to drive out the competition. This is also the criminal offence of **predatory pricing**.

- do not get together with a group of bidders for a project or contract and agree among yourselves beforehand whose bid will be the lowest. This is the criminal offence of **bid-rigging**.

- do not make an agreement with your competitors to restrict the free operation of the market place, for example, by agreeing not to sell a particular product at all or not in a certain geographic area. This is the criminal offence of **conspiracy**.

Record Keeping

Take care of your records, even the ones you'd prefer to forget about:

- don't destroy or conceal any official document (including one showing ownership of land or goods) for a fraudulent purpose. This is the crime of **destroying documents of title** under the *Criminal Code*.

- do not falsify your books or other documents for the purpose of defrauding someone (especially the tax authorities). This is the crime of **falsifying books and documents** under the *Criminal Code*.

CHAPTER TWENTY

TORTS

In the last chapter about unlawful businesses practices, we talked about actions and activities that are forbidden by a federal or provincial statute because they harm the state or the public interest. They are crimes or criminal offences, or federal or provincial offences. A **tort** is different. It is a civil wrong done to an individual rather than to the state. Many crimes and offences are also civil wrongs. For example, the crime of murder is also the tort of wrongful death, and the crime of theft is also the tort of intentional interference with goods. Crimes and provincial offences are created by statutes passed by Parliament and the provincial legislatures. Civil wrongs are created in the common law provinces by judges making court decisions (and are called torts), and in Quebec by the *Civil Code*. If a person commits an act that is forbidden by a statute, she can be charged and prosecuted by the federal or provincial Crown (government). If a person commits a tort or civil wrong, he can be sued civilly by the person harmed. If a person commits an act that is both a crime or offence and a tort or civil wrong, she can be prosecuted criminally *and* sued civilly.

There are many different civil wrongs that you can commit, or that can be committed against you, in the course of carrying on business. If you are successfully sued by a person you have harmed, you may be liable to pay money to that person. Likewise, if you are harmed by someone and you successfully sue, you may be awarded money damages.

In this chapter we discuss the different types of torts you can commit, or that can be committed against you, in the course of different business activities. All of the torts are civil wrongs in Quebec as well.

GETTING GOODS AND SERVICES FROM OTHERS

A person who says (or indicates in any other way) something he knows is untrue in order to get another person to do something (and the other person acts on the statement) commits the tort of **fraud** or **deceit**. For example, a person who gets someone to sell her goods by paying for them with a cheque written on an account that she knows doesn't exist or has no money in it is committing the tort of fraud. A person who knowingly makes an untrue claim in a brochure about a product is committing the tort of fraud if someone who reads the brochure then buys the misrepresented product.

PRODUCING GOODS

A manufacturer who carelessly designs or manufactures a product, or who markets it without clearly warning buyers about known risks of using it, may be held responsible to anyone (not just the buyer) who is injured by the product. This area of tort law is called **product liability**.

A manufacturer who is careless in designing or manufacturing a product cannot avoid responsibility simply by warning consumers about the dangers. The manufacturer must always take reasonable care in making a product, even if that involves choosing a more expensive but safer design or manufacturing process over a cheaper but less safe one. When warning consumers about risks, the manufacturer must warn not only about those that he was aware of before marketing the product, but also about any that become known after the product goes onto the market. The warning has to be specific about the risk or danger, has to be printed on the product's label, and has to be very visible. For example, a drug manufacturer who creates a new drug without properly testing it for side effects, who manufactures it without making sure that it does not become contaminated during processing, or who does not tell doctors who prescribe the drug that it can cause reactions in certain patients, will be held liable to people who are harmed. Those people might be the ones who actually took the drug, but they might also be fetuses in the wombs of mothers taking the drug (for example, as in the case of thalidomide), or complete strangers (for example, a pedestrian hit by a car driven by a man who blacks out because of the drug).

PROVIDING GOODS AND SERVICES

There are several torts that may be committed in the course of providing goods and services.

Product Liability

Product liability doesn't just affect the manufacturer of goods. Others are also required to warn consumers about known risks. A person who sells, prescribes, installs, or repairs a product that was negligently designed or manufactured must warn customers or clients about any known risks or dangers of using it. Anyone who does not do so can be held responsible along with the manufacturer.

Negligence

A person who practices a profession such as law, accounting, architecture, engineering, or medicine claims to have special knowledge and skill just by setting up a practice. So does a person who carries on an occupation such as auto repair, bookkeeping, truck driving, or construction, to name but a few.

Customers and clients are entitled to rely on the competence of people who claim to have special skills and knowledge. Tort law says that professionals and people in skilled occupations—even those who are just beginners—have to be as competent at what they do as any reasonably competent, careful professional or skilled worker in that particular field. Those who fall short of this standard of reasonable competence are committing the tort of (**professional**) **negligence**. Anyone who claims to be a specialist in some particular area (for example, a lawyer who specializes in bankruptcy law, or an auto mechanic who specializes in brake repair) is held to a higher standard of competence than someone who does not claim to be a specialist.

A lawyer was retained by a client to do a real estate deal. The lawyer did all the required paperwork but did not check for prior claims registered against the property, which is standard practice. After the deal closed, the client found out that the seller had mortgaged the property several years earlier. The seller stopped making mortgage payments after the deal closed, and the mortgagee took steps to foreclose on the property. The client sued the lawyer for professional negligence and won.

Negligent Misrepresentation

A businessperson can harm a customer by giving bad advice, as well as by doing bad work. If a professional or businessperson gives advice about facts to a client without making sure that the advice is accurate, and the customer relies on the advice and loses money as a result, he can sue the advisor for **negligent misrepresentation**.

A seller of heavy equipment contacted a credit reporting business for information about a potential buyer. The reporting business gave favourable but inaccurate information about the buyer's credit history. The seller extended credit to the buyer, who stopped making payments after six months with the result that the seller suffered a financial loss. The seller sued the credit reporting business, and won.

DEALING WITH CUSTOMERS, EMPLOYEES, AND OTHER HUMAN BEINGS

People can be harmed physically as well as financially. Business people have to be careful about the products they supply, the work they do, and the advice they give. They also have to be careful not to cause physical harm to individuals, either intentionally or accidentally, and they must not harm the property of others.

Wrongful Interference with Goods

A person who, without the owner's permission, takes, uses, damages (or even touches) goods that belong to someone else is committing a tort. It is a tort to steal someone else's goods, destroy or damage them, or to use them without consent. For example, a person commits a tort by shoplifting, breaking an item on display, vandalizing a vehicle, by "borrowing" and using an item left by the owner for storage or repair (even if it's returned to the owner none the worse for wear), or by refusing to return an item left for storage or repair.

Trespass

A person who comes onto someone else's property without the permission of the owner or tenant of the property is committing the tort of **trespass to land**. If the person comes on with permission, but does not leave when asked to by the owner or tenant, that too is trespass. So is standing outside the property and tossing something (for example, a rock) through the window of a building on the property.

Business premises, including stores, shopping malls, and parking lots, are private property. Although the public has a kind of standing invitation to come in, any person can be asked to leave by the owner, tenant, or their employee, and once asked, as to go. A person who refuses to leave can be removed by force that does not cause unnecessary injury. However, a person cannot be asked to leave business premises simply because of race or colour, or on any other ground that is illegal discrimination under human rights legislation (See p. 194 in Chapter 14).

False Imprisonment

A person who prevents another from leaving a particular place is committing the tort of **false** (meaning wrongful) **imprisonment**, if that person has no lawful authority to hold the other. It is false imprisonment to put someone in a room or a vehicle and prevent her from leaving. It is also false imprisonment to hold onto someone physically and not let him get away.

False Imprisonment and Shoplifting

Tort actions for false imprisonment usually arise out of an accusation of shoplifting. Shoplifting is the crime of theft and at the time it happens it is considered, in law, to be an **indictable** crime, the more serious kind. (The less serious crimes are **summary conviction offences**.) Any person who actually witnesses an indictable crime being committed has the legal right to arrest and detain (imprison) the person committing the crime. For example, anyone who sees a person shoplifting has the right to stop that person and prevent her from leaving the premises. "Anyone" includes a store security guard, store owner, or clerk, another shopper in the store, or a passing stranger. It's not unusual for a shoplifter to be compelled to stay in the store (that is, to be imprisoned). A security guard may hold onto the person, a manager may lock him in an office, or a clerk may just ask him not to leave because the police have been called, and he stays to avoid the embarrassment of being chased all over the shopping mall by the store clerk and the police. There is no false imprisonment in these situations *as long as the person who is being prevented from leaving actually stole something.*

There *is* false imprisonment, however, if the person being prevented from leaving *did not* steal anything and is being prevented from leaving by someone other than a police officer. Here's the story. As we said above, anyone can make a **citizen's arrest** if she actually sees an indictable offence being committed. However, only a **peace officer** (a police officer to you) can arrest a person who is *reasonably suspected* of committing an indictable offence. If it turns out that the person suspected of shoplifting hadn't stolen anything, no one but a police officer had the right to stop and detain her. Anyone else who stopped and detained her had no right to do so and was therefore committing the tort of false imprisonment. People wrongly accused of shoplifting have sued stores for false imprisonment and won.

Defamation, Libel, and Slander

A person who makes an untrue statement that harms another person's reputation or that exposes that other person to hatred or ridicule commits the tort of **defamation**. The untrue statement has to be made to at least one other person besides the one whose reputation is harmed. It is not defamation to make an untrue statement in the course of a lawsuit (in the statement of claim or on the witness stand, for example), or in Parliament or a provincial legislature. It is also not defamation to make an untrue statement in a situation where there is a duty to comment about the person. For example, if you have reason to believe that someone stole something from you, it is not defamation to tell the police. It is not defamation to express an opinion on a subject, for example, to say that a certain politician is leading the province to wrack and ruin, or that a particular work of art could have been painted just as well by a five-year-old.

There are two kinds of defamation: **slander**, if the person making the untrue statement is speaking, and **libel**, if the person making the untrue statement is writing it, or speaking words that are recorded in writing, on film, audio tape, or video tape.

A businesswoman who has just been denied a municipal licence stands in front of a crowd, a newspaper reporter, and a television crew on the steps of city hall and rants that the mayor of the municipality doesn't give licences to honest businesses, only to those that offer bribes. If it is not true that the mayor takes bribes, the businesswoman is slandering the mayor as she speaks to the crowd and is libelling the mayor as she is being filmed by the television cameras and when her words are reported in the newspaper the following day. The mayor can sue the businesswoman for slander and libel, and can also sue for libel the television station that airs her words and the newspaper that prints them.

Negligence

Negligence is not taking the care you should have taken. We've already talked about negligence in the context of:

- product liability—there, negligence meant that the manufacturer didn't take the care it should have in designing or manufacturing a product, or in warning consumers about any risk involved in using it.

- professional or occupational negligence—there, negligence meant that the professional or skilled worker didn't take the care that a reasonably competent person skilled in the field would have taken.

- negligent misrepresentation—there, negligence meant that someone giving advice didn't take reasonable care to check the facts before giving the advice.

Negligence can work its way in anywhere. Whenever a person or business is in a situation where others might foreseeably be harmed by his/her/its activities (or inactivity), that person or business must take as much care to prevent harm as would a reasonably skilled, intelligent, and careful person in the same circumstances. For example, it is negligence:

- to drive in a snowstorm if your windshield wipers don't work
- not to repair the leaking roof of a storage warehouse
- not to refrigerate perishable food products
- to start excavations for a building without locating underground utility lines

Your own life experiences can probably provide you with many other examples of negligence. If a person suffers harm that could have been expected because of someone else's negligent action (or lack of action), that person can sue in negligence for money damages.

Occupier's Liability

Occupier's liability is a particular area of negligence, of special importance to people who have business premises and to those people who come onto business premises. The law of occupier's liability varies considerably from province to province, but for practical purposes the main rule can be stated this way: Every person who occupies premises has to take reasonable care to make sure that anybody who comes onto the premises is reasonably safe. Anyone who is injured on someone else's premises that were not kept reasonably safe can sue the owner or a tenant who occupies the premises. For example, businesses have been held responsible in occupier's liability for:

- not keeping the sidewalk in front of a store free of ice
- not mopping up melted snow or spilled drinks on the floor
- not making sure that stair rails are strong and secure
- not providing enough light for people inside the building to see where they are walking
- not maintaining elevators and escalators in good condition

It is not enough for a business to fix a dangerous condition that a customer or employee happens to notice, or to warn of a known dangerous condition. The occupier has to inspect the premises on a regular basis for dangerous conditions, and then must fix anything that's discovered to be wrong within a reasonable time, which, depending on the danger, could mean immediately. As long as a dangerous condition remains unfixed, people have to be protected from it (for example, by being kept out of the area).

COEXISTING WITH THE NEIGHBOURS

A person who, without permission, parks his car on another's land, leaves garbage in bags for collection on another's land, or who builds even an inch or two over the property line, is committing the tort of **trespass to land**. The car, garbage, and building all have to go if the owner of the land says so. If they don't, the owner can sue for trespass.

A person who uses her land in a way that interferes fairly seriously with a neighbour's use and enjoyment of his land, is committing the tort of **nuisance**. For example, it is nuisance to:

- release pollutants from a factory that drift or flow onto a neighbour's land

- continually make an unreasonable amount of noise that the neighbours can hear

- change the slope of land so that a lot of water collects around the foundation of a neighbour's building after a rainfall

COMPETING WITH OTHER BUSINESSES

In the last chapter, we discovered that although everything may be fair in love and war, not everything is in business. Competition is encouraged in Canada, but only so far. Unfair competition may draw the attention of the federal government, but it may also lead to a lawsuit by another business that has been harmed. The lawsuit can be started against an individual or business that committed a criminal offence under the *Competition Act* or that did not obey an order of the Competition Tribunal or another court.

A lawsuit can also be started against an individual or business that has committed one of these torts:

Passing-off

A person who, knowing that it isn't true, claims or indicates in some way that her goods or services are someone else's, in the hope of attracting customers, commits the tort of **passing-off**. This often involves using someone else's name or trademark, or a confusingly similar name or trademark. For example, it is passing-off to sell knock-off jeans as "Levis" or fake wristwatches marked "Swatch."

Inducing Breach of Contract

A person who persuades another to breach his contract with a third party commits the tort of inducing breach of contract. It is **inducing breach of contract** to convince an employee to leave her present employer and come to work for you. It is also inducing breach of contract to get a supplier to stop providing another customer with goods you want and to sell them to you instead.

Intimidation

If a person threatens another in order to make him do something, and he does do it and suffers harm as a result, this is the tort of **intimidation**. The threat must be to commit some unlawful act, which could include a crime or a tort or a breach of contract. The threat can be made directly against the person whose obedience is desired, or it can be made against a third person. For example, it is intimidation if you suggest to a businessperson that she may frequently find her tires flat unless she stops undercutting your prices, and she then raises her prices and suffers a financial loss as a result.

Slander of Goods

Instead of trading on another business's good reputation or stealing its employees or suppliers, a competing business might try to destroy that business's reputation. A person who makes an untrue statement (in spoken, written, or recorded words) that affects another's goods and causes that other person financial harm by driving customers away, commits the tort of **slander of goods** (sometimes known as **injurious falsehood**). For example, it is slander of goods to say that another business sells contaminated meat, or even to say that one's own product is "the only brand on the market that is pure" (because it strongly suggests that the other brands are impure).

Conspiracy

If two or more people agree to do something for the purpose of harming another, and that other person is harmed, this is the tort of **conspiracy**. What the people agree to do does not have to be illegal if it is being done for the purpose of causing harm. Although it would be conspiracy if two or more people agreed, for example, to firebomb someone else's business or to persuade key employees to leave that business, it would also be conspiracy if two or more people agreed to keep their businesses open (lawfully) on Sunday in order to take away the customers of someone who remained closed on Sunday.

A processing company had contracts with 25 truckers to transport materials to its plant. Fifteen of those truckers had most of the work, and the remaining 10 were only called on by the company as circumstances required. The company decided, and informed all 25 truckers, that it wanted a reduction in rates and that it needed only 15 truckers in total. The 15 truckers who had traditionally got most of the work entered into negotiations with the company and they reached an agreement that the company would limit its transportation contracts to those 15. The 10 truckers who had been left out of the agreement sued the company and the 15 truckers for conspiracy in restraint of trade—and lost. The court found that there was no conspiracy in restraint of trade because limiting the number of truckers was not intended to injure the 10 who were excluded from the agreement, even though it did injure them, and because the agreement did not harm the public.

TORTS COMMITTED BY EMPLOYEES OF A BUSINESS

If an employee of a business commits a tort in the course of work, the person who has been injured (whether physically or financially) has the right to sue the employer. An employer is said to be **vicariously liable** for the wrongful acts that employees commit in the course of carrying out their employment duties. For example, if an employee making deliveries deliberately rams the delivery truck into someone's car, the occupants and owner of the car can sue the employer. If an employee gives advice to a customer that is based on false information that the employee carelessly didn't check, the customer can sue the employer.

THE PERSON WHO WAS HARMED CAN'T WAIT FOREVER TO SUE

The victim of a tort has only a certain period of time to start a lawsuit, and once that time has passed, the victim loses the right to sue. The period of time, called a **limitation period**, varies according to the province and the kind of tort that was committed—typically, it is from one to six years. In some cases there's not only a limitation period but also a **notice period**, in which case the victim of the tort has to give written notice of an intention to sue to the person who committed the tort. These notice periods tend to be very short, usually a matter of days or weeks. There is often a requirement to give notice if the person who committed the tort is part of a municipal, provincial, or federal government.

> **T**
> **I**
> **P**
>
> Whenever you suffer harm because of someone's act or omission—even if you think there's only a *possibility* that you've suffered harm—you should immediately contact a lawyer experienced in litigation. Your lawyer will be able to tell you if you have to take action right away in order to preserve your right to sue.
>
> T I P

For more information about what happens when you sue or are sued, see Chapter 21.

HOW MUCH?

When a court awards compensation (**damages**) to the victim of a tort, it is supposed to be an amount that will put the victim in the position she was in before the harm was done. For example, if goods are destroyed, the court will award an amount that equals their market value immediately before they were destroyed. (The court won't award an amount that equals what it cost to replace the goods.) If goods are damaged, the court will award an amount that will cover the cost of repairing the goods, if the cost of repair is less than the market value of the goods. However, if land or structures are damaged, a court may not award the amount of money it will take to restore the land or buildings, but instead an amount that equals the decrease in the market value of the property. If the victim of the tort suffers physical injury, the court will award an amount that may include:

- the cost of caring for the victim, for as long as he needs care—which can be the rest of his life in serious cases

- wages for the length of time the victim is not able to work

- money the victim missed making when business opportunities were lost because of the injury

- a payment that is supposed to compensate the victim for her pain and suffering—this is obviously something that is very difficult to measure, so Canadian courts (unlike their US counterparts that sometimes award millions of dollars for pain and suffering) give fairly small payments. Top awards for pain and suffering are in the range of $250,000.

Insurance

Your business insurance will cover you if you are sued for defamation or if you are sued for committing a tort that involved being careless (some form of negligence) rather than acting deliberately. Your insurance company will direct you to a particular lawyer and will pay for your defence. If a settlement with the victim of the tort can be reached before trial, your insurance company will pay the amount of the settlement up to the limits of your policy. If you go to trial and lose the lawsuit, your insurance company will pay the amount of the judgment up to the limits of your policy. (We have to tell you that, unfortunately, people sometimes have to sue their insurance company to make them defend and pay.)

Your insurance policy will not cover you for torts you commit intentionally rather than carelessly, such as false imprisonment, trespass, wrongful interference with goods, passing-off, or conspiracy. If you commit one of these torts you will have to pay for your own defence and any award that the court orders.

SUING AND BEING SUED

No sane business person wants to be involved in a lawsuit. Unfortunately, at some point in the life of your business you may well sue or be sued. You may, for example:

- sue a client or customer for non-payment of a bill
- be sued by a supplier for non-payment of a bill
- sue a supplier for providing you with defective materials
- be sued by a customer or client for providing defective merchandise
- sue a former employee for breach of a non-competition clause
- be sued by a former employee for wrongful dismissal
- sue a driver for damaging your business's truck in an accident
- be sued by a customer injured on your premises

These are just a very few of the almost unlimited number of ways that business people can become involved in a lawsuit.

In this chapter we will discuss the factors that will affect your decision to sue, alternatives to litigation, what to do if you're sued, the different levels of courts, the stages of a lawsuit, and doing it yourself in small claims court. For the purpose of this chapter we are assuming that the lawsuit is for money damages, but it is possible to sue for other things (see p. 36-39 in Chapter 3).

SHOULD YOU SUE?

The litigation process, whether you are suing or being sued, is a long, expensive, unpredictable, and emotionally draining way of solving legal disputes, that is probably best avoided. Just because you know you are right does not necessarily mean that you should sue the person who is wrong. In fact, there is an ancient curse: "May you be involved in a lawsuit in which you are right."

A wholesale supplier sued a sole proprietor customer who had ordered several thousand dollars worth of products and hadn't paid the full bill. The lawsuit turned out to be an aggravation from beginning to end. The customer had no real defence to the lawsuit, but put in a statement of defence anyway. When it was time for discoveries, the customer simply didn't show up; the supplier's lawyer had to bring a motion to force him to attend. When he did attend, he refused to answer many of the questions; the supplier's lawyer had to bring another motion to force him to answer the questions. The supplier's legal bill and blood pressure rose together. After making the supplier go through every single stage right up to trial, the customer didn't bother to show up at the trial itself. The supplier got a judgment against the customer including an order that the customer had to pay a good part of the supplier's legal costs—and then he had to find some assets that belonged to the customer so he could enforce the judgment. The customer was self-employed, so it wasn't possible simply to garnish his wages. At a judgment debtor examination the customer refused to admit that he owned any personal or business property or had any income from any source. The supplier hired an investigator to find out whether the customer owned any assets, and the investigator reported that he lived in a nice house and drove a nice car, but both were owned by the customer's wife. After first losing thousands of dollars and then spending thousands of dollars, the supplier finally realized that he was throwing good money after bad and gave up.

Avoiding lawsuits does not mean avoiding lawyers. You should consult your lawyer to help you decide whether or not to sue, based on the following:

- how likely are you to win your lawsuit?—Is the law on your side? Do you have enough evidence to prove your case to a court? How much will you get if you win? Even if the answers are yes, yes, and a lot, there is no sure thing when it comes to a court case. The judge or jury can still find against you.

- how much will it cost to take the matter to court?—Litigation is very, very expensive (if you're not in small claims court, *start* counting in the tens of thousands of dollars), and unless a lawyer agrees to act for you on a contingency basis, you will have to pay her whether you win or not. If you win, the court will probably order the other party to pay some but not all of your legal fees. If you lose, you will have to pay your own lawyer, and you may have to pay some of the other party's legal fees too. Compare the estimated cost of the litigation with the amount of money involved and your chances of winning the lawsuit.

- where will the lawsuit take place?—If the other party lives or carries on business in a different province, you may have to start your lawsuit in that province.

- what are your chances of collecting any money from the other party?—If you win your lawsuit the court will order the other party to pay you money, but it's up to you to collect it. Does the other party have enough money or property to pay your judgment? If not, any judgment you get is not worth the paper it's written on. If the other party lives or carries on business in a different province, the costs of collecting go up and your chances of success go down.

- do you have the time and emotional energy to be involved in a lawsuit?—You will have to spend a great deal of time, usually during your business day, dealing with your lawsuit. You will have to find information and documents for your lawyer, meet with him, attend for questioning before the trial, and be in court for the trial. It may be a year or more before your case gets to court. Most people find the entire litigation process very stressful.

You must weigh all of these factors when you decide whether or not to start a lawsuit. Your lawyer will try to solve the problem first without litigation. If you sue, it does not necessarily mean that the matter will go to court. The vast majority of lawsuits settle before trial.

WHAT ARE THE ALTERNATIVES TO LITIGATION?

Litigation is time-consuming, expensive, and aggravating, and even if you win, there is no guarantee that you'll be able to collect the money you were awarded. Nor is litigation in either party's best interest if there's any desire for a continuing business relationship.

Alternative methods of dispute resolution have become popular as more and more business people look for less expensive and less adversarial ways to resolve their business disagreements. Before you instruct your lawyer to start a lawsuit consider these alternatives to litigation:

- You can do nothing—The amount involved may not be enough to justify the cost of a lawsuit. Or you may not be able to prove your case because important evidence has been lost. Or you may simply lack the time, energy, and emotional strength to take your dispute to court.

- You can try to settle with the other party—Either on your own or with the help of a lawyer, you can negotiate with the other side and try to resolve the dispute without starting a lawsuit. Even after a lawsuit is started, you (or your lawyer) can try to reach a settlement before your case gets to trial. A settlement requires the agreement of both parties—neither you nor your lawyer can force the other party to settle.

- You can try to resolve your dispute by **mediation**—A neutral third party called a mediator will meet with you and the other party to help you try to come to an agreement. The mediator will not take sides and will not judge who is right and who is wrong. If the parties can't agree, no solution is imposed on you. Instead the mediator will help the parties explore the situation to see if there is a solution that can satisfy everyone's needs. There is much more room for flexibility and creativity in a solution arrived at through mediation than in a court-imposed decision, which is usually limited to an order that one party pay the other party money. Mediation is particularly useful if you wish to continue your business relationship with the other party, and it's also faster and cheaper than litigation if it's successful. Mediation is a voluntary process: both parties must agree to it and either may end the process at any time. (For more information read *You Be the Judge* by Norman Ross, published by John Wiley & Sons Canada Ltd.)

• You can resolve your dispute by **arbitration**—A neutral third party, called an arbitrator, is chosen by the parties to hear each side, and makes a decision for the parties. One side will win and the other will lose, just like in a trial. An arbitrator has the power to grant the same kinds of remedies as a court would, and an arbitrator's award is enforceable just like a judge's order. Generally, the decision of an arbitrator is final. In case you're wondering why you would choose arbitration over a court action, it's because it is faster and usually cheaper and you can choose an arbitrator with special expertise in your area. If your dispute involves a contract, the contract may contain a clause stating that you and the other party agree to have any dispute arbitrated.

WHAT IF YOU'RE SUED?

If you are sued or threatened with a lawsuit, doing nothing is generally not an option (although it might be if your business has no assets and you are not personally liable). But you have other choices besides simply going to court. If the other party is merely threatening a lawsuit, you can try to settle the matter, or suggest mediation or arbitration. You can do these things even if a lawsuit has already been started. Consult your lawyer.

THE DIFFERENT LEVELS OF COURT

Every province has courts to deal with civil disputes: a small claims court and a superior court for trials (which court you go to depends on the amount of money involved in the lawsuit), and a court of appeal for appeals.

In addition, the federal government has the Federal Court of Canada, which handles trials and appeals on many matters governed by federal legislation. It also has the Supreme Court of Canada, which is the highest appeal court in the country. It hears appeals from the courts of appeal of all of the provinces and from the appeal division of the Federal Court.

Small Claims Court

Small claims court handles smaller matters, those involving less than a certain amount of money ($3000 to $10,000 depending on the province). Small claims court procedure is simpler and more streamlined than that of the superior courts, and is designed so that parties can handle their own cases, although many parties still choose to be represented by a lawyer, a paralegal, or other agent. (Just because you have decided to go it alone doesn't mean that your opponent won't have a lawyer.) The atmosphere in the courtroom is less formal than in a superior court, and the judge may try to help you if you are representing yourself. However, it is still a court, and you will not win unless your case has a sound basis in law and fact, and you present the evidence to prove it.

If you wish to represent yourself, there are self-help books available with information about preparing the court documents and presenting your case in court. You should consider getting your lawyer to give you some help, especially when you are preparing for the trial.

T
I
P

Before you go to court, practice what you plan to say. When you're in court, speak slowly and clearly, present your case in a logical and organized way, stand whenever you speak to the judge, and be respectful to the judge and polite to the other party.

T I P

The court will probably be very crowded and you may have to wait all day (or even come back another day) before your case is reached.

Superior Court

Every province has a superior court that handles all trial matters involving claims above the small claims court limit. Depending on the province the court is called the Supreme Court, the High Court, Queen's Bench, General Division, or in Quebec, Provincial Court. The procedure in these courts is not designed for parties to handle their own cases, and you cannot generally be represented by a paralegal or other agent in these courts. You should have a lawyer represent you. Your corporation may, by law, have to be represented by a lawyer.

WHAT ARE THE STEPS IN A LAWSUIT?

If you sue or are sued, it is helpful to know how a lawsuit in a superior court proceeds.

Commencing the Action

The person who starts the lawsuit is called the **plaintiff**. The plaintiff's lawyer will draft a document called a **statement of claim** that names the party being sued (the **defendant**) and sets out the nature of the plaintiff's claim, the amount of damages or other relief being asked for, and the facts on which the claim is based. In some provinces the plaintiff's lawyer must first prepare a **writ of summons**, which is a formal statement that a lawsuit has been started. The lawsuit is started when the plaintiff pays a fee to the court to have the statement of claim **issued**. The writ of summons or statement of claim must then be **served** on the defendant, usually by actually handing it to that person.

Defending the Action

After being served with the (writ of summons and) statement of claim, the defendant's lawyer has a limited period of time (a few weeks) in which to defend the action by drafting and serving a **statement of defence** on the plaintiff's lawyer and then filing it with the court. The statement of defence sets out the nature of the defence and the facts on which the defence is based. In some provinces the defendant's lawyer will file an **appearance** before or at the same time as the statement of defence. An appearance simply states that the defendant will be defending the action. If the defendant does not serve and file (an appearance and) statement of defence within the time limit, the plaintiff can get a **default judgment** against the defendant.

Mandatory Mediation

After the statement of defence has been filed, in some provinces the parties to certain types of lawsuits are required to meet with the other party and a mediator to see if the matter can be settled. If it cannot, the lawsuit continues.

Discovery

The plaintiff and the defendant are entitled to find out details of each other's case, including the documents and evidence the other party intends to rely upon. The parties are entitled to **discovery of documents**, meaning that each must give the other a list of all documents within her possession or control that are relevant to the case. Each party has the right to look at the documents listed by the other. In addition, each party's lawyer may question the other party under oath either orally in person (**examination for discovery**) or by way of written questions (**discovery by interrogatories**). An examination for discovery takes place before a court reporter who then prepares a written record (a **transcript**) setting out every question and answer. In discovery by interrogatories one party's lawyer submits a list of written questions to the other party, who must answer those questions in writing.

Requesting a Trial Date

When all of the discoveries have been completed, the plaintiff's lawyer will notify the court that the matter is ready to go to trial, and will ask the court to assign a trial date for the case. The date will be a few months or even a year or more away.

Pre-Trial Conference

Once a trial date has been requested, either party may ask for a **pre-trial conference**. In some provinces, this is automatically scheduled. The lawyers for the parties, and often the parties themselves, will appear before a judge who will try to help the parties settle the case. If the case cannot be settled the judge will see if the parties can agree on any matters that might shorten the length of the trial.

Trial and Judgment

The trial will usually take place before a judge only, but in some provinces it can take place before a judge and a jury if one of the parties requests it.

The plaintiff's lawyer presents the plaintiff's case by calling witnesses to testify, and the defendant's lawyer is allowed to **cross-examine** each to try to weaken the witness's evidence or to get the witness to give additional evidence that might help the defendant's case. The defendant's lawyer then presents the defendant's case in the same way, and the plaintiff's lawyer is allowed to cross-examine the defendant's witnesses. After the witnesses for both sides are finished, the lawyers make a presentation to the judge (and jury) to summarize the evidence and the law that applies to the case.

At the end of the case, the judge will decide the case and give **judgment** (or if it's a jury case, the jury will give a **verdict**). If the plaintiff wins, the judge or jury will order the defendant to pay the plaintiff a specified amount of damages. If the defendant wins, he will not have to pay the plaintiff anything. The court will usually order the losing party to pay some of the other party's legal fees.

Appeal

If the losing party thinks the judge or jury was wrong, she may appeal the decision within a limited period of time (a few days or weeks). The appeal will usually be decided by several judges together. The appeal court will not usually hear any witnesses, but will base its decision on a review of the transcript of the trial. An appeal court will usually only overturn a trial decision if it believes that there was a serious error in how the trial court applied the law.

Enforcing the Judgment

A judgment for damages orders one party to pay money to the other. If the losing party does not voluntarily pay those damages, it is up to the winner to try to collect the money. The winning party has the right to question the loser about his income and assets, and may take steps to get the income and assets by doing such things as **garnishing** the loser's wages (requiring the loser's employer to pay a portion of the loser's wages to the winning party) and seizing the loser's real and personal property.

A winner who gets judgment against a loser who lives out of the province or out of the country has to work a little harder to collect the money awarded. The winner may be able to simply register the judgment where the loser lives and then enforce it in the usual way. In some cases, the winner will have to start a lawsuit where the loser lives to enforce the original judgment. As a general rule, other provinces and countries will assist the winner rather than protect the loser.

All of this adds new meaning to the expression winning isn't everything—collecting is!

GOING OUT OF BUSINESS

Sometimes businesses fail. A 1997 Statistics Canada study found that new small businesses run the biggest risk of failure, perhaps because of management inexperience and lack of basic knowledge about running a business. But established businesses can go belly up too, if they overexpand, for example, or if there's an economic downturn.

When a business starts to slide, the final crisis comes when it owes more money than it has in income and assets. In this chapter we're going to tell you what happens to your business when it can't pay its debts. When things reach that point, the fate of your business is in the hands of your creditors—unless you find fresh capital somewhere.

WHAT CAN THE CREDITORS DO?

The creditors of a business can do a number of things to get the money that's owed them, depending on the nature of the debt and the kind of security the creditor holds. Where there are several creditors, they'll probably all be taking action to get their money back at the same time.

It may be worth your while to consult your lawyer about a creditor's actions, despite the fact that you're in financial straits. Even creditors have to obey the law, and that includes both legislation and the terms of your contract for the loan and for any security. Creditors have been known to act before they were legally entitled to, and you may have a chance of beating your creditor off. Don't fight, however, just for the sake of fighting. In the end that strategy will cost you more money, both in your lawyer's fees and in the costs of collecting that the creditor is allowed to pass on to you.

Enforce a Promise to Pay

When you sign a loan agreement or promissory note, you promise contractually to repay the loan with interest. Most term loans (see Chapter 9 on p. 110) have an **acceleration clause** that allows the lender to demand payment of the full outstanding amount of the loan if you default in any way. So if you miss even one payment by more than a few days, the lender can demand that you immediately repay the whole unpaid amount of the loan, not just the payment that you missed.

When you have a loan through a line of credit (see Chapter 9 on p. 115), your agreement with the lender usually states that the outstanding amount of the loan is payable **on demand**, which means that the lender can demand payment in full *at any time*, not just after you've missed a payment. If you don't repay a loan in full once a demand for payment is made, the lender has the right to sue you for the outstanding balance of the loan, plus interest and legal costs.

If you buy goods or services on credit, you give a contractual promise to pay the supplier on a stated date. If you don't pay, the supplier can sue you for the amount of the payment plus interest and legal costs.

Realize on the Security

Instead of, or in addition to, suing you on your promise to pay, a lender can **realize** on the security you gave for the loan, by taking it to sell. Before moving to realize on the security, the lender has to demand payment and allow you a reasonable time to make the payment. The "reasonable time" may not seem all that reasonable to you—think in terms of days, not months. After the reasonable time has passed, generally speaking the lender can seize the asset without further warning. The actual steps that the lender must take to seize and sell a particular asset will depend on the nature of the asset and the terms of the security agreement.

Security under the Personal Property Security Act

If your province has a *Personal Property Security Act*, and you have given security in the form of:

• a chattel mortgage

• a conditional sales agreement

• a purchase money security interest

• a lease with an option to purchase

• an assignment of accounts receivable

• a general security agreement

• a debenture that has been registered under the PPSA

• Bank Act security that has been registered under the PPSA

and you have defaulted on your loan, the rights of the lender and your rights as borrower are as follows:

• The lender has the right to take possession of the secured property. The lender can get possession by physically removing it from your premises or, if the property is very difficult to remove, by disabling it so that you cannot use it. If you make it impossible for the lender to remove the property, it can start a lawsuit to make you give up possession. After taking possession of the secured property, the lender can keep it, or sell it to pay off the debt. If the lender is going to keep the property, it must notify you. If you object within 30 days, the lender has to sell the property instead. (You'd object if the property was worth more than the debt.)

- If the lender wants, or is forced by you, to sell the property, it has to give you at least 15 days' written notice—but less or none if the property is perishable, the cost of storage is very high compared to the value of the property, a receiver/manager is brought into your business to sell the property according to the terms of your security agreement, or you consent to an earlier sale. During the 15-day period you have the right to redeem (buy back) the property by paying the outstanding balance of the loan, plus interest and costs. A lender who sells property must make sure that a fair price is paid, must account to the debtor for the proceeds of the sale, and must pay the debtor any amount left over after the loan (with interest and costs) is paid off. (Note that if you have given *Bank Act* security that has *not* been registered under the PPSA, the secured property must be sold at public auction.)

- The lender has the right to appoint a **receiver/manager** to take possession of the secured property to satisfy the debt, but only if the loan agreement or security document specifically permits this. The lender will often choose to appoint a receiver/manager to enforce its security over inventory and accounts receivable. The receiver will have to account to you, eventually, for the property seized and sold.

- If the lender's security covers all or almost all of the inventory, accounts receivable, or other property used in your business, the lender must give you notice of its intention to enforce the security, and must then wait 10 days before it can take steps to realize on the security. This gives you 10 days to decide whether to file a **proposal** under the *Bankruptcy and Insolvency Act* (see below on p. 311).

Revenue Canada

Revenue Canada has a statutory lien against the property of a taxpayer who does not pay taxes or remittances that are due. This lien allows the government to seize personal property of the taxpayer after giving 30 days' notice.

Mortgage on Real Property

If you gave a mortgage on real estate, in many provinces the mortgagee (the lender) has the right to **foreclose** on the mortgage and become the legal owner of the real estate, or to sell it under court supervision in a **judicial sale** or privately under the mortgage's **power of sale**.

The mortgagee must start a legal action in order to foreclose, and if the action is successful the mortgagee becomes the legal owner of the property. Foreclosure cancels the mortgage debt. If the property is worth more than the unpaid amount of the loan, the mortgagee doesn't owe you anything. If the property is worth less than the unpaid amount, in most provinces the mortgagee can't ask you to pay the difference.

If you are sued for foreclosure and you want to keep the property, you have a range of options. You can:

- pay the whole mortgage or the missed payments—if you pay off the whole mortgage debt, not only is the foreclosure action stopped, but your mortgage is **discharged** (cancelled). In almost every province you can also stop the foreclosure action by simply paying the missed instalments plus a penalty.

- ask to **redeem**—ask for a period of time (usually from two to six months) to come up with the money to pay the mortgage in full.

- ask for a **judicial sale**—if your request is granted the mortgagee must try to sell the property, under court supervision, before it can foreclose. If the property is sold, the proceeds of sale will be used to pay the loan, interest, and the lender's costs. If any money is left over, it's yours. If the proceeds are not enough to pay the loan, interest, and costs, the lender can go after you for the difference. In some provinces a judicial sale does not have to be requested; it happens automatically.

- defend—in rare cases you may be able to defend the action by challenging the lender's legal rights under the mortgage.

In some provinces, instead of foreclosing the lender may start a court action to have your property sold under court supervision. The proceeds of the sale will be used to pay the loan, interest, and the lender's costs. As in a foreclosure action, you can pay the whole mortgage or the missed payments, ask to redeem, or defend.

Almost all mortgages give the lender a power of sale (the right to sell your property without having to go to court). As with a judicial sale, the proceeds from the sale will be used to pay the mortgage, interest, and costs. Before the property can be sold under power of sale the lender must give you written notice of its intention to sell. Once you receive the notice you have a set period of time (about a month) to pay off the mortgage, and in some provinces you may be able simply to make the payments you missed. If you don't pay, the lender can sell the property.

Call on the Guarantor

If you have given a personal guarantee for the debt of your business and your business does not repay the debt, the lender can demand payment from you. If you don't pay up, you can be sued.

Petition into Bankruptcy

A creditor who is owed more than $1000 and has no security from you for that debt can petition your business into **bankruptcy** if your business is **insolvent** and has committed an **act of bankruptcy**. Your business is insolvent if it owes at least $1000 and cannot pay its debts as they become due. There are 10 possible **acts of bankruptcy**; you can choose from the following list of favourites the one that best fits your personal style:

- not paying debts as they come due
- telling creditors that you're going to stop paying debts
- admitting to creditors in writing that the business is insolvent
- removing, hiding, or disposing of property, or transferring property to a third party, to avoid paying a creditor
- not paying an **execution** (a court order to pay a plaintiff who has won a lawsuit)

To petition your business into bankruptcy the creditor has to bring an action in bankruptcy court and persuade the judge to issue a **receiving order** (an order of bankruptcy). See below on p. 313 for a more complete discussion of bankruptcy.

IS THERE ANYTHING YOU CAN DO?

You're in the soup. What you do now depends on whether you want to keep your business afloat or whether you decide to let it go down.

You Can Put Up a Fight

Even though your business can't pay its debts, you may think that if you get a decent break you can get the business back on its feet. In that case, you're going to have to make some kind of arrangement with your creditors. You might ask your creditors to:

• give you more time to pay

• accept partial payment of the debt, for example, 50 cents on the dollar

• take a percentage of the business's future profits instead of getting paid now

• make their claims against only some of your property instead of all of it, so you can keep running the business

---

T I P Generally speaking, your creditors will not be willing to come to terms with you unless you have some fresh source of money for your business.

TIP

If you think your business has a chance, you should probably get advice from a lawyer who specializes in insolvency, or at least from a **trustee in bankruptcy** who is experienced in commercial (rather than consumer) **proposals**. Then start negotiations with your creditors by making an informal or a formal proposal. Making an informal proposal just involves contacting your creditors and talking to them to see if they'll give you some leeway in repayment. If any secured creditors give you notice that they're going to realize on their security you should make a formal proposal under the *Bankruptcy and Insolvency Act*. To make a formal proposal, you have to have a trustee in bankruptcy to help you. The trustee will file with the bankruptcy court a notice of intention to make a proposal. As soon as the notice is filed, your business gets the following protection from all of its creditors, both secured and unsecured, for at least 30 days:

- your creditors can't collect their debts, either by seizing your property or by getting a court order against your property
- companies that supply essential services (electricity, heat, water, telephone) to your business can't cut off service
- no one who has a contract with you can end it, amend (change) it, or enforce accelerated payment provisions in it (leases often have acceleration clauses). However, you have to pay for any supplies you get immediately and in cash. That, of course, could be a bit of a problem.

Once you file your notice of intention, you have 30 days to file the actual proposal, and during that time you continue to be protected against all of your creditors. The protection period can be extended by the bankruptcy court for additional 45-day periods up to a maximum of five months. The proposal must be made to all of your unsecured creditors, and may also be made to your secured creditors. From this point, you'll only be protected from your secured creditors if they are included in your proposal. Keep in mind that your secured creditors are more likely to be your real threat. Most businesses owe far more to their secured creditors than to their unsecured ones, and secured creditors have more power to bring you down because they can realize on their security. Once your equipment and inventory are seized, you're going to have quite a lot of trouble carrying on business.

The creditors must meet within 21 days after the proposal is filed and vote on it. All unsecured creditors get to vote and if a majority of them accept the proposal and the court approves it, you've got a deal to pay them off. If the unsecured creditors reject your proposal, however, your business is considered in law to have made an **assignment in bankruptcy** (a voluntary transfer of property to the trustee in bankruptcy) and you're well on your way to official bankruptcy. Secured creditors only vote if they were included in the proposal, and they vote separately from the unsecured creditors. If the majority of secured creditors vote against the proposal, they are all free to realize on their security, even if the unsecured creditors approve the proposal. Then you're back in the soup even if your unsecured creditors liked your proposal.

A sole proprietor had liabilities of several hundred thousand dollars, and claimed to have no income and no assets. He made a proposal to his creditors that involved paying a few thousand dollars over a period of 12 months—amounting to a few cents on the dollar for each creditor. He offered no security to support the payment and did not identify the source of the funds for payment. The court refused to approve the proposal, saying that it amounted to a bankruptcy that didn't give the trustee or creditors the benefit of any of the investigative procedures that were available in a bankruptcy.

You Can Throw in the Towel

If you decide that your business can't be turned around and that it's better to end the whole mess, your business can go **bankrupt**. Bankruptcy is not the same thing as insolvency. Insolvency is merely the inability to pay one's debts as they fall due. Bankruptcy is a legal state brought about by a court order. If your business is a sole proprietorship or partnership, you will have to make a personal assignment in bankruptcy and go bankrupt personally. If your business is a corporation, the corporation will make the assignment and the corporation will be bankrupt. See the next section.

Why might you choose to go bankrupt? It's true that bankruptcy is embarrassing, and certain aspects of it can be unpleasant. And personal bankruptcy will probably have a dampening effect on your credit rating for a period of time, possibly several years. But the bankruptcy process is designed to provide a person or business drowning in debt with relief, with an opportunity to start with a clean slate (or perhaps we should say with an empty soup pot). As soon as you go bankrupt you don't have to deal directly with most of your creditors; they must all deal with your trustee in bankruptcy. An individual may be discharged from bankruptcy after nine months, and once you are discharged, almost all of your debts will be wiped out. However, a corporation that goes bankrupt is not entitled to a discharge until after all of its debts have been paid.

BANKRUPTCY

A business is bankrupt once a court determines it is. For an insolvent business, this can happen in one of three ways:

- it can make an assignment in bankruptcy
- its creditors can petition it into bankruptcy, by bringing an action in bankruptcy court and persuading the judge to issue a **receiving order** (an order of bankruptcy)
- it can make a formal proposal that is rejected by the creditors

What Happens if Your Business Goes Bankrupt?

Once you've made an assignment in bankruptcy, had your proposal rejected, or been petitioned into bankruptcy, a trustee in bankruptcy will be appointed by the bankruptcy court. If your business is a corporation, all the property it owns that is not covered by a security agreement **vests in** (becomes the legal property of) the trustee, who uses it to pay off your debts. Any creditor who has taken security against an asset of the business continues to have the right to realize on its security, so those assets will not be available to pay off your unsecured creditors. The bankruptcy court may also order that some or all of the business's income be paid to creditors.

Just because your business is a corporation does not mean that you personally will be totally protected if your business goes bankrupt. You may have to use your own assets to pay loans of the corporation that you guaranteed personally, because those loans will not be paid fully (or, let's be realistic, at all) by the corporation once it goes bankrupt. If you are a director of the corporation, you may personally have to pay up to six months' unpaid wages of employees of the corporation, including vacation pay and bonuses, and you may have to pay unpaid remittances to Revenue Canada for Income Tax, CPP, EI, Excise Tax, GST, HST, or provincial sales tax. If these liabilities are very high, you may have to go bankrupt personally as well.

If your business is a sole proprietorship or a partnership you'll have to go bankrupt personally. Not only your business property but also your personal property vests in the trustee. Legislation in your province may let you keep more of your personal property than the federal bankruptcy legislation allows, but if it doesn't, the *Bankruptcy and Insolvency Act* says that your personal assets that go to the trustee include pretty well everything you own, except some clothes ($1000), and furniture ($2000), and "tools of your trade" ($2000). Your business assets will first be used to pay off your business debts and your personal assets, your personal debts. Anything left over from personal assets will then be used to pay off business debts, and vice versa.

It's not all over when the trustee makes off with your assets. You may be required to answer questions about your financial affairs before the **Official Receiver** (a government official). You may also have to answer creditors' questions, and your creditors can appoint an inspector (who may be one of them) to supervise the trustee's work. Your trustee will investigate whether, once you knew your business was in financial trouble, you or your business transferred any property in order to keep it out of the hands of creditors. You might have paid off one creditor (for example, your brother-in-law who lent your business $10,000) and not others, or you might have sold or given away your property to someone who knew what you were up to (for example, you might have transferred land held by your business into your spouse's name alone). In any such case, the trustee can start a court action to force the transferred property to be given to the trustee. You can be charged with an offence if you destroy, conceal, or falsify documents relating to your affairs, if you transfer property to defraud your creditors, or if you don't truthfully answer questions that are asked at any official examination.

An undischarged bankrupt (person or business) cannot borrow more than $500 (that includes buying anything on credit)

unless the bankrupt informs the other party that she is an undischarged bankrupt. Failing to do so is an offence punishable by a
fine or imprisonment. As well, an undischarged bankrupt person
cannot be the director of a corporation.

Discharge from Bankruptcy: The Happy Ending

If you have gone personally bankrupt for the first time, you will
probably be automatically discharged from bankruptcy after nine
months. You may receive an **absolute discharge**, which means
that you're free of the debts you had before you went bankrupt—
except for certain debts that are never cancelled by discharge
from bankruptcy. They include:

• fines, penalties, and restitution orders

• debts that arise out of your criminal activity such as fraud and
  embezzlement

• money a creditor would have been entitled to receive from your
  trustee in bankruptcy, *if* you had told your trustee about that
  creditor (but you didn't)

You may receive a **conditional discharge**, which means that
you'll still have to pay off certain debts you had before you went
bankrupt. For example, if you owe income taxes you probably
won't be able to get out of paying them.

The rules are different for a corporation. It is not entitled to a
discharge from bankruptcy until all of its debts have been paid in
full. Bankrupt corporations are usually put out of their misery, in
technical terms, **wound up**. After a brief period of mourning,
entrepreneurs create a new corporation and get back to business.

CHAPTER TWENTY-THREE

GETTING OUT OF BUSINESS

What's going to happen to your business when you're through with it? Do you want your partners or fellow shareholders to take it over? Do you want members of your family to run it? Or do you just want to sell it to an outsider and take the money and run (or hobble, depending on how old you are when you sell)? The next question is, do you want to put off thinking about this problem until the time comes, or not think about it at all and let others deal with it after you're dead? Or do you want to plan ahead?

There are a number of good reasons for planning ahead. One of them is to make sure that you'll be able to transfer your business to those you want to have it. What happens to your business if you want out will not be yours alone to decide unless you are in business by yourself. If you have associates, either as partners or as fellow shareholders, they will almost certainly have a say in what happens. You may be required to transfer your interest in a partnership or corporation to your partners or fellow shareholders, regardless of whom you'd like to transfer it to. Or your partners or fellow shareholders may have the right to veto your choice of successor.

Another reason to plan ahead is to make sure that you'll be paid for your business interest, if you're not intending to give it away. You'd only sell to an outsider who could pay you fair market value for the business, but if you're selling to your business associates they may dispute what your interest is worth and may not have the money to pay you anyway.

A third, and especially compelling, reason for advance planning is to minimize the tax consequences of the transfer of your business. And there are always tax consequences. Transfer (and not only transfer by sale) of a business interest is usually a **disposition** for tax purposes that can lead to all kinds of things like taxable capital gains and taxable income in the form of recaptured capital cost allowance, dividends, and attributed income. Tax laws are very complicated, and are constantly changing, and the tax situation of every business is different. No matter what your form of business and no matter who you're transferring your interest to, it is very important that you get proper advice from a tax lawyer and/or accountant, not just when you actually dispose of your business, but in some cases years beforehand.

In this chapter, we're going to examine what's involved if:

- you want to, or must, have your partners or fellow shareholders take over the business

- you want members of your family to take over the business

- you want to sell the business to an outsider

TRANSFER YOUR INTEREST TO YOUR PARTNERS

If your business is a partnership and you want to transfer your interest to your partners when you're ready to leave or when you die, you must plan in advance for that to happen. Think again if you think you don't want to sell to your partners, because practically speaking there's no other market for your partnership interest as a going concern, and your partners are the best market for your share of the partnership assets.

If you haven't planned for it—either because you have no partnership agreement or because your agreement doesn't deal with the issue—your partnership will simply dissolve when you leave or die (in Quebec, a general partnership can keep going). Of course, you (or your estate) can negotiate to sell your share of the partnership assets and goodwill to your partners. But there can be a number of problems with leaving the negotiations for this late stage:

• your partners are not required to buy your share of the assets

• you (or your estate) may not be able to get the best price, or even a fair price, and you can't expect to get a better price from an outsider, since the partnership assets have more value to your partners than to anyone else

• you (or your estate) may end up in litigation over how the assets are to be divided and/or valued

• even if your partners want to buy your share of the partnership assets, they may not have the money

How do you plan ahead? You do it by having a partnership agreement that deals with what happens when a partner wants to leave, retires, or dies. Most partnership agreements have a buy-sell clause that comes into play if one partner wants out. Under the clause, your partners buy you out, or you buy them out. If no one is willing to buy, then the partnership is usually dissolved. In a large partnership, the clause will probably only require the other partners to buy you out—you won't have to buy them out. If your partnership agreement has a mandatory retirement clause, it will require the other partners to buy you out when you retire. If there's a buy-out or buy-sell clause, it should state how your partnership interest is to be valued and how and when you are to be paid.

T I P The partnership agreement should have a clause that requires the partners to have life and disability insurance on each other. The insurance proceeds can help fund a buy-out triggered by the death or disability of a partner. Obviously insurance will not fund a buy-out if a partner wants to leave while alive and in good health. The other partners may have to borrow the money to fund a buy-out in that case.

T I P

In rare cases a partnership agreement will allow you to sell your partnership interest to an outsider, but only if the other partners approve of the new partner. However, the market for your partnership interest could be very limited.

TRANSFER YOUR INTEREST TO YOUR FELLOW SHAREHOLDERS

If your business is incorporated and you want to transfer your interest to your fellow shareholders by selling your shares to them or back to the corporation, again you must plan in advance. If you don't think you want to transfer your interest to your fellow shareholders, you should remember that the market for a minority interest in a privately held corporation is practically non-existent. Besides, the shareholders and/or the directors of a privately held corporation must approve any sale or transfer of shares.

Although the corporation will continue to exist if you leave or die, there can be problems if you don't plan ahead:

- the other shareholders are not automatically required to buy your shares, and neither is the corporation

- you (or your estate) may not be able to get the best price, or even a fair price, if you leave the negotiations until you want out or after you die

- even if the corporation and/or the shareholders want to buy your shares, they may not have enough money

- you may have to start court proceedings to have the corporation wound up (see below on p. 326) or to force purchase of your shares, and you may not succeed

A man and a woman started a small incorporated courier business. In addition to their business relationship they lived together in a "common law" relationship. Because they got along so well in their personal relationship, they never bothered to enter into a shareholder's agreement. Over the years the business prospered, but their relationship did not. Finally they decided to end their personal relationship. The man decided that he did not want to stay in business with the woman and insisted that she buy him out. She thought he was asking too much money and told him to buy her out instead. They each hired lawyers and negotiated back and forth. Finally they agreed to try to sell the business, but then fought over every detail. The business was neglected and started to go down in value. By the time the business was sold and the lawyers paid, there was very little left for either of them.

If you want to make sure that your fellow shareholders or the corporation will buy your shares when the time comes, how do you plan in advance? You have to have a shareholders' agreement that requires the other shareholders or the corporation to buy shares from a shareholder who wants to sell, and/or requires them to buy your shares from your estate on your death. The agreement should state how the price for your shares will be calculated and how and when the price is to be paid. The shareholders should have life and disability insurance on each other (or the corporation should have it on the shareholders) to fund the purchase of the shares. Insurance will not be helpful if a shareholder leaves the business for any other reason—the corporation or the shareholders may have to borrow money to fund the share purchase. You might also want the agreement to provide that you have the right to have the corporation wound up or dissolved if the other shareholders or the corporation can't or don't buy your shares, so that you can get your portion of the corporation's assets.

TRANSFER YOUR INTEREST TO YOUR FAMILY

You may want someone in your family to take over your business as a going concern, either as a gift while you are alive or in your will. You'll want to plan ahead for tax reasons. When you give your business to a family member you want to reduce taxes not only for your own sake but for the sake of the business and your family. If you are giving your business to your spouse, the **spousal rollover** provisions of the *Income Tax Act* allow you to do so without triggering a capital gain for yourself. But if you give your business to a child, there will be a capital gain on which you have to pay tax (unless your business has gone down in value since you acquired it).

Planning ahead can help you reduce the tax you will pay at the time of the transfer, if you're transferring to your child. You can use an **estate freeze** to transfer some or all of the future growth in the business to your child now, while you keep control of, and the income from, the business until you are ready to hand over the reins sometime in the future. If you transfer an interest in the current value of the business, you may have to pay capital gains tax. But future increases in value belong to your child and are not taxable in your hands. Your child will not have to pay any tax on that increase in value until he disposes of the business. If you simply intend to transfer your business on your death, as part of your planning for tax purposes you may want to take out life insurance to help pay any taxes that arise as a result of that transfer.

The specific plans you make will depend on whether the business is a sole proprietorship, partnership, or corporation. Whatever you do, make sure that you get expert tax advice from an accountant and a tax lawyer.

Sole Proprietorship

If you want to hand over your business to a family member during your lifetime, you'll have to transfer ownership of all of the assets of the business. If you want to hand over your business on your death, you will need a properly drafted will leaving the assets of the business to your chosen successor.

Unless you are incredibly generous, you want your successor to get not only the assets of the business, but also all of its debts. As a practical matter, most of the debts will go with the business anyway because assets will have been made security for the debts.

T
I
P
The creditors of the business can still go after you personally after you've left the business, so if you are giving your business away while you're still alive, you should get an agreement from your family member that she will pay you back if you have to pay the creditors.

T I P

If you're giving your business away in your will, your estate will be responsible for paying your business debts, which could have the effect of reducing other family members' share of your estate. You may want to take this into account when you are making your will.

If you want your business to go to your child and you want to reduce taxes by using an estate freeze, you may be able to achieve that by taking your child in as a partner or by incorporating a company to own some or all of the assets of the business.

Partnership

It's unlikely that you will be transferring your interest in a partnership to a family member either during your lifetime, or on your death. You can only transfer your partnership interest in an ongoing business to a family member if your partners consent. If you die while still a partner in a business, you can't just leave your partnership interest to your spouse or child and expect them to step into the partnership in your place, unless you have a partnership agreement that specifically allows that (which is highly unlikely despite what you've seen on television). If you have a partnership agreement it probably requires your partners to pay your estate for your interest. If you don't have a partnership agreement, the partnership dissolves on your death, and your family members will inherit your share of the partnership's assets, which they can keep or sell.

Corporation

If you want to give or leave your shares in a private corporation to a family member, your ability to do so depends on whether or not you are the only shareholder. If you are, you don't need anyone's agreement to transfer your shares to anyone you please. You simply sign them over to your family member or leave them in your will. If you are not the only shareholder, it may be difficult or impossible for you to transfer your shares because the consent of the other shareholders and/or directors is needed. If you want to be able to give or leave your shares to a family member, you must have a shareholders' agreement that allows you to do so.

Transferring your shares to a family member other than your spouse will trigger a capital gain or loss. Up to $500,000 of any capital gain may be tax free because there is a capital gains deduction permitted under the *Income Tax Act* for certain small business corporations.

Whether you're the only shareholder or one of several, you can achieve an estate freeze by creating different classes of shares that allow you to keep control of the company while giving away future growth of the company to family members.

SELLING TO AN OUTSIDER

If you want to sell your business to an outsider, there's not a lot you can do to plan ahead other than make sure that you have the right to do so if you are a partner or one of several shareholders. But at the time of the sale, there are a number of things you can do to reduce the tax impact on yourself. For example, you can arrange for the price to be paid to you in instalments spread out over several taxation years. There are other things that you can do to save taxes, depending on the form of your business. Speak to your tax lawyer and accountant.

Sole Proprietorship

When you sell a sole proprietorship, you do so through a sale of assets. Asset purchase and sale is discussed in more detail in Chapter 7 on p. 86.

Partnership

It's unlikely that you will sell just *your* partnership interest to an outsider. If you have no partnership agreement, your partnership dissolves when you leave (unless, again, it's a general partnership in Quebec). If you have a partnership agreement it will probably require you to sell your interest to your partners. If it allows for a sale to an outsider at all, it will only be with the consent of your partners.

If all of the partners want to get out of business at the same time, the sale of the partnership business will be an asset sale, just as for a sole proprietorship. The only additional issue is the division of the sale price among the partners. If there's no partnership agreement, or if there is one but it doesn't address this issue, the proceeds will be divided equally. If there is a partnership agreement and it covers division of the proceeds, the terms of the agreement will govern.

Corporation

You can sell a business corporation either by selling all of its assets or by selling its shares. The choice you make will depend largely on the tax consequences. You should consult your tax lawyer and accountant to find out which is best for you, and how to reduce your tax as much as possible. If you are the only shareholder, you can do whatever you like with the corporation, but if you're not, you will need the consent of other shareholders and/or the directors for either an asset sale or a share sale.

Sale of Shares

You'll probably want to proceed by way of a sale of your shares because it's generally the most advantageous way to sell a corporation. For more about purchase and sale of shares, see Chapter 7 on p. 85. If you have a capital gain on the sale of your shares, up to $500,000 of it may be tax-free because of the capital gains deduction available to some small business corporations.

If you are not the only shareholder and you want to be sure that you can sell your shares, you must have a shareholders' agreement that allows you to do so. Even if you have permission to sell your shares, it's very hard to find an outsider who wants to buy anything less than 100% of the shares of a private corporation.

Sale of Assets

If you decide to proceed by way of a sale of assets, it's the corporation, not you, that's the seller. The corporation receives the sale proceeds, and pays tax on any income or capital gain resulting from the sale. You then get your money from the corporation in the form of a dividend on which you would pay tax as income (up to a maximum tax rate of about 35 per cent).

Termination of the Corporation

After an asset sale is complete, you still have the corporation on your hands and you may want to terminate its existence. If there are no assets left in it at all, you may choose to do nothing and eventually the government that incorporated it may **dissolve** it for not filing documents or not paying fees. If the corporation still has some assets that the shareholders want returned to them, or that have to be used to pay off debts of the corporation, the shareholders can vote for winding up of the corporation or, in some provinces, can vote either for that or for **voluntary dissolution**. When a corporation is wound up, the shareholders appoint a **liquidator** to pay off debts, make arrangements with creditors, and distribute the corporation's remaining property to the shareholders. (The liquidator does not necessarily have to be a professional or an outsider and may be a director, officer, or employee of the corporation.) If there is voluntary dissolution of the corporation instead of winding up, the present directors and officers of the corporation (rather than an appointed liquidator) pay off the creditors and distribute the remaining property. If trouble is foreseen over payment of debts or distribution of property, a creditor or shareholder may make an application to the court for a **court-ordered winding up**. The court will appoint the liquidator and will oversee the process.

Whether a corporation is wound up or dissolved, if a creditor of the corporation cannot be found, the amount of the debt may have to be given to the government that incorporated the company to hold in trust for the creditor. The same is true if a shareholder who is entitled to receive property of the corporation cannot be found. A shareholder who receives property from a corporation that then ends its existence may be liable for a period of years to pay unpaid debts of the corporation, up to the value of the property that the shareholder received.

A provincial corporation may need the consent—given when all corporate taxes have been paid—of the provincial ministry of revenue to terminate.

A federal or provincial corporation should get consent from Revenue Canada before it terminates. This consent is not *required*, but the directors and officers of the corporation may be held personally liable to pay any taxes owing by the corporation, up to the value of all property distributed by the corporation, if the consent is not obtained. (Notice how we managed to give the last word to Revenue Canada?)

T I P

CONCLUSION

Business, like life, is constantly changing. Your business will go through many stages, and with each stage the legal issues you face will be different. Whatever the legal issues though, your approach should always be the same. First, before you act (or decide not to act) inform yourself about the law. Read this book, read other books, read statutes, ask questions. Do your homework, because knowledge is a very powerful tool. Next, look upon your business's lawyer as a valuable resource, and know when to draw upon it. Even though you have to pay for it, timely legal advice will almost always save you money—as well as time and trouble.

As your business changes, the way you deal with lawyers will probably also change. In the early stages of your business you may have to use your lawyer sparingly and do much of the work yourself. We hope that, as your business expands and succeeds, you'll outgrow the need for a legal primer and have legions of lawyers doing your bidding. But even then, we think you will find the basic legal information in this book helpful in dealing with them efficiently and professionally.

We wish you luck and prosperity.

INDEX

HAVE YOU EVER HAD A GREAT BUSINESS IDEA...

...but didn't know what to do with it?

Or perhaps you already run a successful business, but you could always benefit from great ideas shared by other successful entrepreneurs.

Then try **PROFIT**, the Magazine for Canadian Entrepreneurs. It's written for *you*.

Published six times a year, each issue is packed with specialized information and advice designed to take you and your company to new heights of success. This award-winning magazine gives you the entrepreneurial *success stories* that **inspire** you, the *business post mortems* that **guide** you, and the *trends, briefs and strategies* that can help you **achieve** everything you want to with your million dollar idea.

Discover for yourself great advice on ...**Marketing** ... **management** ...**Technology** ...**Finance** ...**Niches** ...**Exporting** ...**Raising capital** . . . **Insightful one-on-one profiles of successful entrepreneurs** ... **The annual PROFIT 100,** our assessment of Canada's fastest-growing companies ...plus much more of value to anyone with a great business idea!